Social Work with Young People in Care

D0230259

Also by Nigel Thomas

Area Child Protection Committees (with Bob Sanders)

On the Move Again? What Works in Creating Stability for Looked After Children
  (with Sonia Jackson)

*Children, Family and the State: Decision-making and Child Participation**

An Introduction to Early Childhood Studies (with Trisha Maynard)

*Also published by Palgrave Macmillan

Social Work with Young People in Care

Looking after children in theory and practice

Nigel Thomas

Consultant Editor. Jo Campling

palgrave
macmillan

First published in 2005 by
PALGRAVE MACMILLAN
Houndmills, Basingstoke, Hampshire RG21 6XS and
175 Fifth Avenue, New York, N.Y. 10010
Companies and representatives throughout the world.

PALGRAVE MACMILLAN is the global academic imprint of the Palgrave Macmillan division of St. Martin's Press, LLC and of Palgrave Macmillan Ltd. Macmillan® is a registered trademark in the United States, United Kingdom and other countries. Palgrave is a registered trademark in the European Union and other countries.

ISBN-13: 978 1–4039–2050–8 paperback
ISBN-10: 1–4039–2050–8 paperback

This book is printed on paper suitable for recycling and made from fully managed and sustained forest sources.

A catalogue record for this book is available from the British Library.

10 9 8 7 6 5 4 3 2 1
14 13 12 11 10 09 08 07 06 05

Printed in China

For Terry, Billy, Ian and Alan, Hilda, Annie, Vicky and all the others

Contents

List of boxes, exercises and figures

Boxes

Exercises

Figures

Acknowledgements

I am grateful to the following for their help with this book: Jo Campling for being such a supportive consulting editor; Catherine Gray and her colleagues at Palgrave Macmillan, and the anonymous but very helpful reviewers of the first draft; my informal advisers and 'keepers up-to-date' Carys Davies, Eirian Davies, John Evans, Sophie Hughes, Frances Lewis and Mary Romaine; my colleagues when I was in practice, and the children, young people and families with whom I worked; and the ten cohorts of social work students at Swansea on whom many of the ideas in this book were first tried out. (I should also perhaps acknowledge that, had the University not surprised me with a period free of teaching and administration, this book would undoubtedly have been longer in the writing.) Finally, I must pay tribute to my family and friends, who have stuck by me through some difficult patches. I of course am completely responsible for the results, good or bad.

Acknowledgements are due to the following for permission to include extracts from published material: British Association for Adoption and Fostering for permission to reproduce Chart D, 'People's Needs' from Bryer, *Planning in Child Care: A Guide for Team Leaders and their Teams* (1988) (reproduced as Figure 2.1, page 14), and for extracts from Barn, *Working with Black Children and Adolescents in Need* (Banks 1999), Fahlberg, *A Child's Journey Through Placement* (1994), Hess and Proch, *Contact: Managing Visits to Children Who Are Looked After Away from Home* (1993), and Ince, *Making it Alone* (1998); Charles C. Thomas Inc. for permission to reproduce Figure 6 on page 199 of Plumer, *When You Place a Child* (1992) (reproduced as Figure 7.1, page 91); Research in Practice for extracts from Wade, *Leaving Care: Quality Protects Research Briefing* (2003); Save the Children for extract from West, *You're on Your Own: young people's research on leaving care* (1995); HMSO for permission to reproduce Figure 20.1 on page 251 of Biehal, Clayden, Stein and Wade, *Moving On: Young People and Leaving Care Schemes* (1995) (reproduced as Figure 10.1, page 161); Russell House Publishing Ltd for extracts from Wheal, *The RHP Companion to Leaving Care* (Kidane 2002).

Unfortunately it has not been possible to contact the copyright holder for permission to use the extract from Hitchman (1966) *The King of the Barbareens*, although Penguin Books Ltd have indicated that as the publishers they have no objection to the use of the material in question.

A note on terminology

Readers will notice that the title of this book refers to 'young people in care' – not 'children looked after' as contemporary English or Welsh readers might expect. It may be worth briefly explaining why this is.

First, 'children' and 'young people'. The Children Act 1989 refers to anyone under age 18 as a child, as does the United Nations Convention on the Rights of the Child. However, people in their teenage years do not generally refer to themselves as children – nor do they particularly like others to refer to them in this way. The phrase 'children and young people' is one in common use to cover everyone in the age range up to 18 and sometimes beyond, to the mid 20s, and I frequently use this phrase in this book – in fact, it is a macro on my word processor! I also use 'children' alone sometimes when it seems more relevant or simply easier. However, the phrase 'children and young people' may suggest, if we reflect on it, that children are a separate category from people, even young ones. Iona Opie, when she was conducting her famous research in school playgrounds, noticed that children, even quite young children, usually refer to each other simply as 'people'. For this reason I sometimes in this book speak simply of 'young people', and I have done so in the title. After all, even the smallest child is actually a young *person*.

Second, 'care' and 'in care'. In Britain the terms 'accommodated' and 'looked after' have been introduced as alternatives – for the best of reasons, as I explain in Chapter 5. ('Care' is still used in England and Wales, but not in Scotland, for situations of compulsion.) However, these terms are not catchy, and they have certainly not caught on among children and families. Nor are they likely to be meaningful to a non-British professional readership. So 'care' it is.

Otherwise, many of the terms used in this book, whether technical terms in law and policy or words used to refer to particular social groups, are those current and accepted at the time of writing. My apologies to any later readers who find that these terms have dated.

PART I

Theory

Introduction: themes and key principles

Introduction

Working with children and their families can be one of the most stressful, and most controversial, areas of social work practice. It can also be one of the most rewarding.

It is stressful and controversial because of the nature of the responsibilities that social workers carry for the lives of children and young people, because of the importance which our society attaches to the development and the protection of children and young people, and because of the frequent difficulty in knowing what is the right decision to make – and the often serious consequences of making the wrong one. It is rewarding because of the satisfaction that can ensue when things do work out, for instance when a child's life that was insecure and disrupted is placed on a sound foundation. It is also rewarding because, for many adults, working with children themselves can be hugely enjoyable.

The stresses and hazards are probably greatest in child protection work. However, the rewards are perhaps greatest in work with children and young people who are looked after. Of course these two areas of practice overlap considerably – more than half the children in the care system at any one time are there because of child protection concerns. On the other hand, the rest are there for other reasons, and that includes most of the children coming into and out of the system, often for short periods. This means that work with children who are 'looked after' also involves a great deal of work to support families.

In a sense then, it is artificial to separate work with children in care, or 'looked after', from work with children and families in general. Books that introduce or explain work with children and families in general can be very useful, and this book is not intended to be a substitute for them. However, there is enough that is distinctive about this area of practice to justify giving it separate attention; and that is why I hope this book will be useful too.

The aim of this book is to enable the reader to develop a sound understanding of the field of social work with children and young people who are looked after and their families, in order to provide a foundation for ethical and effective practice. This will involve looking at the political and legal context in which children and young people are looked after away from home, and at the social and ethical context. It will also involve getting to grips with the range of service provision for children and their families, and the research evidence for what kinds of services produce the most desirable outcomes. Finally, it will involve studying what happens in working relationships between social work practitioners and children and their families, what are the skills needed for this work and how they can be developed.

The purpose of all this is to lay the groundwork for developing practice skills and knowledge in work with children and young people who are looked after, and with their families. This is a process which does not begin, or end, with this book. My aim in this book is to enable the reader to use and build on whatever existing knowledge s/he may bring to the subject, and most importantly to provide a basis for further study and professional development in practice.

This book has, I hope, a clear theoretical and ethical foundation. In this chapter I introduce a set of core themes, which will be developed in the rest of the book as we look together at different aspects of social work with children and young people who are looked after. The first is concerned with ideas of children's needs and 'best interests', and the ways in which they are used. The second is about the importance of listening to children and young people, and of recognising that they have rights as well as needs. The third is about working with difference and oppression. The last is to do with conceptions of parenting and parental responsibility, and the relationships between children, families, communities and the state.

Children's needs and 'best interests'

These two concepts were both used for the first time in relation to children during the twentieth century. Psychologists in the 1920s began using 'needs' in the sense of human drives or wants, and developmental psychologists applied the concept in a particular way to children; while lawyers developed the concept of 'best interests' in order to promote the idea that the law, in dealing with matters concerning children, should consider what was best for them. Both concepts are useful, but both need to be handled with care, as we shall see.

Children's needs

Much discussion of services relating to children is now expressed in terms of 'children's needs'. The concept is used both to suggest that all children have needs which must be met if they are to develop into healthy adults, and to point practitioners to identifying the particular needs of individual children. In some respects the concept is clearly a progressive one. Putting 'what children need' at the centre of concern is arguably an advance on earlier preoccupations with moral decline, or with the costs of dealing with troublesome and destitute children. However, there have also been criticisms of the concept and the way it is used. Martin Woodhead (1997) has pointed out how statements about needs mix up fact and value. When we make a statement of the form 'a child needs A' what we really mean is 'a child needs A in order to achieve B, and B is something desirable and important'. However, these steps in the argument are left unsaid, and so cannot be questioned. The result is that the 'need' is constituted as an inherent part of children's nature, rather than as a means to a particular end, which may be promoted by some groups and accorded less priority by others.

According to Martin Woodhead, 'need' may refer to children's psychological nature, as evidenced by drives such as those for sustenance or attachment (or by the known pathological consequences of childhood experiences such as institutionalisation). On the other hand 'need' may also represent 'a judgment about which childhood experiences are most culturally adaptive', or 'a prescription about which childhood experiences are most highly valued' (1997, p. 75). Because it is not always clear in which sense the word is being used, it can be easy to overlook the extent to which statements about 'children's needs' contain assumptions that are culturally specific or based on particular sets of values. At the most basic level, contemporary Western culture seems to set a high value on having an enquiring and independent mind, while other cultures may set much greater store by being compliant and obedient.

Woodhead even suggests that the concept of 'children's needs' is so muddled that it might be better to do away with it. In this book we will use the concept, but we will try to do so in a critical spirit and be aware of the pitfalls. In particular we will try to remember two things:

(1) that many assumptions about children's needs are dependent on a cultural context, and there is often room for more than one view of them;
(2) that although children's needs are usually discussed in developmental terms, children are people living in the present, not simply pre-adults in the process of development.

When we look more closely at children's developmental needs in Chapter 2, we will need to bear these points clearly in mind.

'Best interests'

The same caution applies to the notion of children's 'best interests'. It is now common for laws and conventions to refer to children's 'best interests' and to suggest that they should be given priority over other considerations. Examples include the Children Act 1989 in England and Wales, and the United Nations Convention on the Rights of the Child. Section 1 of the Children Act makes the child's welfare the 'paramount consideration' in all court proceedings about the care or upbringing of children. Article 3 of the United Nations Convention says that 'in all actions concerning children ... the child's best interests shall be the primary consideration'.

As with the concept of 'children's needs', this represents progress compared with a past in which the law was mainly concerned with children as property. However, it assumes that it is possible to know objectively what is in a child's 'best interests', and this is questionable. First, however good our research evidence of outcomes for children, its application to individual cases can be tricky. Second, there may be conflict between the short and long term interests of children, and deciding which comes first may be a matter of values rather than objective fact. Third, different cultures will carry different assumptions about what is in the best interests of children. Finally, there is the question of *who decides* what is in a child's best interests – experts or family members? adults or children themselves? It has been argued that it is vain for the state to try to calculate what is in the interests of an individual child, and that it is better to follow some simple general principles such as the value of continuity – or even to give children themselves a role in determining what happens.

The issue of what weight should be placed on children's interests as against other factors can be a difficult one, and can cause misunderstanding. For instance, it is a common misconception that the Children Act 1989 makes the child's welfare the *paramount* consideration in all matters governed by the Act, including local authority services to children and families. In fact it only does so in relation to court proceedings about the care of children. A little reflection shows why it would create difficulties if the paramountcy principle applied to other matters. 'Paramount' means 'supreme over all other considerations'. If, for example, a local authority providing services for thousands of people was required to treat each child's interest as paramount, it could be very difficult to set aside resources for all its other responsibilities such as maintaining highways or collecting rubbish, and impossible for it to take decisions over conflicts of interest between different children and their families. That is why, as we shall see, the local authority's duty to children in its care or accommodated under the Children Act is *to safeguard and promote their welfare* – but not to put an individual child's interests over all others. (In the Republic of Ireland the Child Care Act 1991 actually requires a Health Board, the equivalent in this respect of a local authority, to 'regard the welfare of the child as the first and paramount consideration'; but this applies only when 'having regard to the rights and duties of parents' and not in relation to all issues of service provision.)

'Best interests', then, is another concept which will be used with care in this book. It is a powerful tool, and so can be dangerous when misused

Listening to children and children's rights

Listening to children and young people is a central theme of this book. As a phrase it may sound trite or obvious, but it has real content, and if understood properly presents one of the greatest challenges to social work practice with children and families. The theoretical basis for it is twofold.

One is that above all else *a child is a person*. In Lord Justice Butler Sloss's famous words in the Cleveland inquiry report, 'a child is a person, not an object of concern'. That is a moral, or even a political, statement; but it also connects with themes in the study of childhood by sociologists and psychologists, who have emphasised the need to see children as active participants in social life and in their own development, not just as passive recipients of 'socialisation'. Psychologists building on the tradition of Piaget and Vygotsky have emphasised the extent to which children make their own development in social interaction (see for instance Trevarthen 1995; Woodhead 1999). Sociologists and anthropologists have moved on from studying socialisation and 'upbringing', and now study children as social actors in their own right, even having their own cultures. They also analyse the ways in which childhood is 'socially constructed' rather than being simply a natural phenomenon (see James and Prout 1997; James, Jenks and Prout 1998). If we accept that this perspective is right, then in practical terms it means that we must respond to children as persons, not just as the objects of our caring, and involve them actively in making choices about their own care.

The other part of the theoretical basis for listening to children is that they have *rights*, both individually and collectively. There has been a great deal of debate among lawyers and philosophers about whether children have rights, and also about whether they have the same rights as adults or whether there are distinctive children's rights. (See my own summary in Thomas 2002, Chapter 3.) However, since the adoption of the United Nations Convention on the Rights of the Child there has developed a widespread agreement that children have rights to certain kinds of provision and protection such as a family life, education and health care, freedom from abuse and exploitation. Furthermore, although the extent to which children have the right to determine their own lives is still a matter of debate, there is also general agreement that children have a right to be heard and consulted about such decisions. This principle, based on Article 12 of the UN Convention (see Chapter 3), has become part of the accepted ideology of child welfare. It is not always easy to follow through in practice, and sometimes it receives more lip-service than actual practical implementation. However, it is certainly one of the principles on which this book is based, and in the chapters that follow we will look at some of the ways in which it can be made effective.

The practical implications of seeing children and young people as having rights to certain kinds of provision and protection, and also having rights to be heard and consulted, is that their views about what happens to them, about where they live, and about the plans that are made for them, should be actively sought by those providing care – whether they are parents, foster carers, social workers, or whoever. 'Listening' is a shorthand for this – sometimes children and young people don't have much to say, at least in words – but this does not mean that their wishes and feelings are any less important. It is not just a matter of individual children, either. Children as a group have collective rights, and the views of children and young people in general about the services provided (or not provided) for them should also be sought actively – and notice taken of them. In Chapter 3 we will look at some of the ways in which we can listen to children, both individually and also in groups.

Working with difference and oppression

The third theme that deserves a chapter to itself, and which we will therefore deal with only briefly here, is that of working with difference and oppression. The diversity of background of children and young people who come into care is one obvious reason for this to be a major concern for practitioners.

Whatever our own background, much of the time we will be work with children, young people and their families who are from different backgrounds, sometimes very different indeed. This is the first challenge – to understand these differences, the meanings they have for people, and the effects they may have on their lives.

Another reason for this to be a concern is that any child who comes into care is by definition at a disadvantage, and that in most cases their life chances and those of their families have already been limited by factors that are outside their control – whether that be poverty, mental illness or whatever. Most social workers do not come from disadvantaged backgrounds – although many do, and have overcome them by routes that may be different in each case. A second challenge for each of us in working with children and young people who are disadvantaged is to understand these different patterns of disadvantage and the ways in which people may be discriminated against or oppressed – including ways in which they may be discriminated against or oppressed by the very services we think we have set up to help them.

These issues provide the focus of Chapter 4, and will be explored in some depth there. They will inevitably recur in the second part of the book.

Parenting and the state

Much of this book is about parenting, in different ways. For the children and young people we are considering, parenting is likely to be a major issue. Most of them have their own birth parents, even if they have not lived with them for years. Many of them have parents who are separated, and many have step-parents. Most children looked after are placed at one time or another with foster carers or 'foster parents', and some acquire new parents through legal adoption. For many, a key issue in planning their future is that of whether the parenting provided to them is 'good enough' parenting. For all children and young people who are looked after by the state – or by voluntary or private organisations – 'corporate parenting' is an important part of their lives. It is therefore essential to be clear about what we mean by parenting, who can be a parent, how far and in what ways it may be shared, and what counts as *good enough parenting*.

There seem to be two distinct meanings of 'parent':

- someone from whom one has one's origin;
- someone who takes responsibility for upbringing – who takes care;
  This second meaning can be further divided into three components –
- caring;
- intimacy or connectedness;
- responsibility for outcomes.

Theorists such as Goldstein, Freud and Solnit (1973) have argued that only one or two people can provide what they call 'psychological parenting'. However, it is generally accepted that children can establish significant connections with more people than this, especially if those people have good relationships with each other (see Richards 1986; Fahlberg 1994). At the same time it appears from attachment research that these emotional aspects of parenting are of crucial importance for the development of a healthy personality. These are major issues for anyone involved in planning children's care, or in making decisions about who should look after children and young people.

There is also a question about whether the state can in any real sense be a parent. Does it really make sense to talk about 'corporate parenting'? It is hard to see how the state, or a local authority as a corporate body, can ever provide the elements of intimacy and connectedness that seem crucial to a concept of 'psychological parenting'. Instead, it should be the job of such agencies to see that each child or young person has someone with whom they can establish that kind of relationship. However, the state does arguably have a direct role both in providing care and in assuming responsibility for outcomes.

Fox Harding (1997) identifies four competing value positions in relation to the state's interventions in parenting. These she describes as *laissez-faire*, state paternalism, parents' rights and children's rights. Although the four positions are in ideological conflict, they are often found to co-exist, in that the same legal or policy system may contain elements that represent more than one of these value positions. Linked with these longstanding conflicts over values is a debate about what standard of upbringing children looked after by the state should receive. It is an argument that dates back to the Poor Law and is still very much alive now. At bottom it asks whether children in care are to be compared with other children in the class or community where they originated, or with more privileged groups – in short, whether the care system should or should not be a vehicle for social mobility

There are no easy answers to questions about what constitutes good enough parenting, about who can or should parent a child, or about what should be the precise role of the state in relation to parents and children. At the same time they are questions that cannot be ducked in practice, even if we have not finally resolved them in theory. In Chapter 5 we look a little more closely at how parenting and the relationship between parents and the state are handled in particular legal systems. Issues about the quality of parenting and who provides it will recur in the second part of the book.

Conclusion – working together

The first part of this book is about the theories and principles that should underpin social work practice with children and young people. In the second part, starting with Chapter 6, we look at how these theories and principles work in different aspects of practice. There are some common threads that run through all this, of which one is the idea of *partnership* or working together.

As I said in the introduction to this chapter, working with children and their families can be one of the most stressful and controversial areas of social work practice, because of the importance of the responsibilities involved and the difficulty in making the right decision. Fortunately, these responsibilities are not usually carried alone. As we see in Chapter 5, partnership is a key principle in work with children and young people in care. For social workers that means partnership with one's own departmental colleagues, with other workers such as foster carers and volunteers, and with professionals from other agencies and disciplines. Sharing difficult decisions with managers and within teams is crucially important given the nature of some of the decisions we have to take. Interagency working is increasingly acknowledged as important in all areas of social work practice, and this is no exception. There is increasing recognition too of the multidisciplinary and corporate nature of responsibility for the welfare of children and young people, especially if we really start to see their needs for care, health, education and community in a holistic way.

Finally, of course, partnership means working together with parents and other family members, and with children and young people themselves.

GUIDE TO FURTHER READING

Helpful introductions to social work with children and families in general include Butler and Roberts (1997, 2003), Brandon, Schofield and Trinder (1998) and Colton, Sanders and Williams (2001). Also useful is Thompson (2002), based on the study guide for the all-Wales Postqualifying Child Care Award.

Those interested in exploring further the use of the concept of 'best interests' might consult Alston (1994); see also Thomas (2002). Guidance on further reading on the other key themes of this book is to be found in the next four chapters.

CHAPTER 2

The needs of children and young people who come into care

Introduction

Let's start with some personal reflection. Find a relaxed setting, and try the following exercise in your own time.

Exercise 2.1 Making it personal

Imagine that a child known to you personally is in a situation in which she or he needs to be cared for away from home. You may choose to think about your own child, in the present or in the past, or a child belonging to a relative or friend; but you should think about an *actual* child. You can imagine that s/he needs to be cared for either on a temporary or on a more permanent basis, for whatever reason.

Whatever the circumstances, the task for this exercise is the same. Think about what you would want for the child you have chosen, in terms of the care arrangements to be made. What sort of placement would you want the child to have? What services would you want to see provided? What sort of processes would be necessary to plan and make decisions? Above all, what sort of experience would you want the child to have, and what would be necessary to provide this?

Take ten minutes to reflect on these questions; jot down some notes. Afterwards, if you wish, discuss your thoughts with a colleague or fellow student.

The above exercise is likely to have raised a lot of issues about how children and young people are cared for, many of which we will return to in later chapters of this book. One of the first issues it should raise is to do with what we think children and young people *need* – both in general and as individuals.

An influential use of the concept of 'children's needs' was in the book *The Needs of Children* (Kellmer Pringle 1974, 1986). The author characterised children's developmental needs as

(a) 'the need for love and security' – the child needs to experience loving relationships, consistency and familiarity;
(b) 'the need for new experiences' – the child must have opportunities to explore and to master a succession of tasks;
(c) 'the need for praise and recognition' – encouragement is of crucial importance;
(d) 'the need for responsibility' – children should have increasing independence within a secure framework.

You may notice that this is a highly selective list. For instance, it is noteworthy that Kellmer Pringle does not include physical needs for warmth and sustenance – indeed, she deliberately leaves them out. 'Since physical ones are not only more clearly understood but also more easily and now more generally met, the emphasis will be on psycho-social needs' (1986, p. 34). Kellmer Pringle's approach to children's needs is very focused. Her book was originally commissioned by the Department of Health and Social Security, and is written as advice for parents, teachers and social workers.

A broader approach is adopted by Margaret Bryer in *Planning in Child Care* (Bryer 1988), another book that was commissioned for a specific purpose (as advice to social work team leaders and their teams). Bryer's comprehensive list of 'people's needs' is organised under five headings – physical, social, emotional, educational or intellectual, and ethical. Within these are a total of 87 different categories of need (see Figure 2.1). Bryer's argument – like Kellmer

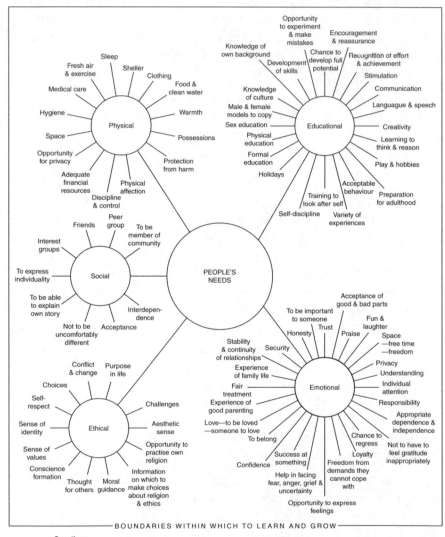

Source: Bryer (1988), p. 32

Figure 2.1 People's needs

Pringle's – is that these needs have to be met both in childhood and through-out life. Bryer also draws a helpful distinction between the general needs that all children have, and the 'priority needs' or 'unmet needs' of individual children in difficulties. Although her book predates the child care legislation of 1989 and afterwards, it is based on similar principles, and its practicality means that we will continue to use it in this book. Other descriptions of children's needs are to be found in basic texts on child development, some of which are referred to in the Guide to Further Reading at the end of this chapter.

The concept of 'children's needs' as an organising principle for work with children and families is now very well established, being central to guides to practice such as the *Framework for the Assessment of Children in Need and their Families* (Department of Health et al. 2000) and associated publications (Cleaver et al. 1999; Horwath 2001). As we saw in the opening chapter, a degree of caution is necessary when we look at statements about children's 'needs'. I concluded the earlier discussion by suggesting that, when talking about children's needs, we should remember that many assumptions about what children need depend on a cultural context, and also recognise that children are not simply adults in the process of development. If we see children and young people solely in developmental terms, there is a risk that we will not see them fully as people living in the present, and as citizens.

At the same time, an understanding of children's development is of central importance to social work practice, and there is knowledge available which we neglect at our peril, and at the peril of children and young people.

Knowledge of child development

There are several reasons why a sound knowledge of child development is necessary for social work with young people in care. First, it enables us to have a better understanding of children's lives at different ages – what skills and capacities they may have, what particular needs they may have, what conflicts they may be dealing with, and so on. Second, it enables us to identify children and young people who are not developing 'normally', and to enquire into possible reasons for that. Third, a good knowledge of child development enables us to plan to meet children's needs, and to advise parents and carers. Finally, it puts us in a position where we can engage in constructive dialogue with other professionals, including psychologists and doctors, and advise courts making decisions about children's welfare and 'best interests'.

What do we mean by 'a sound knowledge of child development' in this context? It is not simply an account of 'ages and stages', of prescribed weights and heights, standard indicators of language development, and so on. There have been enough critiques of 'developmentalism' to make us see that this is not by any means the whole story. First, because people are different, as individuals and as members of cultural and ethnic groups, and we do not all follow the same fixed pattern. Second, because children and young people are not to be defined developmentally, in terms of what they will become; their lives **now** are of central importance. Third, because childhood is itself a socially constructed phenomenon, and many aspects of children's lives are not determined by fixed biological processes, but are produced in social interaction.

However, there are biological processes at work, subtle and complex ones, and we cannot ignore them. The physical growth of children and young people tends to follow certain patterns, although these patterns are affected by individual genetic variation as well as by environmental factors such as nutrition. The development of muscular control in infancy tends to follow a set pattern. The physical structure of the brain appears to develop in predictable ways, and this structural development of the brain continues into adulthood. Environmental factors can impede or facilitate this growth, but they cannot apparently change the basic pattern.

These biological patterns have obvious practical consequences. The normal age of onset of behaviour such as walking or talking tends to be the same in different societies, despite wide cultural variation in child care practice and in other aspects of infant behaviour. If a child does not fit these particular patterns, this at least indicates a need to enquire whether there may be a problem.

In Chapter 1 we noted Woodhead's observation that statements about 'children's needs' may refer to basic drives such as those for sustenance or closeness to people, or to the pathological consequences of particular childhood experiences, or they may refer to judgments about which childhood experiences are most culturally adaptive or which childhood experiences are most highly valued in society. As well as knowing about basic biological patterns of development, we need to know about cultural patterns of development too – not in order to impose the patterns of one culture on all children, but on the contrary in order to understand what is 'normal' in different communities or social contexts, so that we can meet the particular needs of different children in appropriate ways and so that we can engage with children and families from different communities in working to improve children's life chances.

It is not the purpose of this book to provide a detailed guide to what is known about child development, or to the different theoretical models that have been proposed. There are many good sources of information on the subject, some of which are mentioned in the Guide to Further Reading at the end of this chapter. It is worth consulting several rather than depending on a single source. It is also worth reading critically – some authors are better than others at using the concept of 'development' in a sceptical way and at stepping outside their own culture. The focus in this chapter will be on particular aspects of developmental theory, and on the relevance of these for social work with young people in care.

The 'ecological' model

One of the most useful insights in developmental theory, particularly for social workers, is the idea that development is not simply a matter of studying what happens in the individual child, or the child in his or her family, but that there are different levels of analysis that contribute to an understanding of how children develop and the factors that influence this. The classical statement of the 'ecological model' is that made by Bronfenbrenner (1979). He uses a systems analysis to distinguish between: 'microsystem' – the immediate settings such as family, school or peer group within which individuals live and develop; 'mesosystem' – the interaction between these settings; 'exosystem' – wider social institutions such as neighbourhood, government and media; and 'macrosystem' – the broader context of social and economic systems, law, ideology and culture.

There are dangers in using a model such as this too tightly. It can lead to a picture of the individual child as simply a product of external systems, rather than as an active participant in her or his own development. Used flexibly, however, it can help to remind us that there are many different factors that have a bearing on the lives of children and young people, and that they are not all in the child's immediate social environment (see Exercise 2.2). The model has been used by Jack (2001) and others to illuminate social work practice, as we see in a later chapter, in particular by integrating a wider community perspective with the usual focus on the child and family.

Exercise 2.2   Mapping children's needs

Think again about the child you chose for Exercise 2.1. Using the chart in Figure 2.1, try to identify some of the key influences on that child's situation in the microsystem, the mesosystem, the exosystem and the macrosystem.

Developmental pathways

One way to help understand the relationship between biological and cultural factors in child development is through the concept of 'developmental pathways'. This concept is useful in that it reminds us that there is more than one way to grow up, and that more than one way may be 'right' in terms of outcomes. It also reminds us that a child's future as an adult is not wholly predetermined for good or ill by what happens in early childhood.

The concept of 'developmental pathway' is used slightly differently by different authors. It can refer to the opportunities provided for children by different cultures (see Weisner 2002), or sometimes to the pathways foll-owed by particular young people that lead to poor outcomes. Daniel, Wassell and Gilligan (1999) use the analogy of a sailing yacht to show how a child's progress through life may be affected by a succession of factors, some of which may blow the child's development 'off course' while others help to put it back on track. This connects with the concept of *resilience* which I discuss below.

What children need in order to develop

The ecological model suggests that in order to develop fulfilled and healthy lives – whatever we mean by that – children and young people need certain resources to be available, both in their immediate environment and in the wider world around them. Clearly these resources include the fundamentals of warmth, shelter and sustenance, human contact and care – not just at a basic level of survival, but of a quality to provide good life chances. Other funda-mentals, highly relevant for many of the world's children, include freedom from war and violence, displacement, exploitation and other natural or human-made disasters.

Children also need opportunities to form meaningful and positive relation-ships with others – so the social environment in which they grow up is import-ant, both in the family and outside. This is frequently understood in terms of *attachment*, which I discuss further in the following section. Children need opportunities to develop their linguistic and cognitive skills, and this requires a rich and stimulating physical, as well as a social, environment. For some child-ren these opportunities for learning are readily available within the family; others are more dependent on outside institutions such as school, although for all children it is best if both settings work together to offer a learning environ-ment. Media such as television and computers are also important sources of information and of opportunities to develop skills in using it.

Above all, children and young people do not develop in isolation but in a *cultural* context. Indeed, the research psychologist Colwyn Trevarthen (1995) has characterised child development as a process of 'learning a culture'. This refers both to the wider culture of the society in which the child lives – its value systems, scientific beliefs, social expectations – and also to the specific culture of the social group to which the child belongs, which is best defined in terms of ethnicity and class – its traditions, beliefs and ways of doing things. Children's cultural learning comes from all the sources to which I have already referred – family, school, other social settings, communication media. It is important for children to feel that their own particular culture is valued and worthy of respect, alongside others.

Attachment

In recent years attachment theory has come to dominate the discussion of child development in social work, for good reasons. Daniel et al. explain it well:

> Attachment theory … asserts that there is a biological imperative for infants to form attachments and that they exhibit attachment behaviours to promote attachment. In this sense attachment behaviour can be viewed as survival behaviour. The theory relates the quality of such early attachment relationships to emotional functioning throughout life. That is, it asserts that the development of self as a socio-emotional being is mediated by relationships with other people, which in turn are mediated through communication.
>
> Daniel, Wassell and Gilligan (1999), p. 14

They add:

> Attachment theory also relates language, cognitive and moral development to the quality of early attachment relationships. An understanding of the theory of these developmental dimensions should therefore provide a good basis for assessing the possible effects on a child's development when attachment relationships are inadequate … An understanding of the theoretical and empirical links between patterns of attachment and healthy development should help social workers in assessing the quality of a child's relationships.
>
> p. 15

Attachment theory is not just about what happens in early childhood. As a conceptual framework it is also relevant for work with older children and young people, and with adults. Patterns of attachment laid down in infancy as a result of parental behaviour tend to persist (both because parental behaviour persists anyway and because children's behaviour tends to reinforce it for better or worse). It is thought that gradually these patterns become internalised in the child's model of self, and govern the developmental pathway along which the individual will travel. Research has found that both children and adults with secure attachment histories also tend to be better able to give coherent narratives of their lives (Holmes 1993).

David Howe and others have promoted the use of attachment theory in social work with children and families, arguing that 'children need to secure permanent selective attachments to one or more loving and responsive caregivers if they are to achieve healthy psychological development', and that 'social workers have to consider how to maintain, strengthen or provide affectional bonds and good quality attachment experiences for children' (Howe 1996, p. 15).

Jane Aldgate (1991) argues that an attachment perspective has several implications for social work practice with children and young people in care. It points to the importance of work that supports existing attachments rather than disrupting them, for instance by judicious use of respite care. For some children, careful work may be needed to ensure that new attachments to carers develop alongside existing relationships and complement them. For others, where existing attachment relationships are damaging the child's emotional development or have broken down, a new attachment to a permanent alternative family will be needed. Attachment theory is also highly relevant to work with children moving on from one care placement to another, as the work of Fahlberg (1994) has shown. Fahlberg refers to situations where a child feels a strong attachment to a parent that is not reciprocated by the parent 'bonding' with the child. Social workers may mistakenly see this an attachment that needs to be preserved, rather than as an anxious attachment that can prevent the child's needs from being met unless the failure of the parent to bond is addressed and resolved.

Resilience

Another concept that has become increasingly influential in thinking about work with children and young people is that of *resilience*. Gilligan (2000a) defines resilience as 'a set of qualities that helps a person to withstand many of the negative effects of adversity'. It seems likely that some children are naturally more resilient than others; but there are also environmental factors that can enhance natural resilience.

Kirstie Maclean (2003) identifies the 'qualities associated with resilience which develop through children's life experiences' as *self-esteem* (enhanced by acceptance and achievement); belief in one's own *self-efficacy* (enhanced by taking responsibility and making decisions); *initiative* (ability and willingness to take action); *faith and morality* (as Daniel et al. note, 'a belief in a broader value system can help the child to persist in problem solving or in surviving a set of challenging life circumstances' (1999, p. 67)); *trust* in others; *attachment* (as Maclean says, 'one sign of resilience in children is the ability to "recruit" caring adults who take a particular interest in them'); a *secure base*, not just in terms of primary attachment but in the wider sense of a consistent and stable place to live and continuity of wider relationships; *meaningful roles* such as proficiency at school, sport, work, volunteering, caring for siblings and domestic responsibilities (provided they are not excessive); *autonomy*; *identity*; *insight*; and *humour*.

There is a great deal that can be done to develop the resilience of children and young people in care, to build on their strengths rather than simply focusing on problems. This can include providing social and emotional support, encouragement and support in education (critically important for many young people who succeed), encouragement with activities and hobbies, promoting contacts with friends or supportive adults. We will look further at some of this later in the book, and there are useful guides listed in the suggested reading at the end of this chapter.

Family and social circumstances of children coming into care

In thinking about the needs of children and young people in care, we have to consider the needs they have in common with all children, as well as the needs that stem from their membership of a particular group. We also have to consider the circumstances from which children tend to come into the care system, which have their own implications in terms of assessing their needs.

An often-quoted piece of research is that of Bebbington and Miles (1989) who analysed the origins of children in care in the UK compared with the wider population, in terms of factors such as social class, ethnicity, family and household composition. They found that a number of factors were good predictors of which children were at risk of coming into state care, especially when they were analysed in combination. They calculated that a child of mixed ethnic origin, living with three or more other children and a single adult in privately rented accommodation with more than one person to a room, and dependent on supplementary benefit, stood a one-in-ten chance of being received into care, whilst a white child in a smaller two-parent family, in an owner-occupied home with more rooms than people, stood a chance of one in seven thousand.

These statistics tell us several things. They tell us that children in adverse circumstances and with few resources available to them are far more likely to come into care than their contemporaries whose situations are more favourable. They also tell us that even where children are in the least favourable circumstances as defined here, the overwhelming majority of them do *not* come into care (which means it is worth enquiring into what it is that enables these children and their families to manage at home – and at what cost). Especially importantly for our purposes here, they tell us that many of the children and young people who enter the care system bring with them a history of relative disadvantage and associated problems, which we must add to the other needs we have identified.

Abuse and neglect

An additional factor is that a high proportion of children and young people in care have been neglected or abused. Indeed, in the UK the majority (something around 60 per cent) of children in the care system at any time are recorded as being there *because of* abuse or neglect. (This is not the same if we look at admissions to care over a period, when we find that a majority of admissions are related to parental difficulties or relationship problems.)

The fact that so many children in care, and especially the long stayers, have a history of ill treatment has very obvious implications in terms of their needs – implications for placement planning, for the type of care and treatment needed, and for the kind of things that may go wrong. Children who have been abused or neglected may have both physical and psychological consequences to deal with. Their growth may have been impaired. Their self-esteem is likely to be poor. They may have difficulties with attachment or with trust. These and other factors will create problems for the individual child and for those living with her or him. Unless these difficulties are successfully managed, the child's passage through care is likely to be rough and her or his resilience, and ability to face life successfully, further damaged.

Needs of disabled children

There are many groups of children in the care system who have particular needs in addition to the needs which all children have. Some of the issues in providing for a diverse population are discussed further in Chapter 4. At this point I want to focus briefly on one especially important group, that of children who are disabled.

It is common to distinguish between *impairment*, or the actual physical, sensory or intellectual lack or disorder which causes someone to be disabled, and *disability*, seen as the result of socially constructed barriers that stand in the way of people leading full lives. Disabled children therefore have a range of needs, some of which are based on the nature of their impairment, others on how those around them respond to it.

Children with physical or sensory impairments will need a physical environment at home and school that enables them to be as autonomous as possible, and additional help in overcoming barriers to access in the wider world. Children with intellectual impairments will need support in learning to the maximum and perhaps in negotiating relationships with the outside world. Children in both groups may have difficulties in communication, and in this case it is critically important that they are with people who can communicate with them and that they are enabled to overcome these barriers as far as possible.

Children with emotional and behavioural difficulties, which may stem from innate factors or may be the result of accident or abuse, may have difficulties in managing many aspects of daily life or relationships with others, and often demand a great deal of understanding, patience and skill from those caring for them.

In addition, all disabled children are likely to face discrimination and prejudice, and will need help in overcoming and challenging this. Some are particularly vulnerable to abuse, whether before admission to care or after, and may have difficulty in reporting it when it occurs.

Education and health

It is very easy when working with children and young people in care, especially in a busy, overworked department, to be preoccupied by the demands of finding and managing placements, negotiating contact arrangements, and on on — in other words, to focus on the needs that have brought a child into the care system, and in the process fail to attend to the other needs that apply to all children in our society.

All children need good health care, and children who come from disadvantaged backgrounds, who have had problems of a nature and degree that require state care, and who may then pass through a series of more or less stable and appropriate placements, are likely to stand in more need of good health care and supervision than most. As we see later, some research evidence suggests that they may actually get less.

All children and young people need opportunities to learn, as we have noted. In a modern complex society this almost always means schooling. Some families are able to meet their children's needs for education outside the school system, but the families whose children come into care are rarely in this category – in fact it is more likely that their children have relied on school for some of the conversation, stimulation and learning that most children get at home. We have noted in relation to *resilience* that educational success can be one of the key factors that make a difference to how young people manage difficulties and overcome adversity to succeed in life. However, research suggests that children and young people in care often fail to overcome their initial disadvantages, and are highly vulnerable to failure and exclusion at school which has the effect of making things worse. This is a theme to which we will return throughout this book.

Summary and conclusion

We have seen how a working knowledge of child development is indispensable for good practice with children and young people in care. We have looked at some of the important models and concepts, including the 'ecological' approach, developmental pathways, attachment and resilience. We have considered the family and social circumstances of children coming into care, the consequences of abuse and neglect and the needs of disabled children. Finally we have thought about the health and education of children in care – and this brings me to the final message of this chapter, which is the need to respond to children and young people in a holistic way, and not to compartmentalise them. If there is one thing of value in the contemporary concept of 'children's needs', it is that a child or young person must been seen, and treated, as a whole, not as a collection of parts.

GUIDE TO FURTHER READING

There are many books on child development, aimed at different readerships. Probably the most useful introduction for social workers is Daniel, Wassell and Gilligan (1999). For greater depth and detail, especially on problems in development, I recommend Herbert (2002) and in relation to disability Lewis (2003). On attachment, Howe (1995, 1996) and Howe et al. (1999) are all useful, as is Cairns (2002a). Cairns (2002a), Gilligan (2001), Fraser (1997) and Grotberg (1997) are helpful on theories of resilience and strategies for promoting it. On the social background of children and young people in care, Bebbington and Miles (1989) is an excellent starting point, as also is Hayden et al. (1999). On abuse and neglect, Beckett (2003) is a good introduction, and Corby (1993) is also very informative.

CHAPTER 3

Listening to children and young people

CONTENTS OF CHAPTER

Introduction

Aunt Ada and I were shown into Miss Hayhurst's office at the Ministry and after a short conversation Aunt Ada just turned and went. She didn't say 'good-bye' or even look at me, and I suddenly realised with a hopeless sense of finality that she was gone. I set up a loud wailing that rose and increased on the chance that somehow I could reach Aunt Ada and bring her back. Miss Hayhurst just went on writing as if I and my crying were non-existent. Another woman was shown in. Putting down her shopping-bag, she came straight across to me, ignoring Miss Hayhurst who had risen and was holding out her hand.

'Don't you take on now, my mawther,' said the woman, kissing me. 'You'll be all right along o' me. Do you know what I got back home? Why, three old pussy cats, and look you here.' From her pocket she brought out a little poke-bag of sweets, of the kind known as butter balls. I can still recall the salty sweet taste of them. The salt was from my tears which continued to flow, though quietly.

Then the woman turned her attention to Miss Hayhurst, and together they filled in the indispensable forms, while I studied my new foster-mother.

The King of the Barbareens (Hitchman 1966), p. 49

I have been here about four months, but I didn't have much choice. The very first time I went, they didn't let me visit or anything. They just took me there.

Boy aged nine

What foster homes ... like they choose it, but I can say whether I like it or not. That is what every social worker has done ... Well I have had most say in it really because they won't put me anywhere if I don't like it.

Boy aged twelve

Thomas and O'Kane (1999b), p. 375

These quotations give very different pictures of children's involvement in moves in foster care. Elsie's experience in 1924, as related by her adult self Janet Hitchman, was not untypical of that period. The interviews from which the second and third quotations are drawn took place in 1996, and by then it was much more common for children to be consulted about their placements. However, as the quote from the nine-year-old suggests, it was still by no means universal.

In this chapter we will look at why listening to children and young people is important, what it means, and how it can be done ethically and effectively – not only with young people in their teens, but also with younger children.

Why listen to children and young people?

As I said in Chapter 1, listening to children and young people should be part of the foundations of social work practice with children and families. There are three main arguments underlying this principle.

The first argument, as I said in Chapter 1, is that children and young people are persons with a *right* to be heard and to have a say in decisions about their own lives. This is now widely accepted in principle, and is notably expressed in Article 12 of the United Nations Convention on the Rights of the Child, which says that

States Parties shall ensure to the child who is capable of forming his or her own views the right to express those views freely in all matters affecting the child, the views of the child being given due weight in accordance with the age and maturity of the child.

'All matters affecting the child' clearly includes matters concerning the child's personal life, such as where s/he lives or goes to school.

The second argument is that it is in the *interests* of children and young people that their wishes be understood and their views taken into account. There is considerable evidence from psychological research that having a sense of control over our lives is associated with other measures of wellbeing, both for adults and for children as young as babies (see Maccoby 1980). Many children grow up feeling that they have little control, or that important decisions about their lives are being taken without really consulting them or even explaining to them what is happening. This applies especially to children who find themselves in public care. Taking the time to explain things properly to children, giving them a chance to express their own thoughts and feelings, and creating opportunities for them to influence what happens, can give them a feeling of being more in control, and enable them to move on successfully in other areas of their lives.

The third argument is that listening to children and young people actually leads to *better decisions*. It is generally the case that plans and decisions are better if they are based on the knowledge and opinions of those directly involved, and this surely applies where children are concerned. There is even some research evidence that allowing children to influence decisions that affect them can improve the quality of those decisions. Children, like adults, are experts in their own lives, and it would be foolish to ignore that expertise when making difficult decisions.

'Listening to children and young people' is of course a shorthand expression. If we take it too literally, we may risk forgetting three key points:

(1) that children's non-verbal communication can be just as important and revealing as the words they say;
(2) that communication is a dialogue, and what workers say to children – especially in terms of explanation – is important as well as what children say;
(3) that listening to children is a precursor to action, not a substitute for it – children and young people expect us to do something about what they tell us, and soon become cynical or disillusioned if this does not happen.

'Wishes and feelings'

The Children Act 1989 requires a local authority to ascertain and consider the 'wishes and feelings' of a child whom they propose to look after. The same expression was used earlier in the 1975 Children Act. This suggests that when we communicate with children about their care we need to have a dual focus:

- first, on what they want – on the child's views and thoughts about her/his situation, and in particular on what s/he would like to happen;
- second, on how they are feeling – and on the impact of the child's experiences on her/his happiness, security and sense of self.

In what follows it will be important to keep this dual focus in mind. We should respond to what children have to say, include them as participants in decision-making processes, respect their *rights*. At the same time we must remember that they are young people in vulnerable situations who may have undergone traumatic experiences, and who may be bewildered, overwhelmed or frightened – we must respond to their *needs* on a *feeling* level.

Communicating with children

Communicating with children and young people is not necessarily very different from communicating with adults. Where people are in need, the basic requirements always apply – warmth, empathy, trust, and sensitivity to the person's verbal and non-verbal language and style of communication. However, children and young people may bring particular issues to such encounters. They may be relatively uncomfortable with straightforward verbal conversations, perhaps because their verbal skills are limited, because they are distressed, or because they are simply unused to talking about such matters with an adult – especially a strange adult. On the other hand, they may be able to communicate through play or drawing in ways that many adults might find much more difficult. This applies especially to younger children. Older children and young people may have adolescent inhibitions about talking freely with adults, or may have learned not to trust people who say they want to help them.

O'Quigley (2000, pp. 28–9) reviewed the research on what makes for successful listening to children. She identified the following factors, among others:

- Confidentiality 'is empowering and allows the child to speak freely'. She also notes that 'if unconditional confidentiality cannot be guaranteed then this should be made clear at the outset so that the child does not feel that confidences have been betrayed'.
- Age 'should be disregarded as far as possible' – children are often more competent than adults expect, and while being *aware* of developmental and cultural factors one should not use them to make assumptions about individual children.

- A friendly and non-intrusive style of interviewing, that allows children space to develop their opinions, is more effective than a protective or controlling approach.
- Information is crucial if children are to explore options and express coherent views.
- Reassuring the child that there are no 'right' and 'wrong' answers frees the child to voice her or his own opinions.
- Adults should be non-judgemental and open-minded about children's views, and allow them to explore their own agendas.
- Children's competencies are *different* from adults rather than *lesser*. Drawing and other practical supports for communication may help to elicit this competence.
- It is important to recognise that some children may not want to participate in decision making.

Although O'Quigley's focus was on children involved in divorce and separation proceedings, who may be interviewed by relative strangers such as lawyers and guardians, her review of the research was careful and many of the lessons she draws are applicable to other settings such as the care system.

Talking to children and young people is one of the core activities in this area of social work practice. Of course, some practitioners are more confident than others – but we all have to do it, and it is our individual responsibility to become as skilled as we can in this work. There are some good resources around to support this work, some of which are mentioned in the Guide to Further Reading at the end of this chapter. One particularly useful resource is Naomi Richman's book *Communicating with Children: helping children in distress* (Richman 2000). It was commissioned by Save the Children and written specifically for people working with 'children in situations of social crisis or conflict' – this may include refugee and displaced children, street children, as well as those who are in foster homes or residential care. Although the circumstances of children displaced by civil war are very different from those of children in a more stable society whose own families are in difficulty, many of their needs are similar, as are the skills needed to communicate with them. Clear and straightforward, the book has chapters on verbal and non-verbal communication, on establishing trust, on working with children individually, in groups and in families, on barriers to communication and on working with acute distress as well as bereavement. Each chapter ends with some practical exercises, designed to help develop skills in a group.

Box 3.1 offers a way to remember some of the key points about communicating with children and young people. It is based on the findings of research with children in care.

Box 3.1 'TRANSACTS' – key points in communicating with children and young people

Time – it is essential to have enough time to spend with a child; they do not necessarily want to talk 'by appointment'. Time also means working at the child's pace, allowing them to stay in control.

Relationship, trust and honesty – children communicate best with people with whom they have relationships of warmth and trust. It is important to be friendly and open, empathic and above all 'straight' with children.

Active listening – the skills of 'active listening' developed in counselling can be helpful in work with children. This means responding to cues, restating and drawing out the meaning of what the child is saying, combined with the expression of warmth, empathy and acceptance.

Non-verbal communication – an adult's tone of voice, facial expression, body language and even style of dress can affect how children communicate.

Support and encouragement – children need support and active encouragement to speak up, especially when they have something difficult or negative to express. An adult may sometimes need to offer to express a child's views for them. Children don't like it when they feel they are being judged or criticised, and they don't like to be put 'on the spot'.

Activities – many children find it very boring to 'just sit and talk'. Games, writing, drawing and other activities can be used to make the process more interesting. *Life story work* can be an excellent way to involve children in reflecting on their situation (see Ryan and Walker 1993).

Choice, information and preparation – children must have a choice about whether and how they participate in a decision-making process. They are more able to have their say if they have been prepared for the discussion and given time to think about things beforehand.

The child's agenda – it is important to give children space to talk about issues that concern them, rather than just having to respond to adults' questions.

Serious fun! – the fact that serious matters are being discussed doesn't mean that everyone has to be po-faced. Most children find this alienating; some find it threatening. If decision-making processes can be made more enjoyable, children are more likely to get involved.

Based on Thomas and O'Kane (1998a)

A voice for young people in care

There have always been practitioners who are good at working directly with children, responding to their feelings and enabling them to articulate their wishes. However, many agencies and institutions have not always supported this kind of practice, and children's wishes and feelings have often been effectively disregarded. The demand for positive action to involve children and young people in decisions about their lives in care – and even about their admission to care in the first place – gathered strength in the 1970s and 1980s with the establishment of organisations such as Who Cares? and NAYPIC. By the mid 1980s it was much more common for young people to be invited to planning and review meetings – something that seldom happened in the past – and many of them found it a valuable experience. Fletcher (1993) found that 61 per cent of her respondents felt that people listened to them at meetings, and 84 per cent were asked before plans were made to move them. However, some still felt alienated from the process:

> I never really say anything because I am worried about saying the wrong thing. (15-year-old)
>
> They talk about you as if you are not there, so you just shut up and listen without saying a word. (14-year-old)
>
> Fletcher (1993), pp. 52–3

By the early 1990s it was normal for teenagers to be invited to reviews. However, for children aged 12 and under it was much less common, and only later did social workers and their agencies begin to consider whether those under ten might be able to participate. In 1996–97 our research in South Wales found that 55 per cent of children aged 8–12 were invited to reviews and planning meetings, but this varied markedly with age; from 39 per cent of eight-year-olds to 85 per cent of 12-year-olds, with the sharpest increase at age ten (Thomas and O'Kane 1998a). The research also found that use of the *Looking After Children* forms (see Chapter 6) made it more likely that children would be invited; and that children whose parents were in conflict with the local authority were less likely to attend even when they were invited. Grimshaw and Sinclair (1997) found that attendance was higher for 'accommodated' children (see Chapter 5) than for those in care.

The reform of child care law through legislation such as the Children Act 1989 and the Children (Scotland) Act 1995 undoubtedly gave an impetus to young people's participation. The establishment and publicising of systems for responding to complaints, and the development of advocacy services, have continued this process. Practices such as the involvement of young people in the selection of staff, and in arrangements for independent inspection of care services, show how much things have moved on since the 1970s, let alone the 1920s. Nevertheless many young people are still unaware of their rights, especially some of those in foster care.

Issues in work with younger children

Although enabling effective participation by adolescents takes skill and commitment, in several ways the inclusion of younger children in decisions about their care offers greater challenges. One challenge is that with younger children it is often necessary to use methods of communication that are very different from the ways in which adults usually communicate with each other. This should not mean that communicating with young children is a highly specialised skill, which most of us are excused from exercising. As social workers, if not simply as citizens, we should be prepared to deal with all people, from the oldest to the youngest, in terms of real human engagement. Every encounter carries challenges as well as rewards, and working with small children is certainly no exception. It is part of the job to face the challenges, and sometimes even to enjoy the rewards.

A further problem experienced by many practitioners is that even when they are personally committed to 'direct work', as it is called, such work often seems to attract a low priority in the allocation of time and resources. Although many agencies are genuinely committed to enabling staff to engage directly with children and young people, in practice this work may be squeezed out by other imperatives – for example, the procedures associated with formal assessments of various kinds.

In addition there are sometimes difficult issues around younger children's competence, and how to assess it. To some extent this is an issue in work with all children, but the younger a child is, the more sharply the question presents itself. When it comes to the crunch, are young children competent to have a view on what should happen to them?

Children's competence

Understanding of children's cognitive development has been dominated by the theories of Piaget. In his model, children's understanding is incomplete and inferior to adult thinking. It is proposed that as children grow older their patterns of thinking develop through a series of stages which are 'global' – that is, at a particular stage of development all a child's cognitive processes are limited to a particular pattern, until the child moves on to the next stage. It has been argued that Piaget underestimated children's abilities at different stages. Donaldson (1978) revised Piaget with the insight that children's thinking is embedded in social contexts, and that their understanding of a concept depends on whether the situation in which it is used makes 'human sense' to them. More recently, the idea of global stages has been questioned by models that suggest that competence in one area is not necessarily associated with competence in another, and by research that shows how practical experience can enhance mental skills in particular areas. However, physical changes in the structure and organisation of the brain undoubtedly continue until puberty and even beyond, and such changes must affect mental functioning.

The basic question of whether there are fundamental differences between children's thinking and adults' thinking, or inherent limits on what children can understand at different ages, is very hard to answer in precise terms. This means that it is unwise to make many assumptions of the 'children below the age of eleven cannot …' variety, and also unwise to expect children to show a full range of cognitive skills regardless of age. Even if the superior skills of adolescents and adults are attributable to experience and practice, this does not mean that they are not significant. In early and middle childhood some important conceptual frameworks may be fragile and need support to function effectively. Lloyd (1990), looking at the ability of primary-school-age children to communicate complicated instructions, found that they tended to understand ambiguity but not to express it verbally, and that they needed support in dealing with unclarity or misunderstanding.

Garbarino et al. (1992) put it well:

Recent research indicates that Piaget probably exaggerated the differences in children's thinking at different stages of development. However, there is ample evidence to demonstrate that there are important differences in how children think, know, and understand and that children are not simply ignorant or inexperienced adults. Rather than describing them as stages, it may be more useful to think of developmental differences as reflecting gradual but perceptible shifts in ways of participating in and understanding experience. Thus, it is important for adults to try to understand that a child's interpretation and understanding of a situation may be quite different from their own.

p. 41

There is also some evidence that emotional development affects cognitive skills. On one hand, emotional turmoil or stress can affect cognitive development adversely; for example, children who have had emotionally upsetting experiences such as separation from a parent appear to do less well at school. On the other hand, children's reasoning ability sometimes appears to advance most in situations which are emotionally charged (Dunn 1988). Dunn's research was conducted in stable and happy families with warm and positive relationships between parents and children, and the situation may be different for children who come into care, who may have had very adverse experiences. However, it would certainly be wrong to assume that children in care are disabled by their experiences from taking part in decisions about their future. Sometimes the experience of dealing with change, on perhaps of taking responsibility at an early age, can make children better prepared to take part in decisions.

As well as the psychological understanding of children's competence, there is a sociological discourse in which competence is seen as something that is negotiated in social context. In this view the social competence of children is to be seen as a practical achievement: that is, it is not something which is accorded to children by adults, like a right, and can thus be redefined or removed … But it is an achievement that is bounded by structural features of the milieux in which children live their lives.

Hutchby and Moran-Ellis (1998), p. 16

The implications for policy and practice of taking a different view of competence are important. It means that the basic question is how we can design processes of decision making in such a way as to *elicit* and *enable* children's competence. Underlying this must be the recognition of the child's right to take part. As Eugen Verhellen puts it, 'the recognition of self-determination in children is essential in order to make them more competent and vice versa' (Verhellen 1992, p. 81). In other words, social workers have a vitally important job to do in *empowering* children, especially younger children, to take an engaged, informed and active part in decisions about their own care.

Listening to children and promoting their 'best interests'

Is there a conflict between listening to – and taking account of – children and young people's wishes and feelings and promoting their best interests? Both are legal obligations, so it would be helpful if there were no conflict between them. In practice, however, there can be difficult situations where a choice has to be made between giving full weight to a child's own view of things and following adults' prescriptions of what is in the child's interests.

In our research (Thomas and O'Kane 1998b) we found that these conflicts arose in relation to differences of opinion over placement, over family contact, over school and over children's leisure activities. Differences over placement usually involved conflict between a child wishing to return home and the view of social workers or carers that this was against the child's interests. Differences over contact might involve children wanting more family contact, or less. Differences over school included a boy of ten with learning disability who wanted to go to a mainstream school when his carers wanted him to go to a special school, a boy of eleven whose mother wanted him to go to a Catholic school when he did not, and a girl of ten who wanted to change schools because she was 'picked on', when adults thought a move would not help. Differences over leisure time mainly concerned children who wanted to go off with friends in circumstances when parents or carers thought this was inappropriate.

Some social workers and carers were very clear about their responsibility on occasion to override the child's wishes in the interests of their welfare. Others were less confident of their own ability to make the right decision, or more willing to allow the child a substantial role in the process. A third group went for a balance between protecting the child from harm and allowing them to learn by taking risks.

Some children were assertive about their wishes and feelings and wanted to be heard. A 12-year-old boy said 'I don't need, well I do need sometimes, but most of the time I don't need people to say what is best for me.' Others were more self-effacing or submissive to adult judgement – for instance the ten-year-old girl who said 'They care about you – they want you to do what is best.'

It is easy to say that the answer is to achieve a balance between these two obligations. In practice, finding that balance can be very difficult. Gerison Lansdown has suggested that the nature of the balance varies according to the perceived competence of the child in relation to a particular decision. She suggests that 'if the child lacks the competence to understand the implications of the decision, a parent should only override the child if to do so is necessary to protect the child or to promote his or her best interests', whereas if the child is competent a stronger test should apply, in that a parent should only override a competent child 'if failure to do so would result in serious harm to the child'. She also proposes that 'in all cases where the child's wishes are overridden, the child is entitled to an explanation of the reasons and acknowledgement of their concerns' (Lansdown 1995, p. 26).

Listening to children and young people collectively

As we noted in the opening chapter, children and young people have rights as a group as well as individually. They also may have views collectively about the ways in which they are treated and about the services provided for them. Some agencies have developed skills in communicating with children and young people as a group about these issues – through questionnaires and surveys, through open forums, or through representative organisations. This is easier to do with some groups than with others – for instance with teenagers in residential homes rather than with younger children in foster care. It is also easier to include children who are vocal and articulate than children who have communication barriers of one kind or another. However, there are ways of overcoming these difficulties, and when it works the communication can be very rewarding for children and for professionals.

Summary and conclusion

We have looked at some of the reasons for listening to children and young people and taking account of their wishes and feelings. We have thought about some of the more effective ways of communicating with children, and we have looked at how young people in care have begun to get their voices heard. We have considered some of the issues that arise in work with younger children, and at the vexed question of children's competence. We have thought about the conflicts that arise between listening to children and promoting their 'best interests'. Finally we have begun to think about some of the ways in which we can listen to children and young people collectively. What is perhaps most important in this aspect of social work practice is a real commitment to involving children and young people in making decisions about their own lives. Also critically important are three principles that will be a major feature of the next chapter – namely respect, recognition and openness.

GUIDE TO FURTHER READING

There has been a substantial growth in the literature available on this topic in the last ten years, and readers will no doubt find good material themselves. I reviewed some of the theory in Thomas (2002), and Thomas (2000) may also be helpful. For the practice of listening to children, helpful texts are Daniel et al. (1999), Luxmoore (2000), O'Quigley (2000), Richman (2000) and Jones (2003) – the last by an expert on communicating with abused children. There are also a number of useful resource packs for agencies and teams, which contain various combinations of training exercises and direct work materials: for instance National Society for the Prevention of Cruelty to Children (1997) and Thomas et al. (1999). The British Association for Adoption and Fostering is a good source of material that can help in working with children in different situations – see www.baaf.org.uk

The organisation Voice for the Child in Care produces some very useful material, including their recent publication *Start with the Child, Stay with the Child: a blueprint for a child-centred approach to children and young people in public care* (see the website at www.vcc-uk.org). It can also be very helpful to read accounts by young people who have experienced the care system, such as *The Cornflake Kid* (Riddell 1996). Fictional accounts such as *The Story of Tracy Beaker* (Wilson 1991) can illuminate a child's point of view in an accessible way.

CHAPTER 4

Caring for young people from different backgrounds

Working with difference and oppression

As we saw in Chapter 2, there is enormous diversity among children and young people who come into care – reflecting the diversity of the general population, although not at all in the same proportions. Social work with young people in care, like other fields of social work practice, is crucially about working with difference and diversity. Recognising and responding to this difference and diversity must be core elements of ethical social work practice, although the nature of this response, and the words used, have not always been the same. Indeed, social work has sometimes been accused, in practice if not in theory, of imposing uniformity on diverse groups (see O'Hagan 2001).

In addition, children and young people who come into care are very largely drawn from groups in society who are in some degree disadvantaged or oppressed – because they are disabled, because they are from minority ethnic groups, above all because they are poor. This oppression and disadvantage present two key challenges for social workers:

(1) How do we avoid repeating this oppression in our own practice?
(2) What can we do to help overcome the effects of oppression and disadvantage?

In this chapter we will look at how these challenges present themselves in relation to particular groups. First, however, I will try to clarify what are the key principles that I think we should follow in working with difference and diversity. These may be summed up as respect, recognition and openness.

Respect means respecting each person as an individual for who they are. It means respecting their background, their experience of life, their family and their culture. It means accepting that other people may look different, live differently, have different abilities, hold different beliefs and values from those which are familiar to us, but that they are still entitled to our respect as human beings. It also means respecting people who have not made a success of their lives, whether this is because of personal difficulties or because they are part of a disadvantaged group.

Recognition means above all noticing difference and responding to it. It is no part of ethical social work to pretend that everyone is the same or that differences do not matter. People are different, and those differences demand to be recognised and acknowledged if people are to have equal chances. A good example is the issue of ethnic monitoring, where unfair treatment of people of different background or skin colour has only been revealed when note is taken of these characteristics and records kept. Another example is the issue of access to public buildings, where an assumption that everyone is 'able-bodied' has the effect of excluding people who cannot physically climb stairs unaided.

Openness means being prepared to learn about other people's lives and experiences, their cultures, histories, beliefs and languages. It means accepting that others may have something to teach us, even when they come from groups who seem strange or who appear to have lower social status. It means being prepared to find new ways of working in order to make our services accessible to people who may have different needs, different expectations, different assumptions or different ways of communicating.

In what follows we will see how these principles apply in working with particular groups of children and young people. We will consider in particular those who are disabled and those who are from minority ethnic groups. We will also consider children and young people who use minority languages, whose sexual orientation is unconventional, who are from disadvantaged social classes or are poor, or who have come from another country seeking refuge.

In speaking of 'different groups' we should not allow ourselves to think of these groups as in any way mutually exclusive. Nor should we think in terms of minority groups who are 'different' and a majority who somehow represent the norm. We are all different. We all have our own mix of physical and mental characteristics and abilities, and we all have a culture, a language, a gender, a social class, a sexual orientation. Some of these features may mean that we are disadvantaged or discriminated against, and some people – some children and young people – may be doubly or trebly disadvantaged because of their membership of minority groups. The principles of respect, recognition and openness to difference and diversity apply to everyone. The challenges of combating disadvantage and oppression apply to some more than to others.

Disability and disabled children

The meaning of disability

Disability is a field that is fraught with disputes about terminology. Both the words used to refer to particular kinds of disability and the words for disability in general have frequently changed, usually because the words previously used came to be seen as disrespectful or demeaning. As we noted in Chapter 2, a distinction is often drawn between disability and impairment, where 'impairment' means the underlying physical or neurological factor and 'disability' refers to the effects of society's failure to accommodate to the effects of this. As for children, until recently it was conventional to refer to 'children with disability', but more recently people committed to a rights-based approach have argued that 'disabled children' is actually preferable as a term, because it emphasises that disability is something that is done to children rather than something inherent in them.

Disabled children in care

Children and young people in care may be impaired, and as a consequence disabled, in many different ways. They may have obvious physical impairments which reduce their mobility, their dexterity or their ability to communicate – or they may have less visible neurological damage with similar effects. They may have sensory impairments which mean that they cannot see or hear as well as others, or not at all. They may have physical impairments that make them look very different and to which other people react in unpredictable ways. They may have neurological damage that limits their intellectual ability, sometimes profoundly. They may have learned behaviour that creates more or less severe difficulties for them in social relationships.

Children and young people with all these kinds of impairment are represented in the population in care, and to a greater extent than in the general population. Looking after a disabled child can in itself present additional challenges for parents, increasing the risk of children coming into care. Families with a disabled member are also statistically more likely to have lower income, which again means a higher risk of reception into care. Children with emotional and behavioural difficulties, increasingly recognised as a category of disability, are especially highly represented in the care population – not only because children with these difficulties are more likely to be in situations where their parents feel they cannot cope, but also because children frequently have experiences, before or after coming into care, that trigger or exacerbate such difficulties.

Responding to disability – 'stigma' and access

The way in which we understand disability is fundamentally important to how we treat disabled children. A contrast is frequently drawn between the 'social' and 'medical' models of disability (see for instance Oliver 1990). The medical model sees disability as a disease or disorder of the individual, to be cured or ameliorated if possible, adapted to if not. The social model, by contrast, sees disability as the result of barriers erected by society that exclude people from participating fully in its life and activity.

The sociological theory of stigma was first developed by Goffman (1963), from the biblical term meaning a symbol of disgrace or infamy. Goffman identified stigma as 'an attribute that is deeply discrediting within a particular social interaction'; the person with such an attribute is 'reduced in our minds from a whole and usual person to a tainted, discounted one' (Goffman 1963, p. 3). The concept has come to be widely used in relation to ill-health and disability, as well as to other attributes such as poverty or client status. Although it is arguable that all disabled people suffer some degree of stigma, the theory predicts that people are especially likely to be stigmatised if their impairment is highly visible, if it is not well understood by the public, and if it is seen as a result of some moral failing – hence the outcry some years ago over much-publicised remarks by the England football coach who apparently suggested that disabled people were being punished for sins in a previous life.

One of the tasks of work with disabled children must therefore be to overcome the effects of stigma – by challenging public ignorance, by ensuring that services are provided in ways that reduce stigma rather than adding to it, and by helping disabled children themselves to learn ways to defend themselves against discrimination and prejudice.

A central issue for all disabled people is that of access. This is seen at its most obvious in physical terms, most starkly when someone simply cannot get into a building because the entrance is not adapted to their needs. However, accessibility is a test of public services in many other ways too. Are disabled people able to get to services physically? Are providers of services able to communicate with users in ways that lead to mutual understanding? Are services provided in ways that invite and welcome people with disabilities, rather than exclude and demean them? These questions apply to all kinds of services and facilities, from the local shop to the school. They also apply, of course, to care services.

'Inclusion', attitudes and values

In recent years the emphasis in services for disabled children has been on inclusion. This applies particularly to schooling, where it carries the assumption that all schools should be aiming to meet the individual needs of all children, rather than identifying certain children as having special needs for special schooling. However, the same concept applies to care provision – indeed, the statement in section 23(8) of the Children Act 1989 that accommodation provided for a child who is disabled should be 'not unsuitable' to his particular needs may be read as indicating that ordinary accommodation should be adapted where necessary, rather than providing segregated accommodation for disabled children. Part of the ethos of the Children Act is that disabled children are 'children first' and disabled children second. In other words, the first question to ask when we are providing a care service is 'what does this child need as a child in the context of our legal duties and responsibilities to all children?' and only afterwards do we ask 'what in addition needs to be done to ensure that this child's disability does not put her or him at a disadvantage?'

Laura Middleton argues that the current welfare system

> creates disadvantage for children who are physically different, and it does so by conceptualising them as having 'special needs'.
>
> Middleton (1999), p. 75

She contends that only 'a fundamental review of the welfare system' (p. 76) can overcome this. However, this does not mean that individual professionals are powerless to make a difference. In fact there is a great deal that the practitioner can and should be doing. One is to recognise one's own 'disablist' attitudes:

> Professionals may value disabled children less than those who are not disabled, regard them as objects of pity, or fail to notice their uniqueness. Disabled children are often viewed through the lens of their disabling condition and assumptions made about them on the basis of their physical characteristics. Realisation that they hold unhelpful attitudes can be a painful journey for those who consider themselves caring, tolerant and in

favour of a society based on principles of equality or social justice. This can engender guilt, which some disabled activists might encourage, but such a response is not conducive to constructive change. It is more helpful to develop an understanding of the mechanisms through which we learn disablist attitudes and the means by which they are reinforced. In this way we can acknowledge, resist and revise them.

Middleton (1999), p. 78

Middleton also suggests that an 'unhelpful mystique' (p. 79) has grown up around work with disabled children, and that this can have the effect of deskilling both professionals and family members. This does not mean that skills and knowledge are not needed, but it does mean that there is no excuse for any of us dodging our responsibility to meet the needs of all children and include them in the services we provide.

Culture and ethnicity

One of the most obvious ways in which people are different – and on the basis of which they may be subject to prejudice or unfair discrimination – is in their ethnicity. The term 'race' is used less than it was in the past, because it can be a highly misleading concept. The idea that humanity could be divided into several major groups between which there are profound genetic differences is now known to be wrong. Genetic differences within ethnic groups are much more significant than those between them. Physical differences such as skin colour or hair type are extremely superficial and have not been shown to be associated with differences in character, ability or temperament. Nevertheless the cultural differences between ethnic groups are extremely significant, and the fact that physical appearance is often a marker for such differences means that difference is hard to ignore and can have a profound effect on how people behave towards each other.

Our sense of identity, of who we are, is highly bound up with our ethnicity – with our family history, our group membership and most of all our culture. Particularly for members of minority groups in any given society, preserving cultural beliefs and practices can be critical to the survival of this sense of identity. An understanding of this must underpin effective social work practice with members of minority ethnic groups. For children and young people in care, it is very easy for the connection with the group and the culture to become severed, disjointed or confused.

It is sometimes said that black and ethnic minority children are over-represented in the care system. In fact this is something of a simplification, because in statistical terms some groups such as African-Caribbean children are over-represented while others (for example Indian and Chinese children) are under-represented. Most strongly over-represented are children and young people of mixed heritage – a series of studies have now shown that 'children of mixed parentage are the largest ethnic group among those looked after' (Barn and Sinclair 2001).

There are particular issues in relation to the placement of children and young people from black and ethnic minority groups, especially in foster care and adoption, that have been highly controversial. Most controversial has been the issue of whether children should always be placed with people of 'the same race' and what this means in practice, especially for children and young people of mixed heritage. Barn (1999) argues forcefully that poor practice, and the misuse of research evidence in forming policy, have condemned many young black people to placements that fail to help them build a positive sense of their own identity. These issues are considered further in Chapters 7 and 8.

As Barn points out, however, ethnic and cultural identity are not fixed. People constantly make and remake their cultures, and preserving one's cultural identity is not simply a matter of hanging onto traditional practices – although that may be an important part of it. Children and young people in care, especially those who grow up separated from their families and communities, may need work to be done with them to help them develop a positive sense of their identity. This applies particularly to those who are black or of 'mixed race'. Banks (1999) offers some ways in which social workers and carers can do this, and also explains how it is necessary first to address one's own ethnic identity, history and attitudes (see Box 4.1).

Box 4.1 Nargis

Nargis was a 14-year-old South Asian girl of mixed parentage, i.e. with a white English mother and Pakistani father. Nargis disliked her Muslim name and had adopted the name of Susan. Nargis had come into care at the age of eight when her mother had died in childbirth. Her father's whereabouts were unknown and his family had rejected Nargis because her mother had not been married to him. Her mother's family had also rejected her because of her father's origin.

Nargis had been placed with white English short term foster carers, who subsequently became her long term foster carers. They lived in a white working class area, and had not been trained in meeting the needs of a black child of mixed parentage. Nargis adopted the name Susan to avoid constant questioning by other children and being called 'Paki'. For the same reason she told them that her background was Italian.

In addition to identity difficulties, Nargis had unresolved issues around her mother's sudden death and her abandonment by the rest of her family. The social work department was considering moving her to a South Asian family. She was resisting this because they were elderly, inactive and ate hot spicy food which she did not like. She had also become attached to her white foster carers who had offered her stability at a time of great change.

Adapted from Banks (1999), pp. 27–8

As Banks says, this example illustrates the 'appalling position in which some black children can find themselves when their needs are not sensitively identified and met at the outset'. He points out that the agency is faced with a complex set of tasks if it is to address the problems created by earlier poor decision making, and that forcing a move on the basis of ethnic matching alone is simply going to make matters worse. Nargis needs bereavement counselling before anything else can happen, and she also needs to be actively involved in selecting and assessing a suitable family for her future placement.

As well as direct support in developing a positive identity, children and young people from minority groups have the right to expect that care providers will be sensitive to their needs, whether those are physical needs (such as for skin and hair care) or cultural needs (such as provision for diet, religious festivals, or particular clothing).

So what is required of the social worker with children and young people in care, or in any field, in relation to culture and ethnicity? Clearly s/he cannot be an expert in every culture that s/he is likely to encounter. That is not the nature of the task. Rather, the practitioner should be able to respond to the needs and situations of diverse groups on the basis of our principles of respect, recognition and openness, and should be able to recognise when additional expertise is needed and to develop her/his own skills, or draw on the knowledge of others, as appropriate. The concept of 'cultural competence' has been developed to help think about this task. From research into clients' expectations of professionals, O'Hagan (2001) defines cultural competence as comprising:

- 'respect on initial contact';
- an appreciation of why the client's culture is so important, and awareness of components that the client may regard as crucial;
- 'genuine and friendly curiosity';
- an ability to admit ignorance and respond appropriately to one's mistakes.

O'Hagan (2001), p. 254

O'Hagan's research is with Irish speakers in Northern Ireland, who face discrimination and prejudice within their own society. Garrett (2003) also makes the point that people of Irish origin in Britain face racism, which should not be seen simply as a matter of 'black and white'.

Language

For many people language is a key component of culture, and respect and recognition for the different languages used by children and families are important for this reason. They are also important for practical reasons. Much of the work of social workers with children and young people and with their families, especially where children are looked after away from home, is highly sensitive and concerned with emotions and feelings. It can be very difficult for anyone to talk about such issues in a language that is not their first language or the one they normally use to talk about such matters – no matter how fluent they may be in other respects. An awareness of language is therefore crucial to effective social work practice in this area.

Minority ethnic languages

Most contemporary societies are multilingual – in fact, worldwide most people speak at least two languages. In the United Kingdom the majority are mono-lingual, and this can create disadvantages for members of minority ethnic communities who have a different language. Within the UK, for instance, there are many resident speakers of Gujerati, Punjabi, Hindi, Chinese, Greek; of Somali and other African languages; of French, Spanish and Portuguese; of Vietnamese and other South East Asian languages; as well as growing numbers of speakers of Russian and East European languages. Some schools in London have a score of languages used among the children. In other areas it is rare to find any child whose first language is not English. This makes for different demands on social workers and other professionals, and different patterns of resources with which to meet those demands (for example, the availability of translators and interpreters may vary widely). Within this varied and changing situation, it is important to review constantly one's ability to respond to differ-ent needs that may arise, both for written material and for people who can con-duct conversations with users of different languages.

Yr iaith Gymraeg

In Wales, or Cymru, the Welsh language is not only a central component, perhaps the central component, of culture for a large proportion of the population.

It also has the legal status of an official language. People are entitled to conduct their official business – pay taxes and bills, use the law courts – in either Welsh or English. Public bodies have a duty to make services available through the medium of Welsh as well as English, and must state publicly their policies for achieving this. This applies to social work agencies and care providers, especially local authorities, as much as to any other organisation.

The implications of this for individual practitioners can be considerable. Welsh-speaking children and families must have the choice to deal with a worker who can communicate with them in their preferred language. This means that all agencies should have at least some workers who are completely fluent in Welsh – whether this be in an area where a majority of people have Welsh as their first language, or in an area where very few people use Welsh. Welsh-speaking children and families may also feel more comfortable if any worker with whom they come into contact has at least some familiarity with the language. It does not take a great deal of skill to learn to say 'Bore da' ('Good morning') or even 'Mae'n ddrwg gen i, ond dw i ddim yn siarad Gymraeg' ('I'm sorry, but I don't speak Welsh').

In other parts of the British Isles too there are old languages that are still used – Scots Gaelic and Irish, and to a much lesser extent Manx and Cornish. O'Hagan (2001), although he does not mention Welsh, devotes considerable attention to the resurgence of Irish in Northern Ireland and the attempts to give it greater status by the devolved Assembly. Speakers of these languages sometimes face intolerance from monoglot English speakers, including professionals in the health and welfare services, who see their insistence on using the Celtic language as in some way perverse or politically motivated. However, if we go back to our principles of respect, recognition and openness we see that these apply to the choices indigenous people make about preserving their culture, as much as they do to people who have moved to Britain from other continents.

Sexuality

Children and young people in care who are gay or lesbian have a range of issues to confront, both in relation to their own sense of identity and in terms of the attitudes and reactions of others – including their caregivers. Children may sense at an early age that their sexual feelings are different from those of their peers, and need to be in a social environment where they can be comfortable with this and talk about it if they wish. As they get older they will need advice and information on legal issues as well as on taking care of themselves physically and emotionally, from people who know something about it (whether from personal experience or from training) and who are not afraid to deal with these issues in a relaxed way.

Acceptance is of course the key principle here – accepting children and young people as they are and for who they are, and not trying to force them into a mould created by others' prejudices or expectations. Social workers who are not comfortable in dealing with these situations may need to refer to a colleague or supervisor, or perhaps seek counselling themselves. See Brown (1998) and Mallon (2000) for further discussion of some of these issues.

Poverty and class

Most children and young people who come into the care system are from poor working class families. We have already mentioned the seminal study by Bebbington and Miles (1989). They found that almost three quarters of their sample of 2500 children in care were from families in receipt of income support. Over half the families lived in neighbourhoods that were poor, and four fifths lived in rented housing.

It is common now for discussion to be in terms of 'social exclusion' rather than simply poverty. This concept is useful in thinking about some of the ways in which people who are materially poor often have limited opportunities to participate in many aspects of society and restricted access to a range of social resources or 'social capital' (see Chapter 6). However, it is sometimes used to suggest that the remedy for social exclusion is to develop the skills and personal resources of poor people, or to seek ways to overcome the social barriers between poor families and the wider society. While these objectives may be important, they are not a substitute for tackling low income directly.

Poor people are frequently subject to intense discrimination, prejudice and stigma, exacerbated by the fact that they are often seen as responsible for their own poverty. Although children are more often seen as victims – indeed the political impetus for measures to reduce poverty almost always depends on focusing on child poverty, for this reason – they still cannot escape the stigma. Being poorly dressed and underfed does not add much to one's status in our competitive society. Nor does being poorly educated, in a country where even a rich man, who is intelligent enough to captain a national football team, is routinely mocked for not being an intellectual. All these characteristics are associated with being poor, and this gives children from such a background a mountain to climb in terms of prejudice, invisibility, latent hostility or low expectations.

Again we need to return to our basic principles: respect for children and their families, no matter what their background or circumstances, and for the strategies which they adopt to survive in those circumstances; recognition of the reality of poverty and the barriers it creates to inclusion and participation in society; openness to the potential of poor children and their families to succeed, and to give as well as to receive.

Working with travellers, refugees and asylum seekers

Two groups of children and young people, who have not been mentioned explicitly yet in this chapter, have particular experiences of difference and oppression. Travelling children who belong to traditional Roma or gypsy communities are members of an ethnic group who, as well as being victims of myth and prejudice, are often ignored or excluded by mainstream services. Even when agencies provide for such children, they frequently fail to do so in a way that respects or recognises their culture and language. Another group of modern 'new age' travellers also are vulnerable to prejudice and exclusion, even though the cultural barriers may be less marked. In both cases, the fact that families do not have a conventional settled home in a fixed geographical location tends to fuel misunderstanding, as well as disqualifying them from certain facilities and services. Providing care and accommodation for traveller children can be challenging for all these reasons, and also because when families and communities are moving on it can be difficult to maintain a stable placement with consistent family contact.

Another group who have become increasingly significant in recent years are refugees and asylum seekers. This group are particularly vulnerable for a number of reasons. They are usually from ethnic minority groups which are very different from the host community, and in some cases quite unknown to the host community. Their culture and language may be very different from the host community, and they may not speak the language of the host community at all. This is especially likely if they have arrived as a result of an emergency in their country of origin, when their journey may have been unplanned until the last moment. In addition they may be living in a community where they know little or nothing of where things are or how they work, their entitlement to services and resources may be restricted as a result of government action to 'crack down' on asylum seekers, and they may well be victims of racial attacks or abuse.

Children and young people in these circumstances are exceptionally vulnerable, especially if they have arrived in the host country unaccompanied by a parent or other adult. Many such young people find themselves in the care system, and challenge the ability of the care system and its practitioners to respond to their needs with respect, recognition and openness.

The social work role and interagency working

The responsibility to respond effectively and empathically to difference and oppression does not lie solely with social workers. Doctors, health visitors, teachers, police, housing officials, all have their part to play in ensuring that all members of the community have fair and effective access to services and help when they need it. Indeed, in no other aspect of practice are interagency and multidisciplinary working more important than in how we deal with difference and oppression. Joint training can be vital in creating a shared understanding of the task and shared ideas on how to tackle it. It is good to see that a guide to culturally competent practice such as O'Hagan's is aimed at health and social care professionals in general, not just at social workers.

Summary and conclusion

We began the chapter with the suggestion that working well with difference and oppression depends on three principles of respect, recognition and openness. We then saw how this applies in work with disabled children and young people in care, using the concepts of stigma, access and inclusion. We also saw how it operates in relation to culture and ethnicity, especially in work with black and ethnic minority children. We looked at issues of language and of sexuality, at poverty and class, and at what is involved in working with refugee children and with travellers. Finally, we considered the importance of working together across agencies if we are to counteract oppression in an effective way. Social workers cannot take on the sole responsibility for ridding society of oppression and discrimination. However, by attending carefully to our own practice, by listening to children and young people and their families, and by making alliances and working collaboratively with others, we can make a real contribution.

GUIDE TO FURTHER READING

Middleton (1999) is probably the best starting point for thinking about work with disabled children, and Morris (1995) has lots to say about disabled children living away from home. Read and Clements (2001) is an excellent summary of the law in relation to work in this field, although it already needs some updating. Barn (1999) is very helpful in thinking about work with black children and families, and Gambe et al. (1992) have some useful ideas and exercises. O'Hagan (2001) is good on dealing with culture in general, offering an interesting blend of research, theory and practice. On social work and the Welsh language there are a range of useful resources, many of them produced by the now-defunct Central Council for Education and Training in Social Work. Particularly useful for our purposes is the work of Elaine Davies and her colleagues (Davies 1994; Davies, Siencyn and Owen 1999). On working with gay and lesbian children and young people, Brown (1998) and Mallon (2000) are good starting points. On work with traveller children I recommend Kiddle (1999), and on refugees and asylum seekers Kidane (2001a).

CHAPTER 5

Law, policy and practice in looking after young people

Law, policy and professional practice

In any area of social work practice, there are good reasons for social workers to know about the law. Some laws are important because they impinge on social work clients and their lives: laws on housing, employment, race relations, as well as family law and education law. Other laws are important because they directly govern social work practice. These include community care law, mental health law, criminal justice law, and of course child care law.

There are several ways in which the law governs social work practice. It gives social work agencies their powers and duties; it tells clients what their rights are; it provides a framework for service provision; and it provides the authority for compulsion. Whether social work services are provided by national or by local government, this legal framework is of crucial importance. When services are provided by charities or private companies there is also a

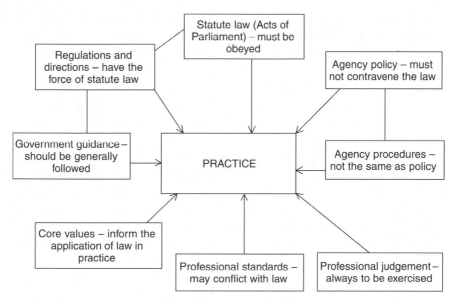

Figure 5.1   Law, policy and practice

need for legal regulation, although these organisations do not generally have statutory duties.

It is important to understand the difference between *powers* and *duties*. Powers *enable* people or organisations to do things which they could not otherwise do; this is important for local government in a state like the United Kingdom, because it is illegal for a local authority to spend public money on purposes for which they are not authorised. Duties, on the other hand, *require* agencies to exercise their functions in specified ways.

It is also important to understand clearly the relationship between law, policy and guidance, to be able to distinguish *statute law* from other kinds of ruling, and to put law in the context of all the other factors that determine good practice (see Figure 5.1).

Statute law, otherwise known as Acts of Parliament, must be obeyed. This applies both to the main sections of an Act and to the accompanying Schedules, which tend to go into more detail. Regulations and directions issued by government in pursuance of an Act of Parliament also have the force of law. Guidance issued by government departments does not have the direct force of law in the same way. However, it should generally be followed, and there is a legal requirement to have regard to such guidance if issued formally under the prescribed legislation. Such 'formal policy guidance' issued in England and Wales under Section 7 of the Local Government Act 1970, cannot be departed from without good reason after due consideration. 'General practice guidance' not issued under Section 7 should certainly not be ignored, but does not have the same force. Brammer (2003) gives a fuller explanation of this distinction.

There has been a tendency in recent years for child care law and policy to become increasingly prescriptive – not content with telling agencies and professionals *what* must be done, it also often specifies *how* it should be done. This was a striking feature of the Children Act 1989 in comparison with preceding legislation – when the Act was implemented in 1991, ten volumes of guidance and regulation were published with it.

The policy of a social work agency does not have legal force, and indeed it must not contravene the law. However, no social worker would want to disregard the official policy of the their employing agency without a very good reason, and the same applies to agency procedures. Procedures are not the same as policies – in general terms, a policy sets out the agency's priorities and objectives, whereas a procedure specifies what steps will be taken to implement them in specific cases.

A social worker practising in a field such as child care therefore has to pay attention to what the law says, to the content of official government guidance, and also to the policies and procedures of her or his employing agency. However, that is not all. It is also necessary to pay attention to the core values that inform the application of law in practice. These include traditional 'bedrock' principles of law such as natural justice, due process, the right to freedom from intrusion and limits on state power, as well as the duty of care held by those providing services, especially when there is an element of compulsion. Finally, as a professional, a social work practitioner has professional standards and professional ethics to follow. These may on occasion conflict with the law, and perhaps more often may conflict with agency policies and procedures. However well thought-out and clear the laws and rules under which we operate, there is no escaping the need for professional judgment. In the sensitive situations and complex decisions that arise when children and young people are in care, such judgement always demands to be exercised.

I argue that the key professional obligations of the social worker operating under the law are:

(1) to use the law to promote ethical and effective practice;
(2) to have regard not just to the letter of the law but to its underlying principles;
(3) to challenge oppression and discrimination.

Law, family policy and national cultures

Legal systems differ in the provision they make for children's welfare and for parenting. These differences may reflect wider differences in the legal systems in different countries. They also reflect differences in social policy towards children and families, and differences in national cultures. Some cultures make no provision for legal adoption. Some legal systems make it very difficult to remove parents' rights over their children, while others will only allow children to come into care if parental rights are removed.

Kamerman and Kahn (1978) suggest that some countries have family policies that are explicit and comprehensive with clear overarching goals, while others only have 'implicit and reluctant' family policies. They include the US and the UK in the latter group, although this may perhaps need some revision now in the case of the UK. As we mentioned in Chapter 1, Fox Harding (1997) argues that child welfare policy in the UK is characterised by four competing value positions: *laissez-faire*, state paternalism, parents' rights and children's rights, but that the dominant elements are parental rights and state paternalism.

Most of the discussion in this book of the law relating to the care of children will be based on the law in the UK, and in particular England and Wales. However, I will try to take note of the different legal arrangements in Scotland and in Northern Ireland, and there will also be occasional mention of legislation in the Irish Republic, in other parts of Europe and in other English-speaking countries of the world. The English-speaking countries tend to have broadly similar legal systems and often similar approaches to decision making about children, even when their family policies are markedly different.

The law governing the care of children and young people

Whatever the national context, modern legal systems dealing with the care of children and young people usually make provision for the following:

- the circumstances in which children are to be cared for voluntarily;
- the circumstances in which children may be removed from home compulsorily;
- the arrangements to be made for children looked after away from home;
- services designed to support children in their own families;
- arrangements for aftercare;
- arrangements for adoption.

In this chapter we will look in particular at how these provisions have been designed in the United Kingdom, and in particular in England and Wales. It is not the aim of this book to give a history of child care policy either in the UK or more widely – the Guide to Further Reading at the end of the chapter gives some suggestions for finding out about this. However, it is worth drawing attention to a couple of key historical moments which have strongly influenced the way in which care services are provided in Britain. The first was the enactment of the Children Act 1948. As part of the postwar settlement of the 'welfare state', this Act established a principle that care could be provided at the request of, and by agreement with, families who were unable temporarily to look after their own children, with a view to their eventual return. It also introduced a principle that the care provided should as far as possible be similar to the care given to children living with their own families. It was followed 15 years later by a law – the Children and Young Persons Act 1963 – that gave local authorities powers and duties to support children in their own homes.

The Children Act 1948 was introduced in part as a response to specific concerns about the ill-treatment of children in foster care, following the death of a young man at the hand of his foster parent, and it placed a strong emphasis on supervision and monitoring of children's welfare. This emphasis continued through the postwar years, in particular from the mid 1970s onwards with a series of official inquiries into the deaths of children in care or under supervision. It is arguable that this reinforced a tendency in British law and policy to concentrate on surveillance and on legalistic, even punitive, responses to the need for child welfare services; see Parton (1991) for a discussion of this.

The approach taken to these matters in other European countries is often different. For instance, there is sometimes a greater emphasis on preventative and therapeutic services, even where children may be being seriously harmed, rather than taking legal action against families. Even when the courts do become involved, this may be in a more conciliatory way than the adversarial approach that is dominant in the UK and other English-speaking countries. There is also a greater emphasis in some European countries on residential care, and on the links between social work and education (see Chapter 11). Although social work theory and practice in the past have tended to look more to the English-speaking world to share ideas, increasingly it will become important to learn from other European countries, especially as laws and institutional practices in the countries of the European Union begin to converge.

The Children Act 1989 in England and Wales

Current legal provision in England and Wales is dominated by the Children Act 1989. The Act is more wide-ranging than previous legislation in that it brings together in a single statutory framework the 'public law' regarding state services to children and child protection and the 'private law' that governs family life and disputes over children's upbringing. This has made it possible for courts to make decisions about children in complex cases without some of the confusion that arose in the past, and it means that where children are placed compulsorily in state care this is done under the same rules and principles in all cases. As well as reforming the ways in which courts intervene in family disputes and the kind of decisions they can make, the Act also reformed the duties and powers of local authorities to children and families and the ways in which services are provided, especially when children are looked after away from home. It did so on the basis of a set of overarching principles contained in Section 1 of the Act and often referred to as the 'welfare principles', of which the chief is that when a court is making a decision about the upbringing of a child it should treat the child's interests as paramount.

Other important principles in the Act include: the concept of 'parental responsibility', which cannot be taken away from a parent except by adoption and means that parents who separate or divorce, or whose children go into care, are expected to remain involved in their children's lives; and the 'presumption of contact' – the presumption that contact is normally in the interests of children and should be positively promoted when a child is separated from parents and other family members, unless there are good and specific reasons to the contrary.

The Children Act and family disputes

The Act provides for disputes between parents and other relatives to be settled under these principles. The assumption is that children's upbringing will be a matter of agreement between those involved, without the need for legal intervention. The court only becomes involved if the parties cannot agree and one of them applies for an order to be made. The orders which can be made by the court under Section 8 of the Act, often referred to as 'Section 8 orders', are:

- a *residence order*, which determines with whom the child is to live (this may be with more than one person);
- a *contact order,* which requires the person who has the care of the child to allow contact between the child and someone else;
- a *prohibited steps order*, which prevents the person with the care of the child from doing certain things which they might otherwise do in their role as a parent;
- a *specific issue order*, which enables the court to resolve a specific issue by a particular order, without disturbing other arrangements for the child's upbringing.

These orders are also available to a court in care proceedings, which means that they can sometimes be used as alternatives to committing a child to care (see below).

The Children Act and support for children and families

There has been some state responsibility for supporting children and families in need since at least the seventeenth century, mainly focused on the provision of accommodation. In 1908 local authorities were first given responsibilities to accommodate children who were removed from home by the courts. In 1948 they were also given a duty to receive into care any child who needed it as a result of the child's parents being unable to provide adequate care. In 1963 there was added a further duty to provide services to children and families to *prevent* reception into care. The legal framework that was introduced in 1989 is different from what went before, in that instead of starting from a child needing care and working backwards to 'prevention' the Children Act starts by defining 'need'.

Section 17 of the Children Act 1989 provides that a child who is unlikely to achieve or maintain a reasonable standard of health or development without the provision of services by the local authority, or whose health or development is likely to be significantly impaired without the provision of services, or who is disabled, is 'in need' for the purposes of the Act. This means that the local authority has duties and powers in relation to the child and his or her family. There is a general duty to safeguard and promote the welfare of such children, and 'so far as is consistent with that duty', to promote their upbringing by their families, by providing a range and level of services appropriate to their needs. There are also specific duties which include providing a range of specific services, assessing children's needs, preventing neglect and abuse, and providing accommodation if it is necessary for the child's welfare.

Equivalent legislation in Scotland and Northern Ireland

The Children (Scotland) Act 1995 fills the same place in Scottish law as does the Children Act 1989 in England and Wales. The Children (Scotland) Act is based on similar principles, although it differs in important respects from the English and Welsh legislation. Scotland has always had its own legal system, and since 1999 has had its own Parliament, although some powers are still reserved to the UK Parliament.

Northern Ireland was under direct rule from London at the time of the reform of child care law, and the Children (Northern Ireland) Order 1995 takes the place of the Children Act there. This Order is in many respects identical to the Children Act, although it also includes provisions relating to child employment, unmarried parents and guardianship. At the time of writing the Northern Ireland Assembly is not fully operational – when it is, child care policy in the province may begin to take a different direction.

Wales has had its own National Assembly since 1999 and some legislation is now specific to Wales – for instance, the Children's Commissioner for Wales Act 2001. However, the Children Act 1989 applies uniformly across England and Wales.

The Irish Republic of course as an independent state has its own completely separate legal provision. Although there are some similarities between the

Child Care Act 1991 in Ireland and the Children Act 1989, the former only deals with the public law – it does not bring together public and private law in the way that the Children Act 1989 and the Children (Scotland) Act 1995 do in their respective jurisdictions.

Care and accommodation under the Children Act

The Children Act 1989 was intended to achieve several objectives in relation to the provision of care and accommodation for children and young people. It sought to reduce the perceived stigma of reception into care, by changing the terminology and by dealing with parents' justified fears that if they 'put' their children in care voluntarily it might be hard to get them back. The Act did this by drawing a clear distinction between 'care' as the outcome of a court order and 'accommodation' provided on a voluntary basis. It sought to improve the way in which family support services were provided in order to make them more access-ible and helpful, by starting from a clear definition of a 'child in need' – and also to make it clear that providing accommodation could be a constructive way to support children and families, rather than a last resort. It clarified the basis on which children could be removed from their parents, with the dual aim of mak-ing the legal process fairer and of enabling children to be protected when they were *at risk* of harm as well as when they had actually suffered harm.

The Act also aimed to improve the quality and rigour of planning and decision making in relation to children being looked after away from home, and to give clear rights to children and parents to take an active part in these processes and to complain when they were aggrieved. These reforms were inspired in part by research in the 1970s and 1980s which showed how poor existing decision-making processes often were in these respects. Underpinning much of the thinking behind the Act, though not specifically mentioned in it, was the idea of *partnership* – between parents, between professionals, and above all between families and agencies.

The Act shared many of these aims with the equivalent legislation in Scotland and other places. Many countries reviewed or reformed their child welfare law at around the same time – for instance Germany, where the new law KJGH was introduced in 1991, and New Zealand, where the Children, Young Persons and their Families Act 1989 is notable for having established 'family group conferences' (see Chapters 6 and 7).

Accommodation

Under Section 20 of the Act a local authority has a duty to provide accommo-dation for any child in need in their area who appears to require it because there is no one with parental responsibility, because the child is lost or abandoned, or because the person with parental responsibility is prevented 'for whatever reason' from providing suitable accommodation or care. Accommodating a child under this section normally requires the agreement of someone with parental responsibility, but a child who is aged 16 years or over can agree to be accommodated in his or her own right.

It should be noted that local authorities also have a duty under Section 21 to accommodate children who are remanded by the court, are subject to an emergency protection order (see below) or have been taken into police protection. In these cases it is not necessary for the child or parents to agree to accommodation being provided – they have little choice.

There is also a power given to local authorities to provide accommodation for any child if this would safeguard or promote the child's welfare. Voluntary organisations may also accommodate children, in which case their duties are the same as those of a local authority.

Care and supervision orders

Part IV of the Children Act 1989 relates to 'care and supervision' of children. It sets out the circumstances in which children may be removed from their families or the powers of parents restricted, and the process by which this may be done. This can only happen if the court is satisfied that the child is suffering or likely to suffer significant harm and that the harm is attributable to the care given to the child not being what it would be reasonable to expect a parent to give to her or him, or to the child being beyond control. 'Harm' is defined as ill-treatment or the impairment of health or development.

Once these threshold criteria have been established, care proceedings become 'family proceedings' in which the 'welfare principles' apply and Section 8 orders are available to the court in addition to care and supervision orders which can only be made in care proceedings. A care order made in such proceedings commits the child to the care of the local authority until the age of 18, and the local authority acquires parental responsibility for the child.

In Part V of the Act provision is also made for emergency intervention and assessment of children thought to be at risk. Orders made under this part of the Act (emergency protection orders and assessment orders) do not mean that a child is 'in care', although she or he may be accommodated for a short period.

'Looked after' children

The Children Act introduced a new category of 'looked after' children. This includes all children who are either accommodated or 'in care'. The agency has a duty to promote the child's welfare, and to ensure that the child is provided with accommodation suitable to her or his needs. This accommodation may be provided by the agency directly or by other people under the agency's supervision.

The local authority also has a number of other duties to children whom they look after: to consult the child, parents and others whose wishes and feelings are relevant before making any decision; to take account of 'the child's religious persuasion, racial origin and cultural and linguistic background' in making decisions; to place and maintain the child in a family, in a community home or in another suitable placement; as far as practicable and consistent with the child's interests, to place the child near to her or his home and with her or his siblings; and to ensure that accommodation provided for a disabled child is 'not unsuitable'.

The agency is also under a duty to 'advise, assist and befriend' the child in order to promote her or his welfare on leaving care, and then to provide after-care; to review the child's case at regular intervals and to hear any complaints and representations from the child, parents or carers. The agency is not entitled to restrict the child's liberty except when authorised by a court or in a specific emergency.

Planning and reviewing

The Children Act 1989 sought to reform the whole process of planning and decision making for children and young people in care. It does this mainly through regulations (the Arrangements for Placement Regulations 1991), which require that any child being looked after should be subject to 'arrangements' and which specify what should be included in these arrangements and how they are to be agreed. In particular it is made clear that the arrangements must be based on a plan, that the plan must be based on a thorough assessment, and that it should take account of the views of the child and the family.

Regulations under the Act also specify the arrangements for monitoring the child's progress and reviewing the plan. They spell out how often reviews are to take place, who is to be involved, and how decisions are to be recorded.

Leaving care and after care

The Children Act 1989 and the Children (Scotland) Act 1995 also aimed to improve services for care leavers, by extending the duties and powers of local authorities. However, these reforms were perceived to be insufficient, and a decade later amending legislation was introduced to deal with this – the Children (Leaving Care) Act 2000 and the Regulation of Care (Scotland) Act 2001. These reforms are discussed more fully in Chapter 10.

The law governing adoption

Adoption, because it involves irrevocable changes to parenting relationships and children's status in families, is often dealt with under legislation that is distinct from that governing other aspects of child welfare. This is the case in England and Wales, where adoption law has tended to develop quite separately since the first Adoption Act in 1926. (The Children Act 1975, unusually, did reform adoption along with other aspects of child care, but this still led to a separate Adoption Act in 1976.)

The intention of the government at the time of the Children Act 1989 was to review adoption law immediately, in order to extend to the field of adoption the welfare principles that underpin the Children Act. However, the subject became something of a political football during the 1990s, and although the review of adoption law was completed by 1993 it was another decade before the law was changed. The Adoption and Children Act 2002 is the result, as we shall see in Chapter 9.

Translating law and policy into practice

In the opening part of this chapter I emphasised the individual responsibility of a social worker in practice with children and families to understand the law relating to this area of practice, and the policies that are associated with the law, and to use professional judgement and professional standards in applying this to actual cases within a framework of agency policy and procedure (see Figure 5.1).

This is of course not the only mechanism by which law and government policy are translated into practice. Agencies such as local authorities and charitable organisations also have systems for ensuring that their working practices reflect the law. Agencies have their own 'take' on what are the most important imperatives to follow, and sometimes on the interpretation they give to the law – as do individual social workers, inevitably.

Governments also have their own view of what are the most important priorities and on how best to apply the law in practice. In recent years governments have increasingly adopted explicit strategies to make sure that the policy imperatives that drive legislation are implemented in agency practice. Social work and social policy in Britain have been characterised by a series of initiatives, as central government becomes more proactive in driving the direction in which services develop and the priorities that are set, and in attempting to improve the perceived quality of practice. Garrett (2003) offers a helpful analysis of the history and politics of these initiatives in the field of child care. In the chapters that follow we will look at the practical and theoretical implications of some of these initiatives.

Relationships between social work responsibilities and those of other agencies

Although much of this discussion has been about social work, social work is never a service that can work in isolation from other agencies and professions. In providing care services for children and young people it is essential to work closely with health and education services, and also with police, housing and a range of other services. These services also have their own distinctive legal powers and duties, and a shared understanding of these is essential to working effectively in collaboration.

As I said in Chapter 2, one of the principles underlying this book is to understand and work with children and young people in a holistic way – not, for instance, putting their care, health and education needs into separate compartments. When the law supports this approach it is of course helpful, but even when it does not it is the responsibility of all professionals working with children and young people to see that they do their best individually and collectively to follow this holistic approach.

Summary and conclusion

We have seen how the law is a crucial underpinning for social work practice with children and families, providing the framework within which services are planned and delivered and the authority for intervention. We have also seen that the law is the result of social and political processes, and reflects prevailing assumptions – for instance, about the relationship between families and the state and about the status of children. We have looked at the assumptions underlying child care law in the United Kingdom, at the objectives of current legislation and at the framework it provides for the care of children and young people. Some of the specifics of this legislation are considered in more detail in later chapters, particularly in relation to leaving care and to adoption. Finally, we looked briefly at the process of translating law and policy into practice, and at the relationships between social work and other professions. It is important to remember that as social workers we can never operate in isolation from the rest of society or from other agencies and disciplines. At the same time we have to take responsibility for our own professional judgement and ethical conduct, and for the way in which we work with vulnerable young people and their families.

GUIDE TO FURTHER READING

On social work law in general there are a number of useful and reasonably up-to-date British texts – for example Ball, McDonald and McGhee (2002), Brammer (2003), Brayne and Carr (2003), Cull and Roche (2001). Slightly older, but still useful on using the law in practice, are Braye and Preston-Shoot (1997) and Dalrymple and Burke (1995).

For child care law specifically, useful practical guides to the Children Act 1989 are Allen (1999) and Ryan (1999); also helpful are Stainton Rogers and Roche (1994). There are number of guides that include the text of the Act and an explanation, of which the most up-to-date at the time of writing is Hershman and McFarlane (2002). The Children (Scotland) Act 1995 is similarly treated in McNorrie (1995).

For similar accounts of adoption law I recommend Bridge and Swindells (2003) for England and Wales, McNeil (1998) for Scotland. On Scottish child care law generally, Plumtree (1997) provides a good brief summary and guide to further reading.

For British readers interested in learning more about European law and policy, Ruxton (1996) is a good introduction; Colton and Hellinckx (1993) provide a focused review of care provision in 12 European countries, and Pringle (1998) offers a broader analysis of patterns of child welfare across Europe. For an interesting discussion of how care is provided in the 'majority world', I recommend Tolfree (1995).

For a brief account of the development of child care services, Hayden et al. (1999) is useful. For a more extended and analytical approach, Hendrick (2003) is authoritative and stimulating. On the relationship between law and policy, Fox Harding (1997) and Parton (1991) have lots of interesting things to say.

Practice

Assessment and planning

Introduction

Individual assessment is not an inevitable part of providing care for children and young people. There are many examples in history of care systems which have allocated placements on a predetermined basis – whether it be to orphanages or other institutions, or to forms of family-based care. Decisions as to what care to provide may be made on the basis of moral and political principles as to what is appropriate for society to provide, or on the basis of economic factors that determine what resources are available. Decisions may also be made according to the social class and status of the child or young person, their age or gender, or the reasons why they need care. All these factors still have a bearing on decisions in contemporary child care systems, as we shall see. However, the idea that each child is entitled to a personalised individual assessment of her or his needs and circumstances is a modern one, largely characteristic of highly developed and affluent societies since the middle of the twentieth century.

In this chapter we will look at how this individualised assessment and planning is done. We will consider first the *content* and then the *processes* of assessment and planning, although it is not always possible or desirable to keep the two completely separate. Through all this we will keep a strong emphasis on the involvement of children and young people in decisions about their care, as well as on partnership with families and with a range of professionals and service providers. We will conclude by looking at some attempts that have been made to introduce more systematic approaches to assessment and planning, such as the *Looking After Children* system.

Milner and O'Byrne (2002) point to the similarity between the activity of assessment and that of qualitative research – especially 'participatory' research. They emphasise the need for social workers to be clear about their intentions, explicit about their assumptions and systematic in their approach to data collection, to think theoretically and clarify and test hypotheses rigorously; and at the same time to be 'actively accountable for their values' (p. 4), to engage with people and listen to how they understand their own worlds. Much of the guidance offered to social workers doing assessment work with children and young people is based on a search for objective answers to questions about children's needs and how they can best be met. This search is important, but it is equally important to remember that there is more than one way of understanding any reality. However we do our assessments, and whatever tools or frameworks we use, we should always be striving to do it *with* people rather than *to* them.

What is being assessed?

Assessment does not happen all at once. Sometimes decisions have to be taken quickly without waiting for a full assessment. Sometimes key information is not available when we first need it, and so has to be fitted into the picture later. All situations change, and assessments usually have to be revised at some point. As the official guidance in England and Wales puts it, assessment is 'a continuing process, not a single event ... Assessment should continue throughout a period of intervention, and intervention may start at the beginning of an assessment' (Department of Health et al. 2000, pp. 14–15).

Assessment is also a dynamic process that involves constantly testing assumptions and hypotheses in the light of emerging understanding – it is arguable that the process begins when a social work relationship begins and does not end until the relationship ends.

In addition, the process of assessment may follow different patterns in different cases, depending on the situation and the people involved. Still, it is useful to have a simple framework or sequence in mind, while recognising that it will not often be followed in strict order. The sequence usually goes something like this:

- collecting information
- analysing the information
- consulting
- preparing a plan
- implementing and reviewing

In this section we will be looking in particular at the collection and analysis of information. It is useful to think of this under something like the following categories:

- the presenting problem or reason for assessment
- the individual child or young person
- the strengths and resources of the immediate and extended family
- the strengths and resources of the community or neighbourhood
- the ability of the family and community to meet the child's needs
- the contribution of health and welfare agencies

The presenting problem or reason for assessment

It is important to be clear from the start about why *this* assessment is being undertaken at *this* time, so that the assessment can focus on the specific issues that need to be resolved – while also looking at the child and her/his life holistically. It is also important to take account of what assessment may already have been done. If a family has already been assessed by other professionals before they meet the social worker, then making sense of what is already known may be more useful than asking the child and family yet more questions. For example, if it has already been established that there are no significant health issues, the assessment may not need to address this dimension.

If it is known in advance that there are particular *risks* that need to be addressed, then it is important to clarify this and ensure that it is understood by everyone involved in the assessment.

The individual child or young person

Every assessment starts with a consideration of the individual child or young person who is its subject – her or his situation, personality and characteristics, and needs. This includes basic information about the child or young person's origins, background and identity, age and gender, social class and ethnicity. It is important to start by collecting this information fully and accurately, if we are to have a rounded – and grounded – understanding of the child in his or her situation.

Our consideration of the individual child or young person also includes looking at her or his patterns of relationships with others, both within the family and outside. We should ask, how does this child engage with the world, and in particular how does this child interact with other people? What messages has s/he already learned about the world and her/his place in it? This should also include a consideration of her/his patterns of attachment (see Chapter 7).

One important aim of this part of the assessment is to get a clear idea of the child or young person's *needs*. Although there are some problems with the concept of children's needs, as we saw in Chapter 3, it is not practical to avoid using the concept in assessment and planning for children and young people. Bryer (1988) distinguishes between the overall needs of a child or young person and the *priority* needs – those, as she puts it, 'which must be met in order that the child's development will not be delayed or damaged' (p. 29). These priority needs may well be the ones which have caused people to consider providing substitute care, and they are likely to be in the forefront of people's minds. It is important to be as clear as possible about these priority needs, so that whatever plan is made can address them effectively. However, it can be all too easy to concentrate on the more dramatic and obvious needs and in the process fail to attend properly to other important aspects of the child's life. This is especially so when children are admitted to care in a crisis, or when they move around repeatedly. Research frequently shows how outcomes for children and young people can be impaired when their basic needs – the needs that all children and young people have – are neglected in the care system. It is partly for this reason that the *Looking After Children* system and the *Framework for the Assessment of Children in Need and their Families*, which we discuss later in this chapter, are built around seven developmental dimensions – health, education, identity, family and social relationships, social presentation, emotional and behavioural development and self-care skills – which reflect these 'ordinary' needs that all children have.

In relation to priority needs (and this also applies to risks), Bryer also points out that 'it is useless to identify what these needs are unless at the same time the cause of each need is identified' (p. 29), because the causation will have implications for the kind of care plan that is required to address the need in question. So from the beginning our investigation of the child's situation demands theory and analysis, for instance about the effects on children and their development of different factors in their background or environment.

Our investigation of the child's situation also demands specificity. We must continually be asking, 'What is life actually like for *this* child or young person? What are *this* child's expectations for the future?' In considering the situation of a child or young person and what are her/his needs, we should thinking both about her/his development into adulthood and also about what life is like for her/him now. Partly for this reason, our assessment of the individual child or young person will be incomplete if we are not able to get in touch with how s/he understands her/his own situation. Never forget that children – like adults – are experts on their own lives, they usually know more about their own lives than anyone else, and they have usually spent more time thinking about their own lives than has anyone else. They can therefore be rich sources of both information and ideas. This is consistent with an approach to assessment that seeks to do it *with* people rather than *to* them.

The strengths and resources of the immediate and extended family

Opinions differ on the relative impact of the family and other social institutions, such as the school or the peer group, on children and young people's lives and development. However, the family is where children spend most of their lives, especially when young, and where they receive most of their day-to-day care. The family therefore has massive potential to do good or harm to a child, and an understanding of the strengths and the resources of the family and of what it has to offer the child is a critically important part of our assessment. In reviewing the present and past, knowledge of family functioning will be a key to explaining the child or young person's situation and to understanding any difficulties. In looking at the future, whether the child or young person is likely to remain living with the family or whether plans are being made for an alternative placement, it will be important to know what can be expected of the family.

A family *history* will provide an indispensable background for the rest of our assessment. What have been the key events in the lives of family members? What is their educational and economic background? What kind of health and other problems have there been? It is particularly important to collect this information in respect of the child's parents or carers, but we also need to understand what has been happening with other family members – brothers and sisters, grandparents, aunts and uncles.

In the same way when we look at family *functioning* – who has what roles, how the family relates together, and how well the needs of family members are met – it is important to look broadly and with an open mind. There are many different family patterns, and different family members may be important to the child either because they provide care or because of their emotional relationships with the child. It is therefore important to consider everyone, and not just focus on the parents – or as often happens, the mother.

Nonetheless, the next step is to look closely at the quality of *parenting* being provided to the child; and the information we have obtained concerning the family history and functioning should inform our assessment of parenting. Our assessment of the quality of parenting is important for two reasons. One is because it may help us to understand the child as he or she is at present, and in particular to understand any difficulties that he or she may have. The other is because in order to make a plan for the child in the future we need to establish what contribution the family can be expected to make. If we are considering leaving or placing the child with the family, we need to know whether they can provide what is needed and what support will be required. If the child is being placed elsewhere, we still need to know whether we should be aiming for her/his eventual return to the family, and what contact arrangements are realistic.

The association between certain problems affecting parents and the quality of care received by children has been well researched – this applies particularly to mental disorder, drug and alcohol problems, and domestic violence (see Cleaver et al. 1999 for a very useful summary). When these problems are found in combination, the effect on children can be especially marked. It is therefore important to have a good understanding of what the parents' own lives are like, in order to be clear about what they can offer the child or young person.

In the end, however, we must look at what the parenting is in reality like for *this* child, and whether it is 'good enough' or can become 'good enough'. In assessing this, we have to take account of all those issues of standards and comparability that we discussed in Chapter 1. That means that we must be aware of cultural variations in patterns of child care, and sensitive to the cultural variations in expectations of children at different ages. It also means that our judgement will in the last analysis be guided by general accepted standards in our society, as well as by the law. A basic question should be, 'What care and upbringing does any child or young person living in this society have a right to expect, and what does that mean in practice for *this* child or young person?'

In considering both the parents and the wider family, we should be thinking about what they can offer the child, bearing in mind what we have learned about the child's needs (see below), and also thinking about any danger that they may present to the child. At the same time we must not forget that family members have needs of their own. The fact that our primary obligation is to 'safeguard and promote the welfare' (in the words of the Children Act 1989) of a particular child does not mean we should not also consider the interests and the wishes of other family members, both children and adults. Difficult issues can arise when more than one child in a family is in need of care, and an assessment of the quality of sibling relationships will be essential in tackling these.

The strengths and resources of the community or neighbourhood

Children do not live only in their families. A large part of a child's welfare is dependent on the neighbourhood and the community. There have been moments in the history of social work when there has been a tendency to neglect this dimension in favour of a concentration on the individual or the family, and this has certainly been true of social work with children and young people. Although it has never completely gone away, in recent years there has been some re-growth of interest in the wider community and its impact on children's welfare, and in 'ecological' approaches that attempt to integrate individual, family, community and sometimes wider society perspectives into our understanding.

Jack (2001) provides a helpful introduction to this way of thinking about child welfare. He points out the value to both parents and children of having reliable relationships outside the family and the importance of a clear assessment of the positive and negative potential of the family's social networks. He also reminds us of the value of 'natural support systems' and of informal sources of support that are based on choice and give opportunities for reciprocation. These supports are sometimes described as *social capital* (Putnam 2000).

Just as with our assessment of the quality of parenting, making an assessment of the strengths and resources of the community is important because it may help us to understand the child as he or she is at present, and because it may help in planning for the future to establish what contribution the community can be expected to make – especially if we are considering leaving or placing the child at home, but also in relation to continuing contact or eventual return.

In this part of the assessment we should be asking:

- What physical resources are available in the local and wider community to support the child and the family? This includes economic opportunities, educational and recreational facilities, transport and shopping, as well as child care resources such as mother and toddler groups, childminders, affordable nurseries, baby-sitting services, youth clubs and activities.
- What social supports are available to the child and family? Are there good networks around and are they in practice accessible to this child and this family? If not, can this be addressed?
- How well integrated are the child and family into their community and neighbourhood? Are their patterns of social relationships helpful to them or are they in themselves problematic?
- What is the quality of the child and family's housing? Do they have sufficient income?

A good model for evaluating how well the wider community can help to meet the needs of children and families is in Penn and Gough (2002). Jack (2001) also points to a number of useful guides to assessing the strengths of networks and to understanding local communities more generally. These ideas are developed further in Jack and Gill (2003).

The ability of the family and community to meet the child's needs

Having collected and analysed our information about the child, the family and the community, we have to ask directly how well *this* family and *this* community, with their identified strengths and weaknesses, can meet the identified needs of *this* child or young person. It can be helpful to tabulate the identified needs, starring with the general needs of this child or young person. These can be expressed in terms of a typology of needs such as that used by Bryer (physical, emotional, social, educational, ethical), or of the dimensions of child's developmental needs used in the *Looking After Children* system (health, education, emotional and behavioural development, identity, family and social relationships, social presentation, self-care skills) – whichever model is used, it is important to have some clarity and consistency in the way in which this is done. It should then be possible to evaluate how, and how well, these needs are currently being met within the family and the community.

Having done this exercise we turn our attention to the child's *priority* needs – both those already identified as such, and any unmet needs identified by the exercise we have just carried out. The task here is to look at how these priority and unmet needs might be met within the child's existing networks of parents, family, friends, neighbours and the wider community. Although the exercise is about assessing a child or young person's needs for care, this does not mean we start by assuming that alternative care arrangements will need to be made. On the contrary, we should always start by looking at how the identified needs can be adequately met within a version of the existing living arrangements – in the words of the Children Act 1989, 'so long as that is consistent with the child's welfare'.

The contribution of health and welfare agencies

At the same time we have to ask critically about the ability of service agencies to meet the child's needs. This follows from what we have just said about the aim of the assessment, and there are three particular reasons why this is important. First, we do not want to make the mistake of planning substitute care for a child on the basis of an assessment of the family's inability to meet the identified needs, without being confident that the alternative is actually going to be significantly better. Second, we do not want to miss the possibility that professional agencies can provide additional help and support which might enable satisfactory care to be provided in the family. Even when parents are unable to change their style of parenting very much, it may be that with enough practical support they can provide a better experience for children than the alternative of being separated from their parents and sometimes from each other, and perhaps facing a series of moves in care. This applies particularly to some parents with learning difficulties, and to large families. Third, even if the conclusion of the assessment is that on balance it is in the child's interests to be placed elsewhere, there may still be needs which can be better met by the family or the community. It is implicit in work based on concepts of 'shared care' and 'partnership' that no party has a monopoly of ability and resources to meet a child's needs.

Processes of assessment and planning

The process of assessment

I mentioned earlier that assessment tends to follow a logical sequence, even if it does not keep strictly to this in chronological terms. In addition to the reasons given earlier, this is because information gathering and analysis cannot be entirely sequential. We are analysing information as soon as we begin to collect it, and this initial analysis affects our view of what other information we need to collect. To an extent, therefore, data collection and analysis go on in parallel with each other. In fact, extending Milner and O'Byrne's (2002) comparison of social work assessment with qualitative research, we might say that this aspect of assessment resembles the model known as 'grounded theory', where analytic categories develop during the analysis of the data as they emerge, rather than a pre-existing hypothetical framework being brought to the research. I would not want to take this analogy too far, because there are many explanatory models relevant to social work assessment with children and families, in addition to our own practice knowledge, which mean that it would not be good practice to start with a completely open mind for each assessment. Nevertheless it is important to preserve an open mind to some degree.

The other general point to make about the process of assessment concerns the relationship between the social worker's professional responsibility for the quality of assessment and for his or her own judgement, and the need to work in partnership with other professionals, with family members, and with children and young people. There has been an increasing emphasis in recent years both on ensuring that children and families are able to express their views and on making assessment multidisciplinary. However, there can be a tension between including a range of professionals in the process and making it genuinely open and accessible to children and families, who may have quite different expectations and styles of communication. The social worker has an important responsibility for ensuring that everyone can contribute appropriately to the process, so that each person's knowledge and views can become part of the overall assessment.

The social worker is also responsible for managing the collection and analysis of information. The collection of information is achieved in several different ways. Some of it will be available in written form – from agency records (which should always be consulted carefully), reports and correspondence. Some of it will depend on observation – for instance, of parents with children, and perhaps of the child in other settings. Much of it will be gathered by talking – and more importantly *listening* – to people, either individually or in groups, and this is a doubly important part of the process because it often in effect combines the collection of information with consultation about the analysis, and sometimes also with the discussion of possible plans.

There are a number of practical tools which can be enormously helpful in getting information about the child and family. These are well used and available from many different sources, which is testament to their usefulness. One is the flow chart, which is a helpful diagrammatic way of showing key events in the history of a child or family. A second is the ecomap, which can be drawn to show the most important relationships and links in a child's current life. The third is the genogram, which is a bit like a family tree and is a good graphic way of describing a set of family relationship and explaining family history. Each of these tools can make the process of collecting information much easier and more comfortable for people, and can also help to draw attention to key elements of a child's situation which might otherwise be missed.

Analysing information is a crucial part of the assessment process. There is no point in collecting masses of information if there is then no attempt to make sense of it. What sometimes happens in practice is that people move straight from collecting the information to formulating a plan, without any systematic reflection. This undoubtedly means that assumptions are being made about the significance of information, but that these assumptions are not really being questioned. When things are done this way it is likely that certain pieces of information will be given a significance that is disproportionate to what is really justified – and the wrong plans will be made! Adcock (2001) distinguishes between different stages of reflection and analysis, which she calls 'putting meaning to the situation', 'reaching an understanding of what is happening' and 'making judgements' (which is different from 'making decisions').

Proper space must therefore be made for analysing all the information that has been collected. Some of this will happen as it is being collected, as we have mentioned – but then it is important to bring it all together in an organised way. It is really helpful to have a proper framework for this, one that is already understood by at least some of the people involved in the assessment, who can then explain it to others. At the conclusion of this chapter, when we review some of the systematic approaches to assessment and planning that have been developed, we will see that there are some useful analytical tools among them.

The process of planning

A key moment in the overall process we are considering in this chapter is the move from 'assessment' to 'planning'. Although in practice the two processes may often happen together, there is an important conceptual distinction between the collection and analysis of information in order to produce a judgement about what needs to be done, and the formation of a consequent plan of action to achieve the objectives that follow from the assessment. In part it is a move from past and present to future – from a consideration of what is happening, of the causes of problems and the meaning of events, to a contemplation of what is to be done and a prediction of what is likely to happen (which is also why we often need contingency plans).

There are different models of planning that are relevant to our purposes here. Models vary in a number of different ways, perhaps most interestingly in the weight they place on participation. At one extreme is a process of planning controlled by one or two professionals – perhaps the social worker and his or her supervisor – with other people being consulted at an appropriate point or points. Conversely, the process can be managed in a much more collaborative way, with what is in effect shared decision making between a group of professionals and family members. This is likely to involve a meeting or series of meetings, and the process is likely to be managed by a chair – who may have a dual responsibility, both to conduct proceedings fairly and see that everyone has a chance to express their view, and to ensure that the eventual outcome is acceptable to the agency. At the other end of this continuum, perhaps, is the family group conference, where the immediate and extended family are the decision takers, within certain constraints and with the advice and support of professionals.

Bryer suggests that the aim of the planning process is to construct what she calls a 'blueprint', specifying what should happen to the child with as much specificity as possible. I am not entirely comfortable with the term 'blueprint', because it seems to me to imply a greater level of detail and definition than is realistic or desirable. However, I think I understand Margaret Bryer's purpose in using it, which is to remind us that when we plan for a child's future we are aiming to build something that will work and that will last – and that just as an architect designing a building, or an engineer designing an aircraft, has to specify exactly what materials to use and how to put them together, we have an equal responsibility to be specific about the components of our plan for the child and confident that they will achieve our stated objectives. Unfortunately, or perhaps fortunately, human beings are rather less predictable than buildings or aeroplanes, which means that we have to be rather modest about what we claim for our blueprints and always allow for things to turn out differently than we expected. None of us has perfect knowledge of the future, and none of us has a monopoly of wisdom.

This is another reason for adopting a collaborative approach to planning. Planning that is done with the child and family, rather than to them, is more likely to be successful both because the plans are likely to be better in themselves and because people are more likely to support them. The same applies to collaboration with other agencies. Seden makes the point that

> If children are viewed ecologically, as individuals in their social and cultural environments, it follows that any action undertaken in their lives should be inter-disciplinary. In addition, if children's development is viewed as multi-dimensional, it is necessary to include the contributions of all professionals to the assessment of need.
>
> Seden (2001), p. 55

Although the social work agency may carry the lead responsibility for promoting the welfare of the child, it is a corporate responsibility of the local authority and one shared in some measure by the health services. Professionals in education, health and housing should therefore be part of the planning process in all cases where this is appropriate.

The process of reviewing

Any plan needs a review at intervals, both to ensure that it is being effectively implemented and to make any changes that have become necessary. Where children and young people are being cared for by the state, this becomes a statutory requirement. As Grimshaw and Sinclair (1997) put it

> A planning process forms part of a developing sequence in which the objectives of the plan and the current needs of the child are reconsidered on the basis of changing circumstances and fresh experiences.
>
> p. 246

They also say that

> A statutory review is a process of considering the whole care plan, concluded by a final child-centred meeting and the completion of all the pertaining records.
>
> p. 250

It is important to ensure that all parties are given a proper opportunity to contribute to the review, and that decisions are made in an open and transparent way so that even if colleagues or family members do not agree with the outcomes, they understand the reasoning behind them.

Enabling children and young people to participate effectively in reviews can be a challenge, because the process is often designed in ways that do not make it readily accessible, especially to younger children. As Claire O'Kane and I wrote some years ago:

> Participation is a dynamic process, and real participation by children requires investment in time, energy and commitment. Children are much more able to contribute when they have been prepared – when they know what the review is for and who will be there, and when they have had time to think about what they want to say. Early preparation can enable adults to work at the child's pace and give children space to talk about the issues that concern them. Carers, social workers, parents and siblings all can play important roles in helping to prepare children ...
>
> Thomas and O'Kane (1999a), p. 228

And

> One of the features that many children found most difficult was that people 'just sat around talking' Many of them referred with approval to the way in which our research interviews used games and activities, and commented that if review meetings were more like that they would enjoy them more. Several children said that reviews should and could be more fun, as did some social workers – one suggested that reviews should take place over the breakfast table in order to be more like ordinary family discussions.
>
> pp. 228–9

What is in a plan?

According to the Department of Health (1991a) a plan for the care of a child should include the following elements:

- the child's needs and how they are to be met;
- the aims and timescale;
- the proposed placement;
- other services to be provided;
- support in the placement and contingency plans;
- arrangements for contact and reunification;
- arrangements for health care and education.

The plan should also specify:

- roles and responsibilities;
- how far the plan takes account of the child's wishes and feelings;
- arrangements for changes to the plan, disagreements and future decision making.

This is a good summary of the key elements that need to go into a plan for the care of a child or young person. It may be helpful to look at each of these elements in turn.

- The *child's needs* have been the central focus of this chapter, and have already been extensively discussed.
- The *aims and timescale* clearly need careful attention, because all the decisions we take have to be based on a clear understanding of what it is we are trying to achieve for *this* child, and on having a clear idea of how long it is expected to take. Timescales of course are critically important for children.
- The *proposed placement* is at the heart of the plan, and this is the main subject of the next chapter.
- *Other services* can include therapeutic work with the child, and advice and support for the birth family.
- *Support in the placement* may mean specialist support for the carers in addition to that normally provided. *Contingency planning* can be crucial – it is important to anticipate things that may change or go wrong, and have a 'plan B' ready to be implemented if the anticipated problems arise. Sometimes carers themselves need planned relief from the work of looking after an especially demanding child or young person, and this should if possible be built in from the start.
- *Contact and reunification* are discussed at length in the next chapter.
- *Health care and education* are crucially important services for every child, and as we have seen they may be neglected when children come into care. It is essential that the health and educational needs of the child, and how they are to be met, are clearly identified in the plan. The educational implications of any proposed placement should feature strongly in all decision making.
- *Roles and responsibilities* may need to be clearly defined from the start if problems are to be avoided in the future. To some extent these may be negotiated, as we shall see.
- It is most important to specify how far the plan takes account of the child's *wishes and feelings*, and when it does not to explain clearly why – so that the child can be given a clear explanation now and in the future, in a way that shows that her or his views and desires were treated with respect.

The content and structure of a plan can usefully be guided by a pre-existing framework, such as those used in some of the systematic approaches to assessment and planning reviewed in the following section. Planning of course does not end with a child's admission to care. Assessment and planning are both continuing processes, and the statutory requirement to hold regular reviews is but one way of reinforcing this. Grimshaw and Sinclair conclude from their research into planning and reviewing that 'a dynamic planning process' is needed, in which professionals and family members continue to feed information and ideas into a continual updating of the assessment and plan for the child (1997, p. 245).

Another way of describing this is in terms of 'only planning as far as you can see':

> For instance, if a child cannot sit in the same room with her parents for more than ten minutes without a row [heated argument], then to plan for a return home in one month is rather pointless. The plan may be to enable them to spend an hour together without a row, then a day together, and so on ...
>
> John Evans (personal communication)

Exercise 6.1 Annie

Annie is ten years old and lives with her mother and younger sister, Sarah aged 4. She has little contact with her father. Annie has mild cerebral palsy which gives her some difficulty in walking and speech. She attends a mainstream school where she has until recently been doing well.

Recently Annie's mother has had several episodes of severe depression. During these episodes her care of the children has been very poor, and arrangements have been made on occasion for them to stay with friends. Annie's mother has now joined a therapeutic programme which she has to attend on a daily basis and which is expected to continue for up to six months. Her psychiatrist has recommended that she is unlikely to benefit from the programme unless she has a break from caring for the children for at least three months. Her sister has offered to look after Sarah but is unwilling to take on both girls. In any case Annie is keen to continue at her school and her aunt lives 30 miles away.

Annie's mother has asked for Annie to be accommodated by the local authority.

What would be the key components of a plan for Annie?
What are her needs, including her priority needs?
What other information do you need?

Systematic approaches to assessment and planning

In recent years there have been a number of attempts to introduce more systematic approaches to assessment and planning for children and families, in order to ensure that all children's needs receive proper and thoughtful attention. Some of these attempts have been prompted by evidence of poor assessment or inconsistent planning in the care system; others by similar evidence in relation to child protection. At their best these systematic frameworks seek to support professional judgement, not to substitute for it. Sometimes they can be experienced by hard-pressed social workers as yet another burden; but used properly they can certainly support good practice and improve the quality of outcomes for children (see Box 6.1 on p. 86). Before leaving the topic of assessment and planning I want to look briefly at four examples of these models, all from the UK, to see what it is that they offer and how they can help.

Planning in Child Care

I have already made reference to Margaret Bryer's work (Bryer 1988), which was commissioned by the British Agencies for Adoption and Fostering and distributed to social work teams in England and Wales by the Department of Health. The purpose of the book was to support the social worker and her/his supervisor in making good plans for children and young people who were in need of care. The approach is based on mapping children's needs in a holistic way, as we have seen, and then on constructing a 'blueprint' which sets out how they are to be met.

Bryer offers helpful advice on the process and content of assessment. Although the book was published just prior to the reforming child care legislation of the late 1980s and early 1990s, it is based on similar principles and much of what it says is still valid. Bryer includes a number of practical tools and materials which can be helpful in making assessments and plans, used where necessary in conjunction with more recent materials issued by government.

'The Orange Book'

At the same time as Bryer's book the Department of Health issued *Protecting Children: a guide to comprehensive assessment for social workers* (Department of Health 1988) – known universally as 'the Orange Book'. Designed for child protection work, the guide was intended to improve the quality of assessments, mainly by ensuring that information was collected in sufficient detail. It includes 167 specific questions about the child and parents, family history and relationships, and the wider environment. It also includes basic working tools such as flow chart, ecomap and genogram, and a copy of Sheridan's guide to developmental milestones.

The introduction of 'the Orange Book' made an important contribution to raising the profile of assessment work in child protection and in child care work generally. However, it was often used rather mechanically – at worst, as a questionnaire administered to parents. Although the guidance does include some tools for analysis, the emphasis often tended to be on collecting information rather than on analysing it. In addition the focus of the guide was on assessing *risk* rather than *need*, which limited its usefulness for care planning. When a few years later attention turned to the demand to 'refocus' child welfare services from a narrow view of child protection to a broader concern with children's welfare, the 'Orange Book' began to seem outmoded.

Looking After Children

The research which informed many of the changes in the Children Act 1989 and related legislation also drew attention to the need to look more carefully at *outcomes* for children and young people who were looked after by the state. It appeared that many local authorities were not mindful enough of their responsibilities as 'corporate parents', and that information about how children were doing in the care system was not consistently collected or organised. There were therefore related issues for research, for management and for practice. A working party chaired by Professor Roy Parker was charged with addressing some of these issues, and its report (Parker et al. 1991) led to the development of a set of tools for assessing and reviewing at intervals the progress of a child or young person and the quality of care being provided, which it was hoped could be used not only to improve the quality of practice but to provide a source of information on the working of the care system.

These tools were the Assessment and Action Records, a set of six questionnaires for children and young people of different ages (0–1, 2–4, 5–9, 10–14, 15–16, 17+). The questionnaires are based on the seven developmental dimensions described earlier, and under each heading a series of specific questions is asked which draws attention to how the child is doing and asks what plans are being made for dealing with any difficulties or gaps in the care provision. Subsequently a set of structured tools for planning and review were developed to accompany the Assessment and Action Records, and the whole package, now known as the *Looking After Children* system, was introduced throughout England and Wales. The system has been very influential and has been adopted or adapted in many other countries, from Canada to Israel (see Ward 1995).

There have been criticisms of the *Looking After Children* system. Knight and Caveney (1998) criticise the system on the basis of 'the normative view of parenting and family life which is seen to be the heart of these documents and the lack of consideration of the resourcing of the action plans' (p. 29). They suggest that contextual considerations relating to race, gender, social and economic factors have been ignored in the Assessment and Action Records – for instance in questions about whether the child is in 'a safe environment', about problematic behaviour in the home or about success in school. Finally they suggest that power issues in the Assessment and Action Records and the 'checklist' approach are inimical to the concept of partnership, that 'discourses around good parenting ... have a strong element of blame attached', that the system symbolises the 'increased professional control of parenting', and that much of the research on parenting that underpins the system is based upon a model of white middle-class parenthood.

Similar themes are taken up by Garrett who criticises the *Looking After Children* system on four grounds: that 'corporate parenting' is an unrealistic concept which does not take into account the diversity of children and young people who are looked after in different settings; that the 'reasonable parent' is a subjective concept; that the system involves unnecessary surveillance in the guise of information gathering – for instance in questions about immigration status; and finally that the system's discourse of parenting is linked with 'authoritarian social policy' represented by initiatives such as compulsory 'parent education' and 'parenting orders' (Garrett 1999a, p. 59; see also Garrett 1999b).

Jackson (1998) has replied to Knight and Caveney, and by implication to Garrett, by pointing out that 'the system is explicitly designed for those looked after by local authorities away from home', and that while 'it is quite true that many children and young people who are not looked after by local authorities also suffer disadvantage and deprivation',

> this is not a reason for failing to provide the best possible care for those par-
> ticularly unfortunate children who are not only disadvantaged and deprived
> but also, in most cases, unable to live with even one parent, and for whom
> the local authority has a special responsibility. The question also arises,
> what should a substitute care system be trying to provide for those children
> whose parents are unable or unfit to look after them? There can surely be
> no question of attempting to reproduce the circumstances in which they
> were previously living, or what would be the point of providing care in the
> first place?
>
> Jackson (1998), p. 48

Jackson also suggests that partnership is a key principle of the *Looking After Children* system. She suggests that the focus on the individual child has the potential to foster corporate responsibility and commitment and highlight under-resourcing, so empowering carers and social workers to fight for resources. Provided that form filling does not become an end in itself, the system should facilitate social workers spending more time with children and young people and establishing better patterns of communication and dialogue.

Followed slavishly, systems like *Looking After Children* can seem burdensome and obtrusive. Used creatively, they can support professional knowledge and skills and enhance good practice. (There are some good training materials around that can help to stimulate creative use of the system – one is mentioned in the Guide to Further Reading.) As a foster carer in one English local authority said of the materials,

> The language on the forms is straightforward and direct. The questions are 'child friendly' so children of four or five years old can understand and enjoy helping to complete the records. Parents and relatives want to know everything that has happened to the child and this shows them how decisions are come to. It stops things being taken for granted. The social worker can use the form to criticise the standards of care but this is right because it is for the benefit of the child. If this system was used in years gone by, many of the children would not have grown up confused about their background and what happened to them.
>
> Quoted in Phillips and Worlock (1996), p. 10

Framework for the Assessment of Children in Need and their Families

While 'the Orange Book' was aimed at child protection services, and the *Looking After Children* system was for children and young people who are looked after, the *Framework for the Assessment of Children in Need and their Families* (Department of Health et al. 2000; National Assembly for Wales 2000) is a structured assessment system for all children 'in need' under the Children Act 1989. The *Framework* incorporates the assessment of risk into a holistic assessment of a child's needs and circumstances. It is based on a triangular model incorporating three 'domains' – children's needs, parenting capacity, and wider family and environmental factors (see Figure 6.1).

Based on a broad review of research into factors that affect children's development (see Cleaver et al. 1999; Department of Health 2001a), the *Framework* is supported by extensive guidance as well as a range of working tools and a specially commissioned training package (Horwath 2001). The guidance and training are aimed first at social workers, but also at workers in other agencies and professions who are expected to contribute both directly and indirectly to the process of assessment.

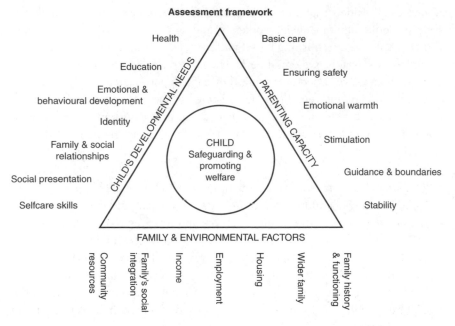

Source: Department of Health, Department of Education and Employment and Home Office (2000), p. 17

Figure 6.1 The three 'domains' of assessment

The working tools that accompany the *Framework* include a set of forms to assist in recording and evaluating information in individual cases. Known as the 'assessment records', they are evidence-based and aim to translate the *Assessment Framework* into a practical tool for social workers, by offering a structured approach for recording and analysing the information gathered during the assessment. There are three types of record, available both in paper and electronic format:

(1) the *referral and initial information record*, whose purpose is to record initial information about the child and family, the reason for the referral and the agency's response;
(2) the *initial assessment record*, designed to assess whether a child is 'in need', what services are needed, and whether a *core assessment* should be undertaken;
(3) the *core assessment record* – this comes in different versions for children of different ages, and is designed to help social workers in undertaking a

more thorough assessment of a child's situation with a view to substantial provision of services.

The aim of the records is to ensure that information is recorded consistently, a plan of action with clear objectives developed, the most effective service identified, and objectives regularly reviewed. The core assessment record also forms the basis for reassessment as a situation changes, and a final section enables local authorities to gather systematically the information about performance required by government under initiatives such as *Quality Protects* in England and *Children First* in Wales.

The working tools also include a number of instruments designed to be helpful in collecting and analysing specific information about children's needs and difficulties and the capacities of parents to respond to them: 'strengths and difficulties questionnaires', the 'parenting daily hassles scale', the 'home conditions scale', the 'adult wellbeing scale', the 'adolescent wellbeing scale', the 'recent life events questionnaire scale', the 'family activity scale' and the 'alcohol scale' (Cox and Bentovim 2000).

The *Framework* was initially intended to be based on a dual model of children's needs and parenting capacity, and the third side of the triangle, 'wider family and environmental factors', was only added at a later stage. This is reflected in the training materials that accompany the model, which are frankly much stronger on the assessment of children's needs and parenting capacity than they are when it comes to wider issues.

The practicality of having one assessment system for children in care and another for children in need in the community is of course questionable, even when there is a degree of consistency between the two systems – which is why the decision was taken to subsume both *Looking After Children* and the *Framework* into an overarching 'integrated children's system' that is intended to provide a context and a set of tools for assessment and planning with all children and families. Following the experience of the *Framework* in stimulating interagency cooperation, the aim is for the integrated children's system to be based very strongly on interagency work, and it also makes much greater use of electronic records. The 2003 'green paper' *Every Child Matters*, which set out the UK government's proposals for reorganising child welfare services in England, announced the development of a 'common assessment framework', drawing on the *Framework for the Assessment of Children in Need and their Families*, the Connexions APIR System, the Youth Justice Board's *Asset* tool, the SEN code of practice and the assessments conducted by health visitors. In developing the new framework the government declared that it intended to look at 'how children can be an active part of the assessment process, and how assessment can identify strengths and opportunities as well as needs and risks' (HM Government 2003, pp. 58–9).

> **Box 6.1**   The use of frameworks – a team manager talking
>
> 'It is too easy to get caught up in the detail and the procedure and lose the sense of what you are doing. It was the same with the Orange Book and is already happening with the Framework. I know of Senior Practitioners who have taken the Core Assessment booklet with them when they visit families and read it out and fill it in. Then they complain that it is just a tick-box exercise that families hate! You need to read the materials and become familiar with them and then put them away and think about what you are doing. It is the same with the Assessment Framework system as with the Looked After Review system, and even with foster carer assessments. All of these are only guides and prompts on how to structure the information in a coherent manner. They should not dictate how you negotiate your relationship with a child or a family.'

Summary and conclusion

We started this chapter by looking at the context and purpose of assessment with children and young people. We then considered the content of assessment in relation to the child, the family and community, and the contribution of health and welfare agencies. We examined the processes of assessment, planning, implementation and review; and we analysed what is in a plan. Finally, we considered some systematic approaches to assessment and planning, including the *Looking After Children* system and the *Framework for the Assessment of Children in Need and their Families*, and the ways in which they can be used to support good professional practice.

Whether these attempts to systematise assessment and planning will be successful in achieving greater integration between different services, and in improving standards and outcomes for children and young people, will depend not just on how cleverly they are designed but on the quality of the training and support that accompany the new systems – and even more so on the level of staffing and resources available to implement them. Systems and practice tools can be an enormous help to good practice, but they are no substitute for well-trained staff who understand what they are doing and have the time and resources to do it properly. It should also not need to be said that, however good the processes of assessment and planning, they are wasted without effective provision of services. However, there is a risk that the very necessary focus on improving assessment and planning may sometimes overshadow the need to ensure that services are available when and where they are identified as being needed, and provided in a way that is acceptable to children and their families.

It is hoped that this chapter will have provided an introduction to the thinking behind good practice in assessment and planning for children in care, and
an overview of this complex and challenging area of work. Many of the themes
will be developed further in the following chapters.

GUIDE TO FURTHER READING

Milner and O'Byrne (2002) is an excellent guide to thinking about
assessment in social work in general. For an overview of assessment
practice with children, both individual and collectively, Ward and Rose (2002)
is invaluable. For a more technical approach to assessment of children and
families, see Wilkinson (1998). Calder and Hackett (2003) is an up-to-date
guide to using frameworks for assessment. Adcock (2001) is very helpful on
the process of analysis.

Howe et al. (1999) offer an excellent explanation and examples of how an
attachment model can be used, particularly in the analytical stage of
assessment. The research review on children's needs and parenting capacity
by Cleaver et al. (1999) is very helpful, as is the review of the literature
relating to assessment of children in need by Seden (2001).

As a guide to planning for children, Bryer (1988) has in some respects
still not been bettered – although it predates the Children Act 1989 and
similar legislation, it is based on very much the same principles. More up to
date is Holland (2004).

Many of the *Looking After Children* publications are very helpful,
particularly the reader edited by Jackson and Kilroe (1996). The pack *Being
Creative with Assessment and Action Records* from Rhondda Cynon Taf
Borough Council (Jenkins and Tudor 1999) is also very useful. Of the many
publications associated with the *Framework for the Assessment of Children
in Need and their Families*, Horwath (2001) is indispensable.

Placement and contact

Introduction

Choosing a placement for a child or young person in care is arguably one of the most important decisions that social workers regularly take. The right placement can ensure that a child is happy and fulfilled, and create a sound basis for her or his development into adulthood. The wrong placement can leave a child unhappy or emotionally 'stuck', can trigger educational or other developmental difficulties, or can lead to a pattern of instability and movement that, at worst, may last through childhood and beyond.

This chapter will begin with a general discussion of the issues in choosing placements for children, before going on to review the types of placement available. We will consider how best to relate children's needs to the capacity of placements to respond, and examine the question of 'who decides' about placement. We will then look particularly at three areas: the implications of what we know about attachment and resilience, the strengths and weaknesses of kinship placements, and the issues of sibling relationships.

Whether children continue living with members of their family or are looked after by strangers, contact with separated family and friends can be crucial to their welfare. The second part of this chapter will concentrate on this aspect of looking after children. We will look specifically at the issues involved in family contact, the purposes of contact, and the principles that should guide the making of arrangements for contact.

In the final section of the chapter we look at some of the practical issues in arranging placements and helping children to make successful moves.

Issues in choosing placements for children

According to Bryer (1988), when we are choosing a placement for a child we should be asking these questions:

- What sort of placement are you seeking for this child?
- What type of care will meet the child's priority needs?
- What are the main tasks required of the carers in order to meet the aims of care?
- What is the expected length of stay in care?
- Proposed contact between child and birth parents/other family members?
- Would a residential or foster care setting be better, and why?
- What particular considerations might affect the choice of placement, e.g. background of child, need for particular location?
- Is it possible to meet all these requirements within the prescribed timetable?
- If not, which criteria will be given priority?
- What options are there?
- Which option offers the most acceptable compromise?
- Who is involved in the decision about choice of placement?
- Have the new carers been given sufficient information about the child and the task they are being asked to do?

(One might want to add to this list a specific question about whether more than one child in the family needs to be placed, and if so what issues this raises.)

The identification of a placement is of course part of the processes of planning that we discussed in the previous chapter, and the choice of a placement should follow closely from our assessment of the child's needs and the resources available. Many children who come into care have deep-seated emotional problems, often as a result of deprivation or abuse. These problems may create initial barriers that can make the process of finding a placement difficult. (On the other hand, such problems may not emerge until the child is settled and feels relatively secure, so that a placement which initially appeared trouble-free begins to come under greater stress.)

When I have lectured qualifying or post-qualifying social workers on placement choice, the initial reaction has sometimes been a hollow laugh. 'What choice?' they ask, remembering or having heard of many situations where the social worker was glad to accept the only placement available. It is important to acknowledge the reality that choice is often very limited, either because of an overall shortage of resources or because resources are badly used. At the same time I usually point out that it is rare for there actually to be only one placement available (as opposed to two, or none), and that to take the first placement offered in an emergency may relieve pressure on staff but is not necessarily in the best interests of the child or young person. In every case a decision has to made as to whether accepting the placement offered will be better for the child than not accepting it, whatever the alternative may be – in the same way that the Children Act 1989 requires courts not to make an order unless it is better for the child than *not* making an order.

The explicit philosophy of many agencies and indeed governments is that the choice of placement for a child, like other issues of care provision, should be 'needs-led' not 'resource-led'. Few would disagree with this as a philosophy, but making it a reality can be more difficult. Even where placement resources are well provided, it is rarely possible to start with a 'blank sheet' for each child; and the first task for a placing social worker is to be well informed about what placement resources are generally available.

Types of placement

In this section we review the main types of placement and draw attention to some of their distinctive qualities. Plumer (1992) uses a model of a 'continuum of care', on which placement types are arranged according to whether they are more or less 'socially restrictive' (see Figure 7.1). Plumer's model does not include certain types of placement, for instance kinship care or secure accommodation, but these can easily be fitted into his scheme. Other placement types are less easy to classify in terms of Plumer's model, such as adoption which is not 'socially restrictive' but is clearly a very major step to

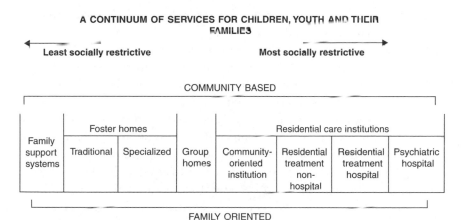

A CONTINUUM OF SERVICES FOR CHILDREN, YOUTH AND THEIR
FAMILIES

← Least socially restrictive   Most socially restrictive →

COMMUNITY BASED

| Family support systems | Foster homes | | Group homes | Residential care institutions | | | |
| | Traditional | Specialized | | Community-oriented institution | Residential treatment non-hospital | Residential treatment hospital | Psychiatric hospital |

FAMILY ORIENTED

Source: Plumer (1992), p. 199

Figure 7.1 The 'continuum of care'

take. For this reason it may also be helpful to classify placements in terms of how far they remove children from their families of origin. The order in which we review different placement types in this section incorporates both of these ways of conceptualising these differences.

Children's own families

The overwhelming majority of children and young people remain with their families of origin throughout their childhood. This is of course the preferred way to bring up children in most societies. For most of the children who come near the care system this will also be the preferred option. Keeping children with, or returning them to, their own families should be the aim in every case where this is consistent with the child's interests, and this is emphasised by much of the legislation we work with. However, this does not simply mean resisting admission to care unless it is unavoidable; a great deal of harm can be done by this kind of strict gatekeeping. It means working positively with children and families to identify what kind of support and intervention may enable children to remain successfully with their own families, and ensuring that services are then provided for long enough to make a real difference. Where children and young people are already in substitute care, it means working to identify situations where they are able to return home, and providing the support and intervention that is needed to make a success of that return. Research by Bullock et al. (1993a) showed that most children and young people eventually return to their families, if only briefly, after leaving the care system. The research lent support to the arguments for maintaining contact and strengthening links, especially when it showed how many families tend to change composition during their children's absence, so that a child who is not in regular contact may quickly lose touch.

There is good evidence that the right kind of family support services can be very effective in enabling children to remain successfully at home. Thoburn (1994) points to research evidence from both the US and UK that shows the value of support services of relatively long duration, services that provide a mixture of both practical and therapeutic help on a basis of participation with families in defining their needs and planning the intervention. Thoburn wrote in 1994 that in Britain, unlike the US, 'it is the exception rather than the rule for well-planned and adequately resourced services to be offered' to families where children are returning home. Unfortunately this continues to be largely true.

A proportion of children and young people remain legally in care while actually placed with their own parents. In the past this was known in England and Wales as being 'home on trial' (see Farmer and Parker 1991). Since the 1980s, following several deaths of children in these situations, placements of this kind have been more tightly regulated. There is some recent research evidence to suggest that failure rates for this type of placement are still relatively high (Aldgate and Statham 2001), but there are always likely to be some children for whom this is the most appropriate arrangement while their parents are unable to take full responsibility for them.

Respite and relief care

One of the ways in which children and families can be supported to remain together is by the provision of 'respite' or 'relief' care. This usually means the child going to a foster carer on a regular or occasional basis, although similar arrangements can also be made in residential children's homes. Much of the respite care provided is for disabled children and young people, including those who are affected by severe or multiple disabilities, who need constant care or supervision, or who present challenging behaviour. Often this care is provided through specialised schemes, run by a local authority or a voluntary organisation, with carers specifically recruited and trained for this task. Care may be planned well in advance to take place at regular intervals, or it may be possible for families to request it as and when they need it.

Less common are schemes for providing regular relief care for non-disabled children in need and their families, although ad hoc arrangements may be set up in particular cases as part of a package of family support. There is evidence that such schemes can be very helpful both to parents and to children (Aldgate et al. 1997).

Respite care arrangements are often designed primarily to help parents and carers – as the terms 'respite' and 'relief' imply. If parents feel supported and find life easier to manage, this is likely to be good for children too. However, there can be a conflict of interests, and it is important to ensure that the experience of going away is also a positive and rewarding one for the child or young person.

Short term foster care

The majority of admissions to the care system involve children and young people going to some form of short term family placement. This may be with relatives or friends of the child and family, and this type of 'kinship' placement is discussed more fully later in the chapter. More commonly the child or young person will be placed with other people who have been approved by an agency as foster carers for this kind of task. There is more than one way to define 'short term'; eight weeks is a commonly used threshold, but so is six months.

Short term foster placements may be used in a number of different ways – for example:

- in an emergency;
- for assessment;
- for a defined short term need, such as a parent's illness;
- to provide care for a child while a longer term placement is sought.

Although we have already emphasised the aim of keeping children within their own families as much as possible, it is also important to recognise that a brief admission to care can sometimes be helpful in the long term.

The carer's tasks in short and long term foster care are very different, as we shall see in the next chapter. Although the matching of personalities that frequently goes into planning of permanent placements may be absent here, careful planning is still needed for a short term placement to ensure that children's needs are well enough met, and that the placement can be stable for the period during which it is needed.

Long term foster care

The majority of children in care at any one time (as opposed to the number of admissions to the care system over a defined period) are in some form of long term foster placement. As with short term placements, these placements may be with relatives or friends of the child or young person, but they are more likely to be with strangers. Long term foster carers may be recruited to care for a particular child, or they may be already approved as potential carers for a category of children, and waiting for a suitable placement.

As with short term placements, there is more than one way to define 'long term', and sometimes a distinction is made between *long term* placements that may be expected to continue for many months or even a few years, but with an eventual end in sight, and *permanent* placements, where the expectation is that the carers will remain on the scene throughout the young person's childhood and even beyond (see Chapter 9).

Specialist foster care

There are also a variety of forms of specialist foster care:

- schemes for fostering adolescents, some of whom may display unusually challenging behaviour;
- schemes for fostering disabled children and young people, some of whom may also display unusually challenging behaviour;
- remand schemes, where foster carers are asked to provide relatively secure care for children and young people who have been remanded by the courts or detained by the police;
- 'mother and baby' placements, for situations where both child and parent need care and supervision.

Specialist schemes typically offer higher allowances combined with a professional fee. Carers may be (but are not necessarily) more highly trained and better qualified, and may take on aspects of work with the child or young person more commonly undertaken by a social worker. These schemes are discussed further in the next chapter.

Residential care

Residential or group care has tended to decline over the years in the numbers of children it accommodates. However, it still remains a very important part of the care system, especially for teenagers and for children and young people with highly specialised needs. Residential care is less likely to be used for younger children, and in many agencies such use is prohibited by local policies.

Because of the decline in numbers of places in group care, it can be difficult to find a placement that is close at hand and able to offer what a particular child or young person needs. Local 'children's homes' take a range of young people who may have very different needs, usually for relatively short periods. Many such homes have explicit policies that set a maximum length of stay. The number of establishments offering more specialised residential care has declined in recent years, but some of this provision remains. This includes community homes providing residential education, and establishments offering particular therapeutic regimes.

Secure accommodation

Some children and young people need to be kept under conditions of security, either for their own protection or for the protection of other people. This may include, for example, a child who is at risk of self-harm, or who is involved in criminal sexual behaviour, or is extremely violent.

Under UK legislation this cannot happen without the specific approval of the court, except for a very limited period in an emergency. Secure accommodation is usually provided on a regional basis, sometimes by a local authority acting as a provider for other agencies. Access to this type of accommodation is strictly controlled.

Adoption

We come to adoption last, not because it is the most 'socially restrictive' in terms of Plumer's model, but because it removes a child or young person permanently from her/his family of origin, and because in doing so it usually amounts to an exit from the care system rather than a further placement. Even though contemporary adoption may involve some continuing contact with the child's family of origin, the fact remains that in law the birth parents cease to be parents, and new people become the child's parents. In this sense adoption is a very radical step to take; however, for many children it can be the most effective way to provide the security and stability they need, as we see in Chapter 9.

Relating children's needs to the capacity of placements to respond

If we have a good picture of the range of placements available and of what each can offer, we will begin to have a sense of what kind of placement might be most appropriate for a particular child. However, choosing a placement is not simply a matter of identifying one of the above categories and slotting the child or young person into it. The task is also to find a particular placement that will meet that child's needs as well as possible. We return therefore to our identification of the child or young person's overall and priority needs, and ask what kind of placement, and which particular placement, will best meet each of these needs.

Part of the answer to this question will relate to features of the situation in which the child or young person needs care – for instance, whether the need is short term or long term, and whether or not the child's family is expected eventually to resume the responsibility for care. Part of it will depend on overt and general characteristics of the child or young person such as his or her age, gender, ethnic and cultural background. A lot of the answer, however, will be to do with individual characteristics of the child or young person and aspects of her or his personal history. It can sometimes be useful to look at this in terms of the 'messages' the child or young person has received from their previous upbringing and the 'messages' that are likely to be helpful to them in the future.

In Boxes 7.1, 7.2 and 7.3 I give three examples of how these different aspects of placement choice may work out in practice.

Who decides?

If the introduction to this chapter seems to imply that choosing a placement is a matter for an individual social worker, that impression is misleading. It is always a matter for discussion and negotiation involving a range of different

---

Box 7.1   Kelly

Kelly is 15 years old and profoundly deaf. Her parents, who both have mild learning disabilities, cannot control her. She has stayed away from home several times without permission, on one occasion apparently staying with a 30-year-old man. Kelly and her parents agree that she should be accommodated. She has an eleven-year-old brother who is settled at home.

The plan for Kelly may well be for an initial admission to care as a basis for work to enable the family to resume living together successfully. However, it has to be acknowledged that this may not work and that Kelly may need care until she is an adult. Young people in similar situations are often admitted to group care, or to a specialist fostering scheme. In Kelly's case close attention to her individual needs and wishes will be necessary to determine the most appropriate placement. It will need to be one where carers are able to exercise appropriate control without driving Kelly further into rebellion. The 'messages' that she has received from her experience at home may well be to do with her being uncontrollable or not worth caring about – this will need further exploration, as will the ability of a proposed placement to give more helpful messages. Kelly's links with the Deaf community also need to be explored – in particular whether this community can offer a suitable placement. This may well be a case where a *family group conference* would be helpful.

Box 7.2 Asha

Asha is two years old and has been removed from home on an emergency protection order because of severe neglect. She is undernourished and has a cleft palate which has not been properly treated. Asha's father is Bangladeshi and her mother is white British. The family have only been in contact with services for a short time, and it is not clear whether with support they will be able to resume caring for Asha. Asha has two older sisters who are now being closely monitored.

It is not possible to say with certainty at this stage whether Asha needs a permanent substitute family, but it is clearly a strong possibility. The primary need at this point is for a placement that will provide safety and good physical care for her while she gets the treatment she needs and the family's resources are assessed. Beyond that there are some difficult issues here in placement choice. Clearly there are advantages for Asha in finding a placement that could if necessary keep her on a permanent basis; but a permanent placement should also be one that can meet her needs as a child of mixed heritage, and a placement now should if possible be one where her sisters could also be accommodated if this becomes necessary. Since all these criteria are unlikely to be met in one placement, difficult choices are likely to have to be made. A team approach to planning is likely to be invaluable in this case, as well as some clear thinking about attachment issues.

Box 7.3 Tomos and Gwilym

Tomos and Gwilym are aged eight and ten, and need accommodation while their father, a widower, has hospital treatment for depression. The prognosis is good and it is expected that they will return home within 2–3 months. The boys both speak Welsh as their first language, as does their father.

Tomos and Gwilym clearly need as a priority a placement close to home that will preserve their links with family, neighbourhood and school. Kinship care ought to be the first option here, but there may also be neighbours or parents of school friends who can offer care to these boys. A placement with family or neighbours may also well be Welsh-speaking, which is highly desirable for the reasons we saw in Chapter 4. Some might argue for a degree of scepticism about the positive prognosis in this case – but at this stage the aim must surely be to work for a speedy return of the boys to their father, perhaps from carers who can provide some ongoing support to the three of them. Tomos and Gwilym are likely to be worried about their father and anxious about the future, and so the quality of emotional support may be a key issue in choosing a placement. (They may also need help in grieving for their mother.)

people. This can include family placement workers, residential care staff, managers and supervisors. It may also include professionals from agencies such as education and health as advisers – and sometimes as contributors to decisions about funding. The decision may involve panels or committees. Sometimes the court may have a part to play in deciding on a placement. Once a potential placement has been identified, those likely to be involved in providing the care will need to be consulted. Above all, the decision must include the child and family, because if they are committed to the placement plan it is much more likely to work successfully.

As with all our planning processes, there is more than one way of including people in decision making, and 'one big meeting' is not necessarily the most effective way. The social worker may need to spend some time talking to peo ple individually about how they view the different options for placement. In the case of the child, and perhaps other members of the family too, this may need to involve visits to proposed placements or face-to-face meetings with possible carers.

Including the child and family effectively in the decision can be difficult when the negotiations required are complex, or when there is pressure to resolve the situation quickly. For this reason it is better if decision-making processes within the agency can be kept as simple as possible.

There are other reasons too for having decision-making processes that ensure a measured reflection on what is likely to be best for the child or young person but which also avoid complex bureaucratic hurdles. June Thoburn reminds us that research in the 1980s suggested 'that the attitude which sees reception into care as something to be avoided becomes a self-fulfilling prophesy in that precipitate and unplanned entries into care caused by this "goal-keeping" policy help to ensure that in many cases care is indeed a distressing and harmful experience', and that 'bureaucratisation of planning' through panels and committees tends to increase the proportion of emergency admissions (Thoburn 1994, pp. 16–17).

Implications of attachment and resilience

We saw in Chapter 2 how useful attachment theory can be in helping us to think about a child or young person's history and her or his needs for future care. In choosing a placement and making the arrangements, it is crucially important to take into account the patterns of attachment the child has developed and how these are likely to be affected by the placement.

The key tasks in relation to attachment will vary according to the child and the situation. In most cases it will be important to ensure that existing attachments are not weakened or threatened unnecessarily by the new arrangements; indeed, in many cases one of our aims will be to strengthen these existing attachments. The task of a short term carer can be difficult – on the one hand, to enable the child to settle in the placement and feel secure, but on the other hand to ensure that existing relationships are not challenged or replaced.

In other cases the aim will be to help the child make healthy new attachments. In these cases the choice of carer will of course assume a special importance, because it must be someone to whom the child or young person is likely to make a good attachment and who is ready to accept this.

Social workers should be supporting placements in ways that allow children to acquire more experience, more skills and resources in making attachments. It is vital to 'ensure that at least one person in a child's life is able to offer a secure base and assist relationship building, so that not all the child's energies are going into trying to understand the bewildering complexities of relating to people and there's some space for fun' (Mary Romaine, personal communication).

Vera Fahlberg is a reliable source of good advice on working with children's attachments. In *A Child's Journey Through Placement* (Fahlberg 1994), she explains how the 'arousal-relaxation cycle', the 'positive interaction cycle' and 'positive claiming' can be used to help children build new attachments. She also gives good advice on managing the relationship between existing and new attachments. As she says,

> If the child cannot be maintained in the birth family and must come into foster care, part of the foster carers' role is to help the child maintain attachments to his or her birth family. Simultaneously, the foster carers must help the child develop healthy and strong new attachments to themselves. When the child leaves their home, foster carers must be willing to actively transfer these attachments to the succeeding permanent primary carers, whether those be birth family members, an adoptive family, or a new foster family. Moves from foster home to foster home should be limited to all but the most unavoidable situations. Every loss adds psychological trauma and interrupts the tasks of child development.
>
> Fahlberg (1994), p. 168

'Kinship care'

Researchers have long been aware that children cared for by relatives or friends often do better than those who are looked after by strangers. Rowe et al. (1984) found that such placements could offer a high degree of security, and this finding has been confirmed by other research. Despite this, foster care with relatives has had variable use in the UK. Research in Hampshire found only 4 per cent of children fostered with relatives, although research in South Wales with children aged 8–12 found over 20 per cent, suggesting geographical variations in practice (Gorin 1997; Thomas and O'Kane 1999a).

Placement with relatives has grown very rapidly in the United States, where it is known as 'kinship care'. In some states the proportion of children in out-of-home care looked after by relatives has risen to 30 per cent, especially among black and Hispanic families. This is partly in response to the sheer numbers of black children being removed from their parents because of drug abuse (Scannapieco 1999). Apart from any other consideration, for children and young people from minority ethnic groups a kinship placement is much more likely to offer continuity and support for the child's ethnic and cultural identity.

Findings of research in the USA are in general very positive. A study of 188 families by the Casey family program found that placement with relatives provided greater stability. Children did better at school and showed fewer behaviour problems. Foster carers who were relatives were more likely to see maintaining contact with the biological family as an important part of their role. There is some suggestion that less support was provided to relatives than to other carers, perhaps because it is not felt to be needed, or perhaps because active intervention by social workers is seen as more intrusive in these circumstances. A number of other studies confirm that placement with relatives is likely to lead to greater stability (although some suggest that it may reduce the chance of successful reunification with birth parents). A retrospective study in Baltimore compared 86 children placed with relatives and 128 placed with non-relatives. Those placed with relatives had fewer problems, better behaviour and fewer changes of placement in childhood, but outcomes in adulthood were similar for both groups. A follow-up study of 525 children placed with relatives in New York State found that the placements were very stable and that a high proportion led to adoption. (Source for the above: Jackson and Thomas (2001); for a fuller account of the US research, see Hegar and Scannapieco (1999).)

If, as research clearly shows, placements with relatives are less likely to break down, the gain in stability may sometimes have to be weighed against quality of care and what practical alternatives are available; however, it may be that if kinship carers were given the same level of support as unrelated foster carers there could be gains both in stability and quality. There are signs that interest in kinship care in the UK is growing, in part alongside the growth of interest in family group conferences (see Broad 2001; Broad et al. 2001).

Sibling relationships and placement

For most of us, our relationships with our brothers and sisters are the most enduring of all. For many children and young people in care, relationships with siblings can be crucial to their sense of stability and belonging. Personal accounts of life in care often reveal that separation from siblings is one of the most painful experiences. There should be no excuse for brothers and sisters to be separated on admission into care, except in rare cases when it is genuinely in their best interests. Yet it often happens, and will continue to happen unless serious commitments are made to prioritise keeping siblings together in placement policy and planning.

Difficult issues can sometimes arise when decisions have to be made about the placement of sibling groups – perhaps because children are admitted at different times, or because a placement that is particularly suited to the special needs of one child cannot cater for a brother or sister. A good assessment of the needs of each child, and of the strengths of the sibling relationship, will help in resolving these issues. In situations where it is not practicable to place brothers and sisters together, robust plans for continuing contact are likely to be needed.

Issues in family contact

There is a general assumption in most contemporary family work that it is good for children to be in contact with their family and friends. This is based in part on research which shows the positive effects on children and young people of continuing contact with people who are important to them but with whom they do not live – whether this is as a result of parental divorce, or admission to care, or for other reasons – and the negative consequences of losing such contact. Some of this research is summarised in *Patterns and Outcomes in Child Placement* (Department of Health 1991a).

The assumption is based, too, on what attachment theory teaches us about the value of affectional bonds in giving us a sense of identity – of who we are, what we are like, and where we belong. It is also, I would argue, based on a value position which assumes that children *ought* to remain in contact with people who are significant to them, and that loss of contact is in itself a bad thing. This may in part be a reaction to a century in which separation and loss have been features of people's lives on a very large scale as a result of wars and other social upheavals, as well as because of a huge increase in the incidence of divorce and separation.

This general assumption is reflected in the law: in case law, where there is a 'presumption of contact in cases of divorce or parental separation' (Cleaver 2000, p. 5), and in legislation such as the Children Act 1989 in England and Wales, where there is an explicit presumption of contact with parents and carers when a child is 'in care' within the meaning of the Act, together with an implicit assumption that contact is desirable in other situations. The United Nations Convention on the Rights of the Child provides for 'the right of the child who is separated from one or both parents to maintain personal relations and direct contact with both parents on a regular basis, except if it is contrary to the child's best interests' (Article 9). This applies to children whose parents reside in different states (Article 10) and to children deprived of liberty (Article 37). The Council of Europe Convention on Contact concerning Children, opened for signature on 15 May 2003 and signed by 12 member states, provides for children and parents to have a right to regular contact, which can be restricted only in the interests of the child. It also provides for children to be informed and consulted, and for contact orders and agreements to be enforced across national boundaries.

The research in the 1980s which showed how frequently children and young people in care lost contact without anyone intending it (for instance Millham et al. 1986) has had a substantial effect on law and practice. As a result far more attention is now paid to the importance of maintaining contact. Hedy Cleaver's review of pre- and post-1989 research, together with her own research, shows that children and young people in care now have more contact with their families of origin, and that social workers 'expend considerable efforts' to ensure that children remain in contact with their families (Cleaver 2000, p. 6). The research showed that the proportion of children seeing a parent at least once a week had risen from 11 per cent to 40 per cent between the mid 1980s and the late 1990s, that the frequency of contact was associated with the frequency of social worker visits to parents, and that social workers did in practice spend time in these visits encouraging parents to remain in contact with their children.

As Cleaver and others have pointed out, once contact becomes the norm it is paradoxically harder to demonstrate its effects on children's wellbeing using comparative research. However, there does appear to be good evidence for an association with placement stability and with general wellbeing, although the picture is less clear for other specific indicators such as educational success (Thoburn 1994; Cleaver 2000). This does not necessarily mean 'the more contact, the better' – rather it means that a good experience of continuing contact with people who are important to the child is associated with success in placement.

Contact arrangements can and should involve many different members of the child or young person's network – brothers and sisters, aunts and uncles, grandparents, friends and neighbours. In many cases these arrangements can be very informal, and the main social work task may be to encourage and support them rather than actively manage them. Nonetheless for some children contact with siblings, with aunts, uncles or grandparents, or with friends and neighbours, may be more important than with parents. For children and young people who have experienced moves in care, contact with previous carers may be especially important, and it easy for these relationships to be neglected if social workers are not 'tuned in' to the importance of keeping them alive. Finally, for some children, especially those who are lonely, isolated or abused, continuing contact with a pet may the most important issue.

However, the contact arrangements most likely to need formalising, and the most liable to tensions and difficulties, tend to be those for contact with parents; and it is on these that we will concentrate in the following discussion. Contact does not of course mean only face to face contact – it can also include letters, telephone calls or e-mails, and sometimes even indirect messages via a third party. However, much of the discussion, and much of the research evidence, concerns face to face contact.

Difficulties with contact

Contact arrangements can be fraught with difficulties, for several reasons. One is simply that maintaining contact with their children can sometimes be an aversive experience for parents. If your child goes to live with strangers because you are not able to provide good enough care for them, it can be hard to see them getting better care from people who may be in a much better position to provide for their needs. This applies even this is only for a short period, and much more so if care is long term and the child is developing new attachments. This is one reason for the unplanned 'withering away' of family links identified in the original research on this topic by Millham et al. (1986). Alongside this there are the sheer practical difficulties for many families of keeping up contact arrangements – transport, childcare, time off work – and the need to manage the contact so as not to disrupt unnecessarily the child's other activities or the lives of the carers. For all these reasons, children's family contact arrangements require active support and often a great deal of sensitivity to make them work well.

Contact can also be an aversive experience for children. Pain associated with separation may be brought to the surface by contact, and this will need to be handled sensitively. If parents or carers feel tense or angry about the situation, this may be communicated to the child in ways that cause upset. If the parent misuses the contact time (see below) or lacks the resources to make it a good experience, then it may become something that the child seeks to avoid or deals with by 'acting out'. To avoid these obstacles to successful contact, attention needs to be paid both to the quality of the experience and to the messages that are being communicated to the child in relation to contact.

Other difficulties apply to those situations where there are fears that contact may have the potential for harm. This may be because the parent has abused the child and there is a risk that abuse may be repeated during contact; these situations demand very careful handling, because it may still be important for the child to maintain a relationship with such a parent but this must be managed in a way that keeps the child safe. In other cases the problem may be that the parent is likely to use the contact visits to disrupt or undermine the care plan in some way. In either of these circumstances part of the answer may lie in closely supervised contact, an artificial situation but one which may sometimes be in the best all-round interests of the child. Supervised contact may also be necessary if the parents are having to learn skills or demonstrate their ability to provide good care.

Taken together these difficulties make working with family contact a challenging aspect of practice, in which it is important to keep a clear head and a clear focus on what is best for the child or young person – and to pay careful attention to what the child is saying, both verbally and non-verbally. Signs of distress should never be ignored, but it should not be assumed that the appropriate response is to stop the contact. Sometimes the distress may be a signal that something that is happening around the contact needs to be looked at; and sometimes it simply means that the child needs to be supported through an experience which is arousing painful feelings.

Purpose of contact

In making plans and arrangements for contact the first step is to ensure that everyone is sufficiently clear as to the purpose of contact for *this* child in *these* circumstances. This will depend in part on what is the overall plan for the child. Is it for return home in the near future? In this case the aim of contact will probably be to maintain active everyday relationships between children, parents and other family members – and perhaps also with neighbours, school friends and so on – in order to keep as much continuity as possible. Is return home perhaps dependent on the parents or family members showing that they can meet the child's needs more effectively than they have done in the past? In this case the arrangements for contact may need to be designed primarily to assess the feasibility of change.

If the plan is for longer term care, on the other hand, the purpose of contact will probably be to keep the child's most important relationships alive in order to help them preserve a sense of continuity in their lives – bearing in mind that most children and young people leaving care do eventually return to their families of origin in one way or another. If permanent substitute care is being arranged, especially through adoption, the main purpose of contact is likely to be to support the child's sense of identity, and the pattern of contact may well be lighter than in other cases. Some of the hardest dilemmas that arise over contact can be those in relation to children for whom the plan is permanent substitute care – especially if the prospective carers do not fully understand or accept the purpose and the value of contact for the child.

In each case, however, being clear about the purpose of contact should help us to think clearly about what *kind* of contact will best meet the needs of the child and of the other people involved. Too often debates about contact, especially when the courts are involved, start with discussion of *how often* and then perhaps *where* – when from the child's point of view, and that of the parents and carers, the most important question may be *what kind* of contact. Fixed intervals and set times may be useful in the short term, especially if there are tensions between the adults in the situation; but in the longer run children need arrangements that are flexible and responsive to changes in their lives – more like ordinary relationships between children and significant people in their lives, such as grandparents.

Making arrangements for contact

Contact should be a good experience for the child or young person. This means it also should if possible be a good experience for the parents and carers. Our starting point should therefore be to ask what kind of contact arrangements will make for a good experience for everyone involved. This criterion should be applied to the 'when', 'where' and 'how' of contact.

Margaret Bryer's foreword to Hess and Proch (1993) is so helpful on this topic that it is worth quoting at some length. She begins by referring to the tendency to over-control contact, which she suggests may be a way of coping with the difficulties of the task. She continues:

One trend is to set rigid contact plans which are not flexible enough to be responsive to the changing needs of the children and parents, or to the progress of the plan ... From the point of view of the social workers, carers, lawyers and other professionals, a timetable for contact seems more manageable and fair than a more flexible plan. Parents and children may be reassured by a clear structure ... Yet timetables can be insensitive to the changing needs of children. A child may need to see a parent for a prolonged visit, or several times in quick succession. A meeting once a month may be spent by both child and parent trying to re-establish where they were the month before, and they may never have time to move forwards before the visit is over and the pattern is repeated. Social workers are constrained by decisions of courts when care orders or contact orders are made. However, the courts rely on information from the social workers and guardians ad litem about the needs and wishes of children and parents. In many cases social workers and lawyers could recommend to courts minimum and maximum amounts of contact. This would give a framework within which there could be flexibility.

Hess and Proch (1993), p. 4

Bryer suggests that within this more flexible approach parents and relatives might sometimes be helped to see that, for example, a longer contact at less frequent intervals could be more satisfying and manageable than a brief weekly visit.

In relation to the 'when', 'where' and 'how' of contact, Bryer goes on:

> There is another worrying trend. Some agencies opt for having contact visits in a 'neutral place', such as a family centre, not just in those cases where this is essential to protect the child and foster carers but as a more general practice. The artificiality of visits may be compounded if they are held in a place where activities are restricted and the parents cannot fulfil any of the basic nurturing tasks of parenthood. In unseparated families, parents inter-act with their children while they are doing domestic jobs, or watching TV, or when they go out together. There will often be other people around. On the contrary, parents and children on contact visits are put in an extraordi-nary position of great intensity, intimacy and stress. It is not surprising that they find it hard to cope and sometimes opt out.

Hess and Proch (1993), pp. 4–5

Bryer concludes:

> People's behaviour under stress can be categorised broadly as approach, avoidance or ambivalence. Some parents and children predominantly show avoidance (withdrawal, rejection, depression), or approach (aggression, over-excitement, swamping with affection or sweets, and certain anti-social behaviours), but most show ambivalence, veering from one behaviour to another. Carers and social workers may feel ambivalent about contact and may not be consistent. Each person's behaviour reflects their attempts to solve a problem; in this instance the practicalities and feeling engen-dered by separation and contact. When parents and children (and carers and social workers) do not manage this very well we are quick to judge. It is hard to see distress as anything but negative, and it is tempting to reduce or end contact rather than try alternative strategies for improving it and making it more authentic.

p. 5

Strategies for 'making it more authentic' could include, for some families, allowing the parties (including children) maximum autonomy to determine their own pattern of contact arrangements. For other families, who need more support, it may mean providing a framework of activities that will help build and sustain relationships (Hess and Proch make some useful suggestions for these), or offering a family aide or other worker to help with visits. In other cases the carers may be willing and able to take on an active role in facilitating contact. There is no universal recipe – the keynote has to be flexibility and adaptability, based on the starting point of 'What will make it a good experience for everyone involved?' Written contact plans are important to make sure that everyone has a clear understanding of what is happening – but they should not be unnecessarily rigid.

Exercise 7.1   Annie again

Return to the example of Annie in the previous chapter. This time, ask:

What are the issues involved in choosing a placement for Annie?
What guidance is most relevant?
What research is most relevant?
What are the realistic options?
What arrangements would you make for contact? Why?

Making a placement – practical issues

Having identified a placement, in conjunction with the child or young person and family, there are a number of further tasks we have to undertake in order to make the placement successfully. We have to complete the process of planning in relation to the placement, building in whatever detailed arrangements are needed for the day-to-day care of the child or young person, as well as the plans for contact. We have to ensure that the child understands exactly what is going to happen, and why, and we have to listen to the child yet again to make sure that we know what s/he is thinking and feeling about what is planned. We also have to ensure that parents and other family members understand what is happening.

In most cases we have to establish a programme of preparation and introduction to the placement. Pre-placement visits should be followed by giving all the parties a chance to voice any misgivings and identify any additional needs for support. Fahlberg suggests that

pre-placement visits can:

- Diminish fears and worries of the unknown
- Be used to transfer attachments
- Initiate the grieving process
- Empower new carers
- Encourage making commitments for the future

Fahlberg (1994), p. 169

Very practically, such visits can give the child a chance to 'check out' what the new household is like and how to find their way around it (and to it), and so begin to imagine what it will be like to live there. Visits can also give carers, parents and social workers an opportunity to identify needs that may have been missed in the rest of the planning process.

It's morning. As you awaken, you look around you. It is an unfamiliar room. You slept little last night. You've always been warned about strangers and here you are, with no one else you know, in the midst of them.

You hear people up and about. What are you supposed to do? Lie in bed until someone comes and tells you to get up? Get up, get dressed, and go downstairs on your own? Did anyone tell you last night what was expected? Your memory is fuzzy.

Where are your parents? When will you see them? Do they know where you are? One question after another engulfs you. Pulling the covers over your head, you try to block them out.

What could be done to make this transition easier? Would you be less frightened if the adults were known to you? Would even having your own teddy bear to hug be of any comfort?

Fahlberg (1994), p. 166

In all this work of course we have to pay attention to feelings – of the child, the family, the carers – because these feelings may be the key to success or failure in the placement. However, we also have to attend to some basic practical issues: How and when is the child actually going to make the move? What will she or he need to take? What will she or he be leaving behind? Who will need to be told about the move? A checklist can be a useful aid to practice here; Thoburn (1994, pp. 52–4) gives quite a good one, which can be adapted for different contexts.

The other key task at the beginning of a placement is to clarify the arrangements for supervision and support. There is plenty of research evidence of the importance of social work input in the early stages of a placement if the child or young person is either to return home as planned or settle successfully in a permanent placement. All parties – carers, birth family and above all the child – need to know what support they can expect, and they need regular contact with the social worker in order to deal with worries or difficulties before they become insuperable. Although there are statutory requirements for visits and reviews, it is also necessary to have an agreed plan for how those are to be carried out in a way that will be most helpful to the child in placement.

Summary and conclusion

Entrance into the foster system is often sudden and without preparation. Once in the child care system, the child's traumatic separation from his or her birth family is frequently allowed to drift into permanent estrangement. Worse still, the maintenance of a bond between the child in interim care and his or her birth family is sometimes actively discouraged. The child's feelings of loss are frequently ignored or glossed over. Contacts between parents and child may be limited or prevented. Children's emotional reactions to visits with their birth families may be misunderstood and misinterpreted. Foster carers may not receive the help they need in dealing with the increased behavioural problems precipitated by the visits. However, the truth is that minimising the trauma of separations and losses and working to facilitate the development of new attachments are complementary, rather than competitive, tasks.

Fahlberg (1994), pp. 167–8

We began this chapter by considering some of the issues that arise in choosing placements for children and by reviewing the types of placement that may be available. We then looked at the process of relating children's needs to what placements can offer, and at issues of participation in decision making. We also considered some of the ways in which thinking about attachment and resilience can helping in making choices about placements, at the contribution of 'kinship care' to the range of options for children and young people, and at the part played by sibling relationships in placement decisions. We then considered a number of issues in relation to family contact for young people in care, the purpose of contact, and some of the difficulties that may arise. Finally, we looked at some aspects of the practical arrangements for placement and contact.

The passage from Fahlberg quoted above brings together many of the themes of this chapter: the importance of attachment and the intense feelings that can be associated with separation; the value of working actively to maintain contact between a child and significant people; the need to listen carefully to the child and understand her or his reactions. The final point that needs adding is the extent to which good placement practice usually starts by asking 'What can we do to keep this child as close to home, in every sense, as possible?'

GUIDE TO FURTHER READING

On placement, the best general text is Thoburn (1994), on which I have drawn at several points in this chapter. An excellent source on keeping children and families together is Marsh and Triseliotis (1993). Broad (2001) is a good up-to-date source on kinship care, while Doolan et al. (2004) offer good practice advice. On sibling relationships, Mullender (1999) and Sanders (2004) are both useful. On contact, Hess and Prosh (1993) and British Agencies for Adoption and Fostering (1999a) are very helpful.

For government guidance and the legal regulations, Department of Health (1991b and 1991c) and Scottish Office (1995) are essential sources. Finally, Fahlberg (1994) is a book which everyone should have – mainly concerned with permanent placement, but full of wisdom and sound advice.

Residential and foster care

Introduction

In this chapter we will look in more detail at the main types of care provision for children and young people – residential or group care, and foster care or family placement.

We will look first at the distinctive characteristics of each of these two broad categories of placement, with some reference to the historical background. We will then consider what skills are involved in each type of care, what factors are linked with success or failure, and what are the respective roles of social workers and carers. This will prepare the ground for going on to consider what might be the advantages and disadvantages of one care type over the other.

After this we will look specifically at the role of the field social worker and at the supervision and inspection of placements. The chapter will conclude with a discussion of abuse in care and how it can be prevented, and of the place of therapeutic work in care.

A word on terminology – in this chapter I generally use the term 'residential care'. Occasionally we will talk about 'group care', and when appropriate 'children's homes'. Likewise the chapter includes references both to 'foster care' and to 'family placement', to 'foster carers' and to 'foster parents'. All of these terms have their advantages as well as their drawbacks, and I do not propose to legislate as to whether some are better than others.

Characteristics of foster care

Background

Foster care or 'boarding out' has always been a feature of substitute care for children. Examples include the practice of placing older children in other people's houses to learn a trade or as a domestic servant, and the use of wet-nursing. Under the Poor Law, officials sometimes placed children with families rather than in institutions. Whether this was primarily to save money, or because they thought it was better for the children, is debatable. Charitable societies made less use of boarding out, either because of their investment in bricks and mortar or because of their mission to 'save' children. However, they did send children abroad on a large scale, and many of these were placed with families. From the 1880s there was a growing campaign both to promote boarding out and to improve the standard of care and supervision, which was mainly done by volunteer visitors. However, large institutions remained the most typical form of substitute care, as we see below.

In Britain the biggest changes occurred after the Second World War, and were at least in part a response to the dislocation which so many children suffered during the war years and to greater awareness of the perceived defects of institutional care. In England and Wales the Children Act 1948 made boarding out the preferred form of child care, consistent with its aim to 'normalise' the experience of children in care as much as possible. At the same time – and partly in response to the then recent death of Dennis O'Neill at the hands of his foster father – the Act created a much more rigorous framework of supervision for children in foster care, with specialist staff originally called 'boarding out visitors' and later renamed 'child care officers'. Detailed regulations introduced in 1955 prescribed the manner and the frequency both of visiting and of reviews of placements.

The assumption of the 1955 'boarding out regulations' was that when a situation arose where a child needed a foster home, an officer who knew the child personally would identify a suitable family for that particular child. By the time the regulations were revised in 1988, the organisation of foster care had changed, and people were thinking much more in terms of a 'foster care service'. Most agencies aimed to recruit and maintain a range of foster placements approved for different purposes – assessment, short term care, long term care, therapeutic work – from which a choice would be made for a particular child. Training programmes for carers developed, allowances were often more realistic, and in addition most areas had some kind of specialist scheme – most commonly for adolescents who in the past might have been in children's homes.

Although the 1988 regulations did not really reflect these changes, new regulations made in 1991 under the Children Act 1989, and in 1996 under the Children (Scotland) Act 1995, did reflect them. Under these regulations local authorities now had a duty to maintain and support a range of foster homes chosen to reflect the needs of children in their area. Carers had to be approved for specified types of care, and were only to be used for the purposes for which they were approved – although the regulations also made provision for emergency placements. The approval of a household was to be reviewed at regular intervals, quite separately from the review of a child placed there, and it was made explicit that on at least some of the regular visits to a placement the child should be seen apart from the carers.

Types of foster care

Triseliotis, Sellick and Short (1995) classify foster care into a number of different types:

(1) Relief care: care offered to provide a periodic break for parents (or for children).
(2) Emergency fostering: provided by carers who undertake to be available whenever needed to take in children pending more planned arrangements.
(3) Short term foster care: either when the need for care is temporary or for assessment, and lasting, suggest Triseliotis et al., 'from a few days to about twelve weeks' (p. 12).
(4) Intermediate or medium-length fostering: this they suggest 'covers the majority of children in foster care' (p. 12), lasts 'from about eight weeks to two years' (p. 13), and is intended to give parents time to sort out difficulties, to help children overcome difficulties, or to protect children.
(5) Long term or permanent fostering: for children who need care for the remainder of their childhood.
(6) Private fostering: Triseliotis et al. include this, but it is quite distinct from all other forms of fostering in that it is arranged by the child's parents although the local authority must be notified.

As I mentioned in the previous chapter, there is more than one way to define short and long term fostering, and Triseliotis et al.'s classification into short, medium and long term is quite helpful. Sellick and Thoburn (2002) divide all family placement into temporary and permanent, or 'supplementary' and 'substitute', which is also a useful way to look at it. The important thing for practitioners to remember is that people may use these terms in different ways, and therefore it is sometimes important to clarify what exactly is meant. Note that Triseliotis et al. do not have a separate category or categories for the various kinds of specialist fostering schemes. These now include *remand fostering*, where young people awaiting court appearances, who in the past would automatically have gone to a residential placement, may now be placed with a family.

Although *private fostering* is not discussed at any length here, it is an important topic affecting thousands of children, and those interested in finding out more about it are referred to Holman (2002) or Philpot (2001).

What sort of people foster?

As one might expect from the range of tasks involved in foster care, a wide range of people undertake them. The most recent survey is by Triseliotis, Borland and Hill (2000) in Scotland, which also took account of data from England and Wales. On the basis of this research it is possible to say that three quarters of carers are aged over 40, although the majority started to foster before they were 40. Most are living in married or other stable relationships, but a significant and growing group are lone carers – mainly divorced or separated, nearly all women, often highly committed to their work as foster carers. The age distribution varies widely from authority to authority, as does the proportion who are alone; but in most areas carers are overwhelmingly white. Most carers have their own children, but do not have more children of their own after starting to foster. Employment patterns vary: the most common arrangement is for one carer to go out to work and one to stay at home, but this is not universal; a third of households have both carers working full or part time, and other foster carers are unemployed or retired.

In some respects the profile of foster carers has not changed very much in the past 30 years, but the number of single carers has increased and the proportion of women going out to work is much greater than it was 30 years ago. The latter is part of a more marked increase in the female population generally, which has tended to make it more difficult to recruit and retain traditional carers and has encouraged 'professionalisation'. Triseliotis, Borland and Hill found that most foster carers explained their wish to foster in terms of 'having something to offer', 'fondness/liking to care for children', or 'awareness of need and wishing to offer something back to the community'.

There has been some controversy over the approval of gay and lesbian people as foster carers. The clear advice from the British Agencies for Adoption and Fostering is that there is no reason why gay and lesbian individuals or couples cannot in principle provide good care for children. As always, the issue is one of choosing the right placement for a particular child based on an assessment of her or his needs and who is best able to meet them. For a discussion of these issues see Hicks and McDermott (1998).

Most foster carers work directly for local authorities, and some for voluntary agencies such as Barnardos (more so in England and Wales than in Scotland). In recent years an increasing number have been engaged by private fostering agencies. For the most part these agencies take more 'hard to place' children and young people, although this may be less true in areas with more severe recruitment crises. Apart from the budgetary implications, some of the private agencies present a real challenge to statutory agencies in the support they provide to carers.

What sort of children and young people are fostered?

When we come to the picture of children in foster care we find that there has been much more change. Again the most up-to-date source is Triseliotis, Borland and Hill (2000) As they point out, the actual numbers in foster care have not changed very much, although as a proportion of children and young people in care they have changed markedly. However, there has been a significant change in the kind of children and young people who are in foster care. As Triseliotis et al. (2000, p. 2) put it, 'Most of those looked after in foster care now would have been in residential care 20 years ago, and those in foster care then are now looked after in their own homes.'

It is arguable that children tend to enter the care system now with more severe problems than in the past, and undeniable that many of those with the most difficulties find themselves in foster care. The effects of physical, sexual and emotional abuse (more readily identified than in the past), emotional and behavioural disorders, the consequences of alcohol and drug misuse, HIV – all are encountered routinely in modern foster care. It's important not to compare the present with an idealised version of the past. It has always been the case that many children in foster care have severe problems and are very difficult to look after well, but the extent and degree of problems does appear to have worsened, and the residential sector no longer operates as a filter or safety net in the way that it used to do.

Many children and young people who come into foster care are from black and ethnic minority groups. When the availability of foster carers is limited, some children are placed with white families in white communities, or with people who in other ways are from a completely different cultural background. Although this is a hotly debated issue, the research evidence is reasonably clear that however successful 'transracial placements' may be in some respects, they frequently fail to support young people in developing a secure and positive sense of their own identity (Gill and Jackson 1983; Maximé 1993).

Working in foster care

Skills needed by foster carers

All these pressures have affected the nature of the fostering task. The aim of foster care has traditionally been to provide as far as possible a normal family life – foster parents undertook to bring up a child as if s/he was their own. This is still a fair description of what foster carers do in many cases, especially for children who are expected to remain with a particular family on a permanent basis. However, it is increasingly recognised that foster care is a skilled task, and one which should arguably be regarded as professional. In addition to dealing with all the difficulties presented by children and young people, most foster carers are now expected to work in partnership with a child's own family and to facilitate regular contact. This is reflected in the shift in terminology from 'foster parent' to 'foster carer'.

Whichever particular fostering task they take on, foster carers have to be able to:

- make warm and effective relationships with children and young people;
- provide good physical and psychological care for them;
- enable children to feel at home, without disrupting their existing attachments;
- prioritise the needs of children and young people with a range of problems, without causing harm to the foster carers' own children;
- work in partnership with social workers and other professionals.

Clearly this demands a lot in terms of skills and personal resources, and good preparation and training is critically important if foster carers are to be successful. Knowledge is also important; Cairns (2002b) writes directly and affectingly of the ways in which theories have helped her in her work as a foster carer. In the UK in recent years, and after extensive consultation, 'national standards' have been introduced for foster carers which specify in some detail what is expected in terms of skills, training and practice, and government has introduced objectives and targets for levels of qualification among carers. Increasingly it is being argued that greater professionalisation and a re-thinking of the role of foster carers are essential if the needs of children and young people in care are to be met effectively (see Ainsworth and Maluccio 2003; Hutchinson 2003).

It is not part of my purpose to look in any depth at recruitment or assessment of prospective foster carers. Those interested in this aspect of practice should look at the material produced by agencies such as the British Agencies for

Adoption and Fostering and Fostering Network (formerly the National Foster Care Association); Triseliotis et al. (2000) is also useful. This work is usually the preserve of specialist teams – but any childcare social worker may be involved in assessing whether particular carers are able to meet the needs of a particular child, and what kind of support they may need, and it is important to have some understanding of what is involved. It may be necessary to look in some depth at the personalities and relationships within the fostering family, as well as at the parenting and other skills which the carers can offer.

Success and failure in foster care

Research into foster care indicates that success is not always easy to predict. Although a number of factors, especially child-related factors, are associated with success and failure in placement, the implications of these findings are not always clear-cut. There are a few exceptions: the finding that fostering a child close in age to the carers' own children carries a high risk of breakdown is a very consistent one. It is also clear that one common characteristic of carers who do well is openness – to experience, to ideas and to people. Carers who are able to accept children and young people as they are and acknowledge their past experiences, who can include them in the foster family without excluding the family of origin, and who have good links with a wider community, tend to last longer as carers and provide better placements.

Care in selecting the right carers for a particular child is important, but can be difficult when choice is often limited – especially for children from minority ethnic backgrounds. Research shows that however good the care which white families may provide for black children, what is usually missing is the chance to grow up with a secure sense of identity and knowledge of their own heritage. For these and other reasons, however well planned the 'fostering service' in an area, it is still sometimes necessary to look for new carers for a particular child or young person.

Transitions and moves can be a testing time for child and family, and the time when a child leaves their foster home is an important transition. Whether it is to another placement, back to the original family, or on to 'independent' living, if the move is managed well and relationships kept alive the child or young person is likely to benefit much more.

Roles and relationships in foster care

In practice a successful placement is a partnership between carer, parent, social worker and child – and sometimes other people as well. There is scope for confusion about roles and responsibilities, and one of the purpose of regular planning meetings is to make these things as clear as possible.

Although the agency's duty is to promote the welfare of the child, there are many interests to be considered, not least those of the foster carers' own children and other children who may be placed with them. Research has shown that while being part of a fostering family can have benefits for foster carers' own children, it can also create difficulties that need to be addressed (see for instance Spears and Cross 2003).

A good working relationship with social workers is usually essential for successful fostering. What carers value most is reliability (including simple things like returning phone calls and visiting when promised), warmth and friendliness, and useful practical knowledge. Research suggests that carers are usually pleased with the service they get from their 'link' workers, but often dissatisfied with the service from the child's social worker. This may be related to inexperience, overwork and high turnover among childcare social workers (see Sellick 1996).

Fisher et al. (2000) found that foster carers valued social workers who exhibited the following qualities:

- show an interest in how carers are managing;
- are easy to contact and responsive when contacted;
- do what they say they are going to do;
- are prepared to listen and offer encouragement;
- take account of the family's needs and circumstances;
- keep them informed and include them in planning;
- ensure that payments, complaints, etc. are processed as soon as possible;
- attend to the child's interests and needs, and involve foster carers in this where appropriate.

Fisher et al. (2000), p. 231

Exercise 8.1   Annie in short term care

Annie has been placed with a family in her home town. Mr and Mrs Farmer have two children of their own, boys aged eight and six. Annie is able to attend the same school, and has some contact with her mother and with Sarah, who is living with their aunt.

   Mr and Mrs Farmer are fond of Annie but find her quite 'clingy'. She appears jealous of the attention they give to their own boys.

What skills do Mr and Mrs Farmer need in order to give good care to Annie and to their own children?
What support are they likely to need?
What issues are likely to arise when the placement is reviewed, and how might they be dealt with?

Characteristics of residential care

Background

Like foster care, residential care for children has a long history: nurseries, residential schools, orphanages and other institutions go back to the Middle Ages and even earlier. Sometimes they are part of the normal pattern of care for entire classes or communities; examples are the Prussian *gymnasia* (modelled on those of ancient Sparta) or the English 'public' school, where a primary purpose of the institution is to ensure that boys over a certain age are looked after by men rather than women. More often, however, the institutions are provided specifically for abandoned or delinquent children.

In Britain in the nineteenth and early twentieth centuries the majority of children looked after by the Poor Law boards or by the childcare charities were in residential institutions (for a brief analytical account of this history, see Parker 1990). As we have seen, foster care was always part of the picture. After 1948 foster care became the placement of choice, in theory at least. However, because of the rise in numbers in care and because of the investment that had already been made in residential establishments, residential care remained numerically very significant until the 1970s and 1980s. In the 1970s residential nurseries disappeared, and residential care ceased to be used much for children of primary school age. During the 1980s a sharp and sustained decline in numbers in care enabled the closure of most residential childcare places. Now residential care is increasingly seen as a short or medium term resource for adolescents, often those who cannot be placed satisfactorily in foster care because of their behaviour or their circumstances.

Types of residential care

To take the example of one country, the figures for England on 31 March 2000 (Department of Health 2001b) show that there were 1146 children's homes at that time, including 672 community homes maintained by local authorities, 103 voluntary homes (some 'controlled' or 'assisted' by local authorities, but the majority independent), 256 private registered children's homes, and 103 registered residential care homes providing personal or nursing care for children who are ill or disabled. The total number of places available was 9164 (of which 6559 were occupied). This does not include facilities such as regional treatment centres that are provided directly by the Department of Health.

It is worth noting that over the period 1995–2000 in England the proportion of local authority homes fell from 65 to 59 per cent, while the proportion of private homes rose from 16 to 22 per cent. At the same time the number of homes accommodating five children or fewer rose sharply, while the number accommodating ten or more showed a marked decline. Only 31 homes had space for more than 20 children. Numbers of homes are not the same as numbers of places, of course, and the aggregated figures suggest that around 40 per cent of places were still in homes accommodating ten children or more.

Within these official categories there are wide variations. Berridge and Brodie (1997) divide their sample into 'local authority homes for adolescents', 'local authority homes for younger children', 'local authority homes offering short term breaks for young people with severe learning disabilities and additional health needs', and 'private children's homes'. Some voluntary or private sector homes may provide highly specialised resources. Some establishments, local authority, voluntary and private, have education on the premises – although this is less common than it used to be. Other specialised facilities, such as secure units, may be provided by one local authority on behalf of others.

What sort of children and young people are in residential care?

The most obvious thing to say about children in group care, as compared to children in care in general, is that they are older. The age pattern is clearly exemplified in the English statistics in Figure 8.1, which show an over-whelming majority (around 80 per cent) aged 12–17, with a marked peak at 15. However, it should also be remarked that one child in five lies outside this age

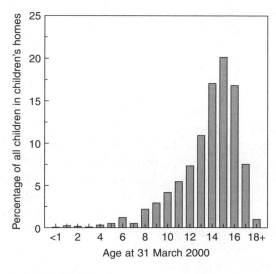

Source: Department of Health (2001b)

Figure 8.1   Children placed in children's homes at 31 March 2000, England, by age

range, and that this includes a small number of very young children. It is also the case that 'most children and young people in residential care are older' does not mean 'most older children and young people are in residential care'; at any one time the majority of children and young people in care of *all* ages are in foster homes.

It would be tempting to assume also that children in residential care tend to have more problems, but this would be to oversimplify. We noted earlier the comment of Triseliotis et al. (2000) that most of those looked after in foster care now would have been in residential care 20 years ago, and to some extent it is also true that children and young people in ordinary children's homes are more 'demanding' or 'difficult' since the decline of more specialist facilities. However, the pattern has been for greater difficulties to emerge (or to be recognised) in every kind of placement. As we see later, there are a number of factors that may influence whether a young person goes into family placement or into group care, and level of difficulty is only one of these.

Children with physical, sensory or learning disabilities are often placed in specialised accommodation, although legislation such as the Children Act 1989 encourages practitioners to think in terms of adapting ordinary accommodation where necessary. Children from minority ethnic groups are slightly more likely to find themselves in residential as opposed to foster care than white children, although this varies between local authorities (Rowe et al. 1989; Department of Health 1998).

Working in residential care

Skills needed in residential care

Residential childcare workers have characteristics in common both with foster carers and with field social workers. Like foster carers they do the 'hands-on' business of actually looking after children from day to day. Like field social workers they are employed directly by the agency and do not normally work in their own homes. They may have the same professional training as field social workers, and to a greater or lesser extent they take responsibility for planning and for negotiating with other agencies and professions.

The profession of residential childcare is not in general a high status one, and many workers are relatively unqualified and inexperienced. However, within the profession there are also very high levels of skill and knowledge. The tasks involved, in addition to the routine (if it can ever be called that) provision of physical and emotional care for children and young people, may include:

- assessment;
- therapeutic work;

- work with group dynamics;
- management of challenging behaviour;
- work to prepare young people for return home;
- work with families;
- preparation for foster care;
- preparation for independence.

These tasks demand a wide range of skills and knowledge. Whitaker, Archer and Hicks (1998) looked closely and analytically at practice in group care, and concluded that the work required the following knowledge, skills and personal qualities:

- *knowledge and understanding* of personal development, transgenerational processes and family dynamics; the positive and negative potentials of group living; networks and network interactions; organisational structures and dynamics;
- *skills* in listening, observing, intervening and assessment, in order to understand emotional reactions and feelings in the young people and themselves;
- *personal qualities* and *values* that are consistent with the aims and philosophy of the establishment.

(summary based on Department of Health (1998);
Whitaker et al. (1998))

Some of this can certainly be acquired in practice, if staff are fortunate enough to work in a setting where there is already good practice and support for learning and development. Some of it can best be learned through formal education and a structure of qualifications. Despite many years of attempts to improve the situation, the majority of residential child care workers in Britain still do not have formal qualifications. In recent years national standards have been introduced for children's homes and managers, together with requirements for increasing numbers of the workforce to hold a relevant National Vocational Qualification; but there is a lot of catching up to be done. This contrasts with the situation in some European countries, where residential care is regarded as a relatively high status profession, and where residential workers may be expected as a matter of course to have qualifications at degree level or beyond in social work, psychology, teaching or 'social pedagogy' (see Chapter 11).

Success and failure in residential care

It is sometimes suggested that residential provision has no place in modern child care. People argue that all children should be in families, that the risks of abuse are too great, or that residential care is not cost-effective. However, not all children want to be in families, and adolescents who have poor relationships with their parents often prefer group living, at least for a time. Abuse also takes place in foster care, perhaps on a greater scale than is suspected. Good quality foster care for the most difficult children can also be expensive. The Utting report (1991) argued strongly that there remains an important place for good, purposeful, professional residential care with proper standards and safeguards.

Assessing success of course depends on what the aims are. Sinclair and Gibbs (1998) studied a range of different kinds of children's homes with the aim of comparing outcomes and explaining the differences, in particular in the social environment of each home and the wellbeing of individual residents. They found that homes in which young people were more likely to behave 'delinquently' also tended to be seen by residents and staff as marked by difficult behaviour and unfriendly relationships between the residents. In these homes residents tended to feel that they had little say in how the home was run, that being in the home was a waste of time and that they were not being helped. Staff morale was typically low and the quality of relationships between staff and young people was poor. The likelihood of a home fitting this description was not related to the previous behaviour of the young people, or to the number and level of training of the staff. Homes were more likely to have a positive social environment if they were small, if the head felt that roles were clear and compatible and that s/he had enough autonomy, and if staff agreed on how the home should be run. Positive change in individual residents was more likely if the head of home had a coherent philosophy of how change could be enabled, and if the turnover in the home was not great. (Summary based on Department of Health 1998.)

Brown, Bullock, Hobson and Little (1998), in a parallel study, found that success was associated with congruence between the structure and goals of the establishment, the staff culture and the child culture. Frost, Mills and Stein (1999) argue that 'the *empowerment* of children and young people should be the central focus of the residential child care task' (p. 39; my italics). They explore the ramifications of this approach for issues such as rules and procedures, planning meetings and reviews, use of sanctions, gender, sexuality, ethnicity and disability. They suggest that empowerment has the potential not just to inform a framework for practice, but to 'restore belief in residential child care' (p. 127).

Roles and relationships in residential care

Residential workers usually operate as members of a team and look after children in shifts, and communication is critically important. Unlike foster carers who live together as members of a family, opportunities for residential workers to exchange information and ideas have to be relatively formalised.

One of the challenges of group care is to ensure that each child or young person has the chance to develop one or two close relationships, and that there is at least someone in the home who has something like the knowledge of the child and her/his situation that a parent might have. 'Key worker' systems are often used as one way to achieve this; but of course the key worker is not always there when a child needs attention, so it is important that the whole team has a shared understanding of how to work with each child or young person.

We see throughout this book how professional childcare must be based on partnership. In particular, a good working relationship between field and residential social worker is fundamental to good care and planning for children and young people who are looked after in children's homes. This can only be based on mutual respect and understanding of each other's roles. The potential for confusion or misunderstanding is probably greater between field and residential workers than between social workers and foster carers. Residential workers may take on work with families or report writing, as well as liaison with other agencies, and it is important to develop a shared understanding of respective roles and mutual expectations. If either party feels either pushed aside or 'dumped on' then the partnership will not be effective, and children and young people will suffer as a result. Where local children's centres have been developed which include 'outreach' and family-based work in addition to residential provision, this can have the effect of breaking down some of the divisions between field and residential social work.

The relationship between residential and foster care

According to a research overview by the Department of Health (1998) of 30,000 children and young people coming into care each year in England and Wales, some 15,000 stayed for less than six weeks and 15,000 for longer. Of the first group about 11,000 were looked after in foster care and 3200 in residential care, while 150 had a combination of placement types. Of the second group 9500 would go into foster care and 3500 into residential care, with 750 experiencing a mixture.

What is it that determines which children go into which type of placement? To some extent clearly it is age, as Figure 8.1 showed. To some extent it is a matter of rules: according to the Department of Health, 56 per cent of children's homes set a minimum age of between 10 and 15, while 36 per cent were able to accommodate younger children. To some extent it is a matter of supply: local authorities are regularly short of foster placements, especially for older children and young people or for those who present behavioural challenges. To some extent it is a matter of client preference: young people or their families may strongly favour family placement, on the one hand, or residential care on the other. If the processes of assessment and planning that we outlined in Chapter 6 are well managed, then it should above all be a considered choice based on an assessment of the child or young person's needs.

A number of studies have compared residential and foster care in terms of the care provided and the outcomes. Colton (1988) found that specialist foster homes were significantly more 'child-centred' than children's homes and that children were more positive about their placements, but that the children's homes were equally successful in a number of respects including addressing problem behaviour and encouraging school performance. Rowe et al. (1989) found that residential placements were assessed by social workers as less successful in meeting their objectives (46 per cent against 53 per cent of foster placements), although the difference tends to disappear once account is taken of age. Cliffe and Berridge (1991) studied the Warwickshire 'experiment' in which all children's homes were closed, and found that most placements appeared to be successful, but less so than in other local authorities and with more placement instability.

Berridge (1994, 1997) reviewed the research and concluded that, once age factors and differences in aims were taken into account, both residential and foster care were equally effective in meeting their objectives for children and young people in care. However, he added, this did not mean that the two services were interchangeable but rather that they were *complementary*:

> Residential environments are not suitable for children to grow up in over long periods: younger children, especially, require more intimate care and greater daily continuity and predictability than residential settings can usually provide. Foster care, therefore, has clear potential advantages in these areas.
>
> Berridge (1994), p. 147

An alternative perspective comes from countries where residential care is viewed and practised differently. In much of Europe residential institutions are traditionally seen as providing stable long term care, with interesting results. For instance, a study of children's villages in France, where placements tended to be extremely stable, found that school achievement was better than for children in traditional foster care or with their own families, especially for children placed under the age of six (Dumaret 1988).

More recent studies by Hayden and Gorin of residential and foster care in three local authorities also illustrate the interdependence of residential and foster care, and the value of having both types of placement available (Hayden et al. 1999). In this way the system is able to respond to children's changing circumstances and also to plan for their future needs. For instance, as we see in the next chapter, for some children permanent family placement may require a period of preparation in residential care.

From a young person's point of view, a foster placement may be more like their family home, or what they might have wished their family home to be like, with their dominant relationship being with parental figures; while in a group care setting their relationships with a group of other young people may be much more important. Which is preferable will depend on the individual young person and what they are looking for from the experience of care; and this may need to carry as much weight as any professional assessment of the young person's needs.

Supporting children and young people in residential and foster care

Roles in relation to placements

We have spoken already of the need for field social workers to work together with both residential staff and foster carers in order to make and support good placements for children and young people. The field social worker will normally have the lead responsibility for ensuring that the agreed plan is implemented (or reviewed if necessary), that tasks are allocated and followed through, and that legal requirements are adhered to. However, this does not mean that the field social worker does all the work, or indeed any particular task. Tasks may be undertaken by residential workers, by foster carers, or by parents. What is important is that everyone understands who is doing what. That is why the *Looking After Children* Assessment and Action records invite one to specify who will undertake each identified task. (It is sometimes thought that under the Children Act 1989 foster carers cannot consent to medical treatment – but the Foster Placement (Children) Regulations 1991 say that one of the matters to be covered in foster placement agreements is 'any arrangements for delegation of responsibility for consent to the medical or dental examination or treatment of the child'; regulation 5(5), schedule 3, item 3.)

Other key players in these relationships may include placement officers and family link workers, supervisors and managers, family aides and support workers, and of course parents and family members. At the centre of course is the child or young person, but what does this mean in practice? Above all it means listening to the child or young person, and thinking about all the arrangements made in terms of what it will mean to them. It means consulting them about what is going on and who is doing what. For the field social worker it means keeping in regular contact with the child or young person and developing a proper working relationship with them. However good the care provided, and however strong the child or young person's relationship with their carers, it can be crucially important for them also to have a trusting relationship outside the home, in order to safeguard and promote their welfare.

It is also important to clarify who has the primary responsibility for supporting the child or young person's education, and to show that everyone is committed to this. Guidance issued in England and Wales is comprehensive and helpful (Department of Health and Department for Education and Employment 2000).

Supervising placements and inspecting placement resources

Regular visiting and regular reviews are both part of the process by which we ensure that children and young people are being properly looked after. For children in foster care this means regular visits by the social worker. These visits have a number of purposes, including keeping contact with the child and supporting or advising the carers. They also have the purpose of ensuring that the child is being well cared for and not being ill-treated – this can easily be forgotten in the desire to make friendly relationships with carers, but it remains a primary purpose of the 'statutory visit'.

Reviews of children in foster care should be held at least at the intervals prescribed by law and guidance – but it should be remembered that these are *maximum* intervals, and reviews should be held more often if the child's needs require it. It is likely that a family placement link worker will also be in regular contact with the foster carers, and from time to time there will also be a review of their terms of approval as carers, quite separate from the child's review.

For children's homes the arrangements are different. Social workers are not legally required to visit at specified intervals, but should be guided by good practice and by the circumstances of the case. The kind of trusting relationship we talked about just now depends on an appropriate pattern of contact, but this pattern will vary with circumstances and with the wishes of the child or young person.

The monitoring of standards of care in the UK is not the responsibility of the social worker, but of an independent inspectorate which visits each establishment and which from time to time will speak to the residents. Responsibility for ensuring the welfare of children and young people in residential care is therefore shared, because the social worker still has a professional responsibility to satisfy her or himself that the child's welfare is being safeguarded and to take appropriate action if not. S/he also has a professional responsibility to take appropriate action if s/he has concerns about the welfare of other children and young people in the same establishment.

Reviews of children in residential care are normally governed by the same regulations as are reviews of children in foster care. In both cases reviews should be managed in such a way as to ensure that the implementation of the plans for the child is properly scrutinised, that plans are revised when necessary, and that all parties – and especially the child or young person – have a real opportunity to take a full part in the process.

Advocates and independent visitors

It is increasingly recognised that if children and young people are to be effectively protected from harm, and their wishes and feelings properly taken into account, then it is not enough to rely either on their own ability to speak up for themselves or on the skills and commitment of those looking after them. Because of the power imbalance between adults and children, and because of the particular vulnerability of children and young people in care, some form of outside support is necessary. The system in England and Wales distinguishes between

- *independent visitors* appointed to befriend a child who has little or no support from her or his own family – there is a duty to do this if the child wishes it and would benefit from it, and
- *advocates* whose job is to speak for the child or to support the child in speaking for her/himself, in a variety of circumstances where the child wishes for this service.

Advocates and visitors may be appointed by the local authority or care provider directly, or by an organisation funded for this purpose. Since the 1990s there has been a substantial expansion in provision of advocacy services of one kind and another. An additional source of advocacy now available to children and young people as an interest group, and to some extent to individual children too, is the office of Children's Commissioner. Following well-established precedents in Scandinavian countries and elsewhere, the first such appointment in the UK was in Wales in 2001, followed over the next few years by similar appointments in Northern Ireland, Scotland and finally England.

Abuse in care and how it can be prevented

Abuse of children in residential care has been the subject of a series of major scandals in recent years, among the most notable being:

- the Staffordshire 'pindown' regime, where children were deprived of normal basic care as part of a supposedly effective professional approach to behaviour management (Kahan and Levy 1991);
- the Leicestershire case, which involved the repeated physical and sexual abuse of children by a powerful and charismatic figure under the cloak of 'regression therapy' (Kirkwood 1993);
- the North Wales case, which involved the operation of a conspiracy to abuse children for the sexual gratification of powerful adults (some of them

working as part of a network) which went undetected or unchallenged for many years (Waterhouse 2000).

The earlier scandals led to reviews of the nature and purpose of residential care and attempts to improve standards, among them the first Utting report *Children in the Public Care* (Utting 1991). At the same time the Warner report (Department of Health 1992) recommended a series of improvements in the recruitment, selection and staffing of homes. The events covered by the Waterhouse inquiry happened in the 1970s and 1980s, and by the time the inquiry took place the system had changed considerably. Children's homes are now subject to much closer outside scrutiny and staff are better trained and supervised (as well as being subject to criminal convictions checks). There is also clearer definition of the purposes of residential care – both in particular establishments and in individual cases; and the general planning of residential provision is integrated into overall children's services planning. However, this does not mean that children are no longer abused.

In general the issues of abuse in foster care have received much less attention than have the same issues in residential care – although the reviews of 'children's safeguards' in England and Wales and in Scotland did consider children in all forms of care (Kent 1997; Utting 1997). It is likely that much abuse in foster care goes undetected. At the same time foster carers often feel vulnerable to unfounded accusations, and if allegations or suspicions are handled badly then good carers may be lost as a result (see Thomas 1995). It is also important to remember how vulnerable foster carers can be when they are caring for a child who has been abused and who has a distorted understanding of how to please adults. Such children's behaviour can be very provocative, and a carer must be mature, experienced and confident in themselves in order to manage such behaviour carefully and sensitively.

For practitioners the important lessons from the earlier inquiries are clear. What they show more than anything else is the importance of listening to children and young people, of creating space in which they can confide in trusted adults, and of ensuring that they have good information about accessible complaints procedures. What they also show is the duty of staff with concerns to speak out, and the danger of allowing any professional to operate without scrutiny or challenge.

Support with difficult behaviour

Managing emotional or behavioural difficulties can be a real challenge for any placement. There is sometimes little congruence between social workers' and foster carers' understanding of the reasons for children's difficult behaviour, and still less about strategies for managing it. Both residential and foster carers may sometimes feel that the behaviour is in some way their fault, or that others may think it is. Golding (2003) describes a project which enabled carers, support workers and therapists to work together to understand and manage children's challenging behaviours. Initial consultations for foster carers helped them better understand children's behaviours as adaptive strategies from their early years which might be long-standing and resistant to change, and not as a product of their poor parenting. Placements which were seen as at risk were sometimes enabled to persist by introducing greater realism about the prospects for change. Sometimes foster carers may themselves need periods of respite from the strain of looking after a particularly demanding child.

Therapeutic work in care

We have already seen that many children in the care system have acute problems with their identity, with their behaviour or with their relationships with other people. Many of them have been abused or neglected and may need help in dealing with the consequences of that. For many children and young people a secure, stable placement with good care provided with warmth and affection will be sufficient for the process of healing and growth to take place, or at least to begin. For some, however, more is needed, including in some cases specialised therapy. The extent to which therapy can be made available as part of a care placement is highly variable, and the distinction between what is care and what is therapy is not always a simple or straightforward one. Some foster carers, and some residential establishments, have particular skills or experience in dealing with particular kinds of difficulties that children may have. In other cases additional therapeutic input – individual psychotherapy, group work, play therapy – may need to be arranged either in the home or elsewhere, often at an outpatient clinic.

What is critically important is not to neglect the needs of some children for therapy. It often seems expensive, and managers may be reluctant to commit large chunks of a limited budget to one child – especially if the placement itself is already costing a lot. However, a moderate investment at the right point can avoid much greater costs later, both in service provision of various kinds and in human unhappiness.

Summary and conclusion

I hope this brief review of residential and foster care has given a helpful picture of the different types of placement and some of the ways in which they can be used for the benefit of children and young people. The most important points to remember are:

- Both types of placement have their strengths, and in the end it is a matter of asking, 'What is going to be the most helpful placement for *this* child or young person?'
- The success of a placement depends to a large extent on the atmosphere of the household or culture of the establishment, and on the commitment of carers to working directly with children and young people.
- All placements must be open to the outside world, to advice, supervision and scrutiny, in order to safeguard and promote the welfare of children and young people.

The focus of this chapter has been on all types of placement for different purposes, short, medium and long term. In the next chapter we will look in more depth at what is involved in achieving permanence for children and young people.

GUIDE TO FURTHER READING

On foster care, the best general sources are probably Triseliotis, Sellick and Short (1995), which is written for social work students, Triseliotis, Borland and Hill (2000) which is more for family placement specialists, and Wheal (1995, 2002) – the former written mainly for foster carers but equally useful for social workers working with them. For reviews of the general foster care research, Berridge (1997) is very useful, and so is Sellick and Thoburn (1996). Some of the research from the 1980s is still worth reading directly – for instance, Berridge and Cleaver (1987). For those involved in assessing foster carers, British Agencies for Adoption and Fostering (1999b) is indispensable. A helpful book for work with 'children who foster' is Camis (2001).

On residential care, Kahan (1994) is indispensable both for residential workers and for anyone seeking to understand their work, and Ward (1993, 2004) is also very helpful. Frost, Mills and Stein (1999) offer a challenging review of the issues in policy and practice, and Berridge (2002) gives a brief but up-to-date review. The most recent research studies commissioned by the Department of Health are helpfully summarised in Department of Health (1998), but the studies are very rich and it is worth looking at them directly – especially perhaps Sinclair and Gibbs (1998) and Whitaker, Archer and Hicks (1998). Berridge and Brodie (1997), a sequel to Berridge (1985), is also fascinating. For a map of earlier research, Bullock, Little and Millham (1993b) is very useful. For an international view Tolfree (1995) is valuable; for a focus on children's rights see Willow (1996).

The British Agencies for Adoption and Fostering, and Fostering Network (formerly the National Foster Care Association) both provide a wide range of valuable material, and their websites are also worth consulting (www.baaf.org.uk and www.thefostering.net); likewise the Children's Residential Care Unit at the National Children's Bureau (www.ncb.org.uk/depts). The audiotapes on family placement and residential care produced by 'Research in Practice' at the Dartington Social Research Unit are also useful – and good for listening to in the car! The 'Research in Practice' website is at www.rip.org.uk.

Adoption and working for permanence

Introduction

We saw in Chapter 2 that, whatever is meant by 'children's needs', in some sense it is true that all children need to experience stability and security as they grow up, in order to have a sense of belonging and a secure identity. For many children who come into care the experience is a relatively short one, and they quickly return to their own families. In most cases it is assumed that their own families are able to provide them with the necessary stability and security. For a high proportion of children and young people, however, it is the task of the care system to meet these long term needs.

It is this group, and this task, which we will be considering in this chapter. We will look first at what is meant by permanence, and how it is related to concepts of attachment and parenting. Then we will consider the different ways of achieving permanence, and the advantages and disadvantages of each for children. We will also examine a model of practice known as 'concurrent planning'. Finally we will take an extended look at the place of adoption in planning for children, and at social work practice with children and families for whom adoption is the preferred route to permanence.

Exercise 9.1   Annie in long term care

Annie has been with Mr and Mrs Farmer for six months, and appears to be happy there, although there are still tensions in her relationship with the Farmers' own children.

   Over a recent bank holiday weekend Annie's mother became severely depressed and took a fatal overdose. It has been agreed that she and Sarah now need permanent placements. Their aunt has offered to continue to foster Sarah with a view to possible adoption, but is unwilling to take on both girls. Annie's father has asked to re-establish contact. He has a new wife and twin babies, and is not offering to care for Annie. Mr and Mrs Farmer would like to keep Annie on a permanent basis, if approved to do so.

What are Annie's needs, in the short and long term?
Who is most likely to be able to provide what she needs?
What legal arrangements are most likely to provide what she needs?
What about Sarah?
How should decisions about Annie's future care be made?

What is 'permanence'?

'Permanence' can mean different things in different contexts, and it is worth trying to be clear about how we are using the term. It is sometimes used to refer only to new placements, but at other times it can include children living with or returning to their own families. Thoburn et al. (1986) define 'permanent family placement' as

> placement with a family – usually, in our context, not the birth family – as a result of which children experience stability, security and a sense of belonging, in confidence that their needs will be met by parents who genuinely care for them as individuals, and with whom, barring unforeseen accidents, they will remain until they are adults – or longer, if they wish or need to.
>
> Thoburn et al. (1986), p. 10

   The term came to prominence in the 1970s, particularly in the USA and the UK in what came to be known as the 'permanence movement', although it took slightly different forms in each country. In the USA it tended to be associated with the concept of 'psychological parenting', and there was probably as much emphasis on reunification work with birth families as there was on finding new families through adoption. The approach has been defined in this way:

> Permanency planning is the systematic process of carrying out, within a brief time-limited period, a set of goal-directed activities designed to help children live in families that offer continuity of relationships with nurturing parents or caretakers and the opportunity to establish lifetime relationships.
>
> Maluccio and Fein (1983): 197, cited in Maluccio, Fein and Olmstead (1986): 5

In the UK there was initially much more concern with finding new families for children who might otherwise move through a series of placements without ever experiencing stability. An influential research study was that by Rowe and Lambert (1973), which exposed the plight of 'children who wait' for a permanent placement without any purposeful action being taken to achieve such an outcome. The point of the 'movement', if that is what it was, was to find new ways of placing such children on a permanent basis. This was achieved in part by redefining the groups of children for whom adoption was possible, and the kind of support given to adopters; but also by using the concept of a 'permanent family placement' to break down the distinction between foster care and adoption and draw attention to the ways in which fostered children could be given a real sense of permanence and belonging. The approach taken to promoting permanence could sometimes be superficial, with local authorities setting arbitrary timescales on planning processes (for instance, ruling that any child who had been looked after for more than six months should be put forward for adoption).

It is now widely accepted that 'permanence', if it is to mean anything useful in childcare practice, must include children living with their birth families as well as those placed with new families. We could even adapt Thoburn et al.'s definition slightly, and define permanence as:

> placement with a family – which may be the birth family – as a result of which children experience stability, security and a sense of belonging, in confidence that their needs will be met by parents who genuinely care for them as individuals, and with whom, barring unforeseen accidents, they will remain until they are adults – or longer, if they wish or need to.

The key elements of the definition are:

- placement with a family;
- the child's *experience* of stability, security and belonging;
- the child's *confidence* in being genuinely cared-for;
- and the expected continuation of the relationship into adult life.

'Psychological parenting'

The concept of the 'psychological parent' is one way of expressing the idea that parenting is not just a matter of genetics, or of legal relationships, but of feelings. A child, it is argued, is entitled to live with someone whom they regard as a 'real' parent because they are attached to them and care for them. This may be a natural parent, a relative, or a foster or adoptive parent. As noted in Chapter 1, it has been argued that a child can only have one 'psychological parent' or set of psychological parents, but evidence from psychological research is contrary to this (Goldstein, Freud and Solnit 1973; Richards 1986). The main points to note for practice are:

(1) that a relationship may need some time to develop into one of 'psychological parenting';
(2) that very often it is only the child who can tell us where s/he feels safe, cared for and a sense of belonging. This may be communicated in words or through behaviour, and it will often require very sensitive 'listening'.

Attachment theory and permanence

In thinking about what permanence means and how to achieve it, it is helpful to return to attachment theory. For some children who do not have secure attachment relationships, a primary objective will be to give them the opportunity to develop these. For others who have strong attachments but who cannot continue to live with the same people, the aim will be to build on these bonds as the child develops new relationships.

As Schofield points out, children bring their 'internal working models' into any new set of relationships, and with children who are in need of permanent substitute care these working models may well 'derive from experiences of anxiety about their own lovability, which the child will then need to defend against':

> Those who have experienced consistent patterns of rejection may have learned to deactivate their proximity-seeking attachment behaviours and demonstrate an avoidant attachment pattern. Those who had insensitive, unpredictable care may have learned to hyperactivate their attachment behaviours and demonstrate an ambivalent/resistant attachment pattern. Many maltreated children who have experienced particular kinds of frightening and unpredictable environments will have developed representations of caregivers as dangerous or neglectful and will have found it impossible to organise a strategy for coping. They may demonstrate a disorganised attachment pattern.
>
> Schofield (2003), p. 8

These different patterns will all have consequences – consequences in terms of the kind of placement that will meet the needs of the child, the kind of preparatory work that will have to be done, and the support that carers will need in placement. This applies equally whether the child is going to live in a foster home, or be adopted, or return to their family of origin.

Some children have a deep-seated mistrust of adults and an ambivalence about whether they will allow themselves to be looked after, perhaps with a history of neglect and failures of care on the part of parents who have serious problems in looking after themselves. If this background is followed by multiple early accommodation experiences such as emergency and short term placements, with foster carers who are unable to cope with the complex needs of these children, then this is likely to lead to deeper mistrust. At the end of such a process, adopters face a very serious challenge and are likely to need a lot of support in caring for the child.

Schofield also makes the point that children are active in adapting to their environment and in making meanings. This reminds us that placement is not something we do *to* a child, but something we do *with* her or him. Each child or young person will have his or her own agenda and own strategies for making sense of the environment, in the light of the child's individual character and what has happened to her or him in the past. Good practice works with the grain of the child's own coping strategies, seeking to modify them when this is necessary and appropriate; it does not impose solutions on the child.

Ways of achieving permanence

Lowe and Murch (2002) found that planning was often characterised by muddled thinking about the meaning of 'permanence', often used unhelpfully as a synonym for adoption. It is of course much more than that. The proposed practice guidance to support the national adoption standards in England and Wales attempts to clarify professional thinking with a clear statement that 'permanence is a framework of emotional, physical and legal conditions that gives a child a sense of security, continuity, commitment and identity'. It continues:

> The objective of planning for permanence is to ensure children have a secure, stable and loving family to support them through childhood and beyond. A spectrum of options exists, all of which can deliver high quality outcomes for individual children. The planning process will identify which option is most likely to meet the needs of the individual child and takes account of their views and feelings. The options include

- Returning home to birth parents.
- Care with wider family or friends.

- Long term fostering.
- Adoption.

Of these options, only the first and last provide legal permanence. However, one of the other options may provide the best chance of emotional and physical permanence for a particular child.

Department of Health (2001d), p. 11

Reunification

Most children and young people experience permanence with their own families. For many children who come into the care system, return home will also offer the best chance of permanence. However, to achieve this may need a great deal of work on the part of family members and those helping them. Parents may need to change their style of parenting or learn new skills. Changes in the family's physical or social circumstances may be needed – better housing, better integration into the neighbourhood, a different neighbourhood. Support from relatives may need to be built into the placement plan. (Alternatively, as we saw in Chapter 7, it may be a relative who provides the care on a permanent basis.) In some cases action may be needed to ensure that members of the family or their social circle who have abused the child are no longer in a position to do so. This may involve court proceedings or voluntary arrangements.

All these preparations for a return home can take time, and for a child time never stands still. While the work is going on, the child may be making new relationships – with temporary carers and their children, perhaps with a new neighbourhood and a new school. S/he may experience changes of placement, which may confirm negative attachment patterns and make an eventual permanent settlement even more difficult. At the same time changes may be taking place in the family – people leaving or arriving, new relationships being formed – which can cause the absent child to feel displaced or alienated from the family. For some parents, the work needed to enable a return may involve an extended programme of treatment – for instance, for mental disorder or addiction – with no guarantee of success.

All these factors can make the planning of a return extremely difficult and stressful for everyone involved – the child, the parents and family, the temporary carers, the caseworker. It can also be very difficult to decide whether or not it is realistic and in the child's interests to plan for return at all, and in a moment we will look at one response to this dilemma in the form of the 'concurrent planning' model.

Despite all these difficulties, return home remains the best way of providing permanence for many children and young people. It builds on existing relationships and networks, and fits with 'the cultural expectation that children will be brought up within their birth families, most usually by one if not both of their birth parents' (Schofield 2003, p. 12). Triseliotis et al. (1995) found that, for the teenagers they studied, on balance living with parents provided a better chance of stability than other forms of placement.

It certainly is not always successful: Farmer and Parker (1991) found that a fifth of placements of children 'home on trial' were unsatisfactory and two fifths broke down at some stage. Children who had spent longer in care experienced less successful outcomes. Some children experienced repeated unsuccessful attempts to return them home, with increasingly poor outcomes and the children becoming increasingly disturbed. However, the authors found that most placements home did meet the child's needs, and did endure. With better planning and decision making and good enough support, the proportion could no doubt be higher.

Permanence with substitute families

In contrast, for many children the route to permanence will be with a new family, whether this is through foster care or through adoption. A permanent substitute family is the preferred option for any child whose parents are never likely to be able to provide good enough care, or who are not likely to be able to provide it within a timescale that is realistic for *this* child.

As we have seen, 'family' in this context may mean different things. It certainly does not necessarily mean a married couple with children of their own although in many cases it will. Unmarried couples, single people, or gay and lesbian couples can in principle provide good permanent homes. What is important is to ensure that the family is right for this particular child – that they will be able to meet her/his identified needs, including the need to form secure attachments, to begin to undo any harm which s/he may have suffered, and to start to experience success.

The task of identifying a family who will be right for a particular child is not a straightforward one. Although there is considerable research evidence as to which kinds of placements are successful, it is not always clear and unambiguous. As Quinton et al. (1998) point out, 'The factors predicting successful and stable placements have remained elusive', and even more so the reasons why these factors are important. For instance, it is well established that later placements are more likely to be unsuccessful, and so are placements where there are children close in age to the child being placed – but we do not know why.

It seems fair to assume that a great deal depends on the subtle interaction between the child and his or her personality and history, the new parents or carers and their family culture and patterns, and the placement itself – the way in which it is planned, managed and supported. There is some evidence to suggest that expectations are important, and in particular the match between children's and carers' expectations of how the placement will develop (Butler and Charles 1998). Schofield's retrospective study of young adults who had been in long term foster care identified seven distinct 'pathways', which she labels 'close and special', 'testing out', 'distant and self-reliant', 'anxious and fearful', 'breakdown and rebuilding', 'rescue, relief and recovery', 'hurt, angry and disappointed'. Without further elaboration, these words in themselves give a flavour of the diverse and intense emotions that can be involved in permanent placements – whether or not they are 'successful'. One of Schofield's findings was that even young people whose placements had 'broken down' might still regard the foster parents as their 'real parents'.

When identifying a permanent placement, it is of course even more important than with a short term placement to take into account the child's ethnic, religious, cultural and linguistic background.

Concurrent planning

A recurring dilemma for social work practice is presented by situations where there are strong arguments for planning for a child to return to the birth family, but where this is dependent on the success of work with the family to enable them to offer good enough care. It is easy to feel torn between the wish to ensure that a child's future is secured without undue delay, and reluctance to miss an opportunity to rebuild the family. Appeals to the obligation to put the child's interests first do not necessarily help, not simply because it is still important to be fair to parents, but because what is actually best for the child may not be clear. Delay may make it harder to place the child successfully in a new family, but precipitate action may be hard to justify until the parents have been given a chance to tackle their problems.

Exercise 9.2   A planning dilemma

Jenny is aged two and has been admitted to care as result of neglect. Lorna, her mother, is a single parent with no other children. She has moderate learning difficulties and attended a special school. It is clear that Lorna has a limited understanding of the needs of a young child, but she is very fond of Jenny and was upset to find that she had not been meeting her needs.

An initial assessment at a family centre suggests that over time Lorna could be helped to give good care to her daughter. The recommended programme is expected to take twelve months. There is of course no guarantee of success.

How would you make a plan for Jenny, bearing in mind her need for permanence?

One answer to this is the model of 'concurrent planning' first developed in Seattle, USA in 1981. In the first place an assessment is done to distinguish families where the chances of children's successful return are remote from those where the prognosis is more hopeful but still poor; this is called 'differential diagnosis'. For children who have little realistic hope of return, immediate permanent placement is sought. Concurrent planning is the method employed for children where it is thought that there may be a reasonable chance of reunification after work with the parents – children like 'Jenny' in Exercise 9.2. While the work for reunification goes on, at the same time an alternative plan is developed for placement with relatives or with foster carers who can adopt. The children are placed with these families from the outset. By 1987 children were moving to permanent homes within 13 months and by the mid 1990s this had fallen to nine months. Although only 15 per cent of the children were able to return home, 93 per cent of those adopted by permanent carers had only one placement (Katz and Robinson 1991; Katz 1996). Much higher rates were recorded by a similar programme in Minnesota (Monck, Reynolds and Wigfall 2003).

The concurrent planning model was introduced into the UK by Manchester Adoption Society, in an explicit attempt to reduce the number of moves experienced by children before they are adopted. Prospective adopters begin as foster carers working with social workers to reunite children with their birth families. If this fails they undertake to adopt the foster child. The project was evaluated alongside similar projects in London and Brighton by Monck, Reynolds and Wigfall (2003), who found that concurrent planning appeared to be successful in obtaining permanent placements for children more quickly.

The success of the model depends on having a pool of prospective families who are willing to care for young children with the hope of adoption, but who are also willing to support the child's birth family, knowing that if they succeed the child may return home. This dual task is of course painful and stressful.

As the Department of Health guidance makes clear, concurrent planning is to be distinguished from 'parallel' or 'twin track' planning, where the child remains with the birth parents or is placed with foster carers, a rehabilitation plan with timescales is in place, and 'at the same time the agency puts in place elements of a plan for an alternative permanence placement if the rehabilitation plan is unsuccessful' (Department of Health (2001d), p. 13).

Long term foster care or adoption?

A permanent family placement may be made using either foster care or adoption. The most important differences between the two types of placement are legal ones. A child in foster care continues to be under the responsibility of her or his parents and of the agency making the placement, while an adopted child is under the sole responsibility of the adoptive parents – who will continue to be the child's legal parents after the age of majority.

The question of which type of placement is 'better' is a contested one. In practice there are always differences between those children placed for adoption and those who are fostered, which makes it difficult to draw conclusions from evidence of which placements succeed. A research review by Triseliotis concludes modestly that

> the weight of the evidence examined suggests that adoption confers significant advantages to children who cannot return to their birth families, especially in terms of emotional security and sense of belonging.
>
> Triseliotis (2002), p. 30

On the other hand, he adds, for some children long term fostering can still be preferable, in particular for:

- children who are clear that they don't want adoption;
- those closely attached to their carers for whom a move would not be in their best interests;
- children where there is a high level of continuous birth family involvement;
- situations where children, especially older ones, and their carers want time to get to know each other before perhaps making a final commitment.

'Other things being equal', Triseliotis concludes, 'the ideal for children in long term fostering who cannot return to their birth parents is to be adopted by their foster parents' (p. 30).

The advantages of adoption seem to have to do in part with the nature of the commitment made, which means that parents are less likely to give up when things go wrong, and that children may feel more secure. However, Thoburn and others have argued forcefully that foster care can also give a sense of security and permanence, especially if the agency responsible for the placement allows the carers real autonomy. It is arguable that one of the most stigmatising aspects of being in care, in the sense that it marks a child out most clearly as different, is the division of responsibility for parenting – among present carers, absent parents, a visiting social worker and his or her distant managers. To the extent that foster carers, or foster parents, can be freed to exercise the authority and responsibility of parents, both they and the child are more likely to feel that they are part of a real and abiding family.

Schofield et al. (2000) comment from their study in depth of 58 placements that long term foster care embraces a wide variety of different patterns and situations. As they put it, this area of practice

> does not respond well to simple categories and regulation. It means living with a paradox around security as defined legally, bureaucratically and

emotionally. This, however, is not an argument for seeing long term foster care as a last resort, a position that can lead to children remaining at home in maltreating families, waiting too long for adoption or drifting in unplanned short term foster care. It is an argument for demanding the highest possible professional standards, interpersonal skills, creative ideas, theoretical knowledge and active commitment from social workers, supported by their managers and agencies. It is an argument for supporting and resourcing this sector of the child care service properly.

pp. 295 6

It is worth briefly noting that there are other legal arrangements which may help to give a greater sense of permanence to foster placements. In England and Wales there have been a series of alternatives, starting with custodianship under the Children Act 1975 (implemented very late and not much used), and continuing with residence orders under the Children Act 1989 and special guardianship orders under the Adoption Act 2002.

Adoption and its place in child care

Background – adoption in contemporary society

Legal adoption, which is the formal transfer of the status of parent in respect of a child or young person to someone who is not the 'birth parent', is not a universal institution. It has only existed in Britain since 1926, and in some countries or cultures it is still not recognised. Legal adoption was introduced in the UK following the First World War, partly in response to the needs of families affected by the death or disappearance of parents and by children being conceived outside marriage. For the next 40 years it was used primarily to provide new homes for babies whose mothers felt unable to keep them because of their circumstances, and babies for couples who were unable to conceive.

This picture changed radically with social changes in the 1960s and 1970s. The greater availability of contraception and safe abortion, and the lessening of stigma attaching to being an 'unmarried mother', meant far fewer babies needing new families. At the same time the increased prevalence of divorce led to a demand for adoption by step-parents – mainly step-fathers – as a way of marking relationships within reconstituted families.

There was also a change in the theory and practice of adoption. Previously the intention in most cases was that the child should grow up as if s/he were the natural child of the new parents, without the outside world – or even the child – knowing that s/he was adopted. Gradually it came more and more to be recognised that this deception could create huge problems for adopted people and their families, and social workers encouraged adopters to explain the situation honestly to children. The Children Act 1975 gave adopted people the right to have access to their original birth records once they reached adulthood, which lent a strong argument to social workers attempting to persuade adopters who were reluctant to reveal the truth to their children.

Since the 1970s the biggest change has been the increase in the number of children being adopted from the care system, in particular older children and disabled children. By the late 1990s in England and Wales the mean age of children adopted from care was $5\frac{1}{2}$ years. A large number of these children have emotional and behavioural difficulties – Quinton et al.'s (1998) study of adoptions of children aged 5–9 found that four fifths had severe and persistent problems.

The characteristics of people seeking to adopt have also changed. The diverse nature of children needing adoption from care has meant that a much wider range of people have tended to come forward or to be recruited as adopters. Many of the more traditional adopters, typified by the infertile couple wanting a healthy baby, have been diverted into intercountry adoption, increasingly sophisticated infertility treatment, or surrogacy.

The main uses of adoption currently are therefore (a) to regularise relationships in reconstituted families and (b) to provide permanency for children in care. In the case of step-parent adoptions this usually begins as a decision by a family to make an application, and becomes the province of social workers when the court appoints a social work agency to inquire and report on the welfare of the child(ren). Because this kind of adoption is not linked to the provision of care for children and young people, this book does not consider it at any length. However, social workers in family placement services may well have responsibility for this work.

Adoption from care on the other hand is a central focus of this chapter, as we have already seen. However, in looking at some of the practice issues it may be helpful to put it in the context of adoption work more generally. This part of the chapter will be based mainly on the law and practice of adoption in England and Wales, with some reference to Scotland. However, much of the content will be applicable to work in other countries.

Adoption services and the legal obligations to provide them

The precise arrangements for adoption services of course vary between countries. In England and Wales until recently the main law was the Adoption Act 1976 as amended by the Children Act 1989. A review of the law was set in train in 1989 but, as we noted in Chapter 5, there were delays in preparing the new law which eventually emerged as the Adoption and Children Act 2002. In Scotland at the time of writing the Adoption (Scotland) Act 1978 still remains in force, as amended by the Children (Scotland) Act 1995.

What all these Acts have in common is that they (a) specify the circumstances in which adoption orders are to be made and the arrangements for making them, and (b) set out the duties and powers of adoption agencies. Adoption agencies may be local authorities or adoption societies, but local authorities have a duty to plan the provision of adoption services in their area, either by themselves directly or by voluntary societies. These include services for children in need of adoption, for parents who seek adoption for their children, and for prospective adopters. Although the Adoption and Children Act 2002 made substantial changes to the law on adoption, this basic structure still applies. The services required may include provision of information, advice and counselling, practical services including accommodation, and of course assessment (of both children and adopters) and eventual placement.

Decisions about the approval of adopters and the placement of children for adoption have to be considered by an independent *adoption panel*, and regulations specify how this is to work.

Good practice in adoption and post-adoption services

Good practice starts, as always, with assessment. The assessment of prospective adopters is not covered in detail in this book. The assessment of children's needs has already been discussed in some depth, and all that we said in general terms about assessing children and their situations applies equally to assessment for adoption.

Placement choice is of course of critical importance. If there is one area of placement practice where it can never be excusable to say 'we had no choice', it is adoption. We are choosing a family for life for a child, and we have to be as confident as we can that they will be really committed to the child and able to offer the care *this* child needs.

Placement for adoption brings additional complications in relation to parental agreement. Whilst in all placement practice the aim should be to work in partnership with the family, in adoption there are specific requirements for parents to agree to their children being adopted. Courts do have the power to order an adoption without agreement, even in the face of parental opposition if the child's welfare requires it. In general, as we know, children are likely to make more successful transitions if they feel that they have 'permission' from those to whom they are attached, but some parents, even when they can see that it is right for a child to be adopted, cannot bring themselves to give their formal consent.

'Contested adoptions', as they are known, can be among the most stressful processes for everyone involved, and an increasing number of adoptions in the UK are contested. Courts in England and Wales are now able to deal with the issue of consent before placement in making a *placement order*, which reduces the problem of a child spending considerable time with adopters in a state of uncertainty as to whether the adoption would eventually be allowed to go ahead – or of parents feeling that the agency has pre-empted the court's decision by allowing the child to establish a bond with the prospective adopters before the issue of consent has been tested. Previously this was dealt with by a step known as 'freeing for adoption', which at the time of writing still applies in Scotland.

When we are placing, or considering placing, children for adoption, information is crucially important. All parties to the 'adoption triangle' – parents and birth family, adopters, and above all children – need to understand what is happening and why.

- Parents need to know as much as possible about the people who will be adopting their child.
- Adopters need to know everything about the child and family's history – including the medical history.
- Children need to know about the adopters, about the process, and about themselves and their families.

For children who are adopted when they are very young, the question of how to tell them about their origins is an important one (see Box 9.1). The adoptive parents should be able to give information and answer questions as

---

Box 9.1 Telling children about their past

'Children often ask for information about quite ordinary things in the history of their family – What colour was my mother's hair? What subjects did she like at school? Where did we live? Adoptive parents often worry about how much to tell their children – I have always said that they should tell them just a little bit more than they can understand. You begin with a bare framework of the story, and begin to fill out the details in response to their questions. Children often do not understand when they are first told, and forget that they have been given this information – which is why you need to keep going over it. The balance to find is that you respond to their questions and interest without ramming it down their throats, or on the other hand creating an atmosphere where it is not OK to ask. One way is for the adoptive parent to build up a *life story book* with the child that is left where the child can get it at any time. The story can be added to and rewritten as the child's understanding becomes more sophisticated.'

John Evans (Team Manager, adoptive father and member of Adoption UK)

and when the child is ready, but will need support from the agency in the form of written material such as letters or a life-story book, photographs and even audio recordings that can fill out the picture of the child's early life. (A life-story book may also be referred to as a 'life journey book' or 'life journey work'; children sometimes take the word 'story' to indicate something fictional.) As the child gets older the question of why they were 'given up' for adoption becomes salient, and an honest but helpful answer to this must be prepared in advance – with the help of the parent(s) if this is possible.

Support after adoption should be carefully planned and agreed, for the child, the adoptive parents and the birth family. Because the adoptive parents now have sole parental responsibility, this does not mean that they should expect to say goodbye to the agency that placed the child. Post-adoption support has always been good practice, and it is now a legal requirement. This should include information, advice and practical support. There are several organisations working in the post-adoption field who have done a great deal over the years in working with families and in promoting better services, and who are still valuable sources of information and advice. Social workers should inform adoptive parents of the availability of support groups. Adoption UK is particularly useful – it is a self-help group, and offers a source of valuable support from others who have had the experience of being adoptive parents themselves.

Where children are adopted from care there is the possibility for a continuing monetary allowance to be paid, to cushion the blow to the child and family of losing the foster care allowance. This is especially important for disabled children, whose care can involve considerable extra expense. Since adoption allowances were first introduced, the number of disabled children adopted has increased substantially. It should be noted that the majority of children adopted from care are *not* adopted by their foster carers.

'Open adoption'

There has been a great deal said and written in the last 20 years or more about 'open adoption'. It is important to clarify what is meant by 'openness'. The word has on occasion in the past been used to indicate adoptions that are openly acknowledged and not kept secret, but that usage is rare now that secrecy is no longer practised – although in some countries, for instance in the former USSR, the issue is still a live one. More commonly 'openness' refers to a degree of contact between the birth family and the adoptive family.

This kind of 'openness' is best thought of in terms of a continuum. It does not necessarily involve face-to-face contact between the child and the birth family. At a minimum, 'openness' may imply merely that the child is actively aware of the existence and whereabouts of the birth parents or other family

---

Box 9.2   Contact after adoption

'The issue of face-to face contact is a complex one. Some would say that it difficult enough for a child to make new attachments anyway without the complication of loosening existing ties. There are two crucial factors:

- the attitude of the birth-parents to the fact of the adoption. If they are unable to accept the adoption and give permission for the child to accept the new carers they will continually be undermining the new carers, upsetting the children and themselves
- the nature of the disorganised attachment pattern for the child/ren.

For some children contact with their birth parents can be beneficial – for others it is not. Once again, careful assessment is the key. Many adoptive parents are fearful of the idea of contact, but in my experience thoughtful discussion of the issues can enable them to take a far more realistic and sensitive position whereby the needs of the child are central to any decision-making. Their ability to contact the birth parent may be critical in enabling them to answer some of the questions the child may have about their background – questions that even the best case record-keeping will not encompass.'

John Evans (Team Manager, adoptive father and member of Adoption UK)

---

members. Greater 'openness' may include the regular exchange of letters, photographs or news. Families where there is actually regular face-to-face contact are rare in the UK, but more common in New Zealand and Australia where there has been some investment in developing this approach to adoption. The aim is to build a relaxed and friendly relationship between the birth parent(s) and the new family from the start, in which continuing social relationships are possible (see Box 9.2). Advocates of this approach to adoption argue that it produces a situation that is healthier for all, especially the child, and in which the rights of birth parents are better respected. Ryburn's (1992) review of research suggests that contact between children and their birth families after adoption can be beneficial, but Quinton et al. (1998) argue that the picture is more complex. A study by Neil (2003) found that some face-to-face contact helped birth parents to accept the adoption.

Policy and political issues in adoption

Adoption has been one of the more politically charged aspects of childcare in recent years – which is one reason why the law in the UK has taken so long to reform. There have been heated debates over the issue of who should be able to adopt – social workers and medical advisers have been accused of being 'politically correct' when they object to adopters who are overweight or smoke heavily, or even when they seek to place children with families of similar ethnic background. Perhaps the best way to look at the issue is to bear in mind that no one is *entitled* to adopt, and that the purpose of the adoption service is to find suitable families for children in need, not to provide babies for childless couples. On the other hand, everyone is entitled to be treated fairly and to receive genuine consideration for what they have to offer.

Along with the myth that social workers have been preventing people from adopting through 'political correctness', there has been concern that not enough children from care are being adopted. The drive to increase the use of adoption has been led in the UK by the Prime Minister's office, spurred by the large disparities in adoption rates between different local authorities and by evidence of the length of time that children wait before achieving a permanent home (Ivaldi 1998). There are some indications that practice is becoming more consistent and that waiting times are being reduced.

There is also perhaps a greater public acceptance now of the importance of thorough vetting of prospective adopters, following the publicity given to cases like that of the Kilshaws (see Box 9.3), where the story was clearly presented as one of an inappropriate placement being prevented by the intervention of social workers, rather than one of officiousness and bureaucracy.

Intercountry adoption

The 1980s and 1990s saw a large increase in applications for adoption of children across national borders. In part this was another response to the decline in numbers of babies needing adoption in countries like the UK, and to the careful vetting that was required of prospective adopters. In part it was an emotional response to the well-publicised plight of abandoned or neglected children in crisis-ridden countries such as Romania.

For a time this area of practice was largely unregulated, and there was concern that children were being adopted without proper parental consent or by couples who did not have the right skills or attitude to make a success of it. There is still a wider political concern that attention should be given to improving conditions in their countries of origin, rather than taking children away to be brought up in a different culture. This of course is not just an objection to intercountry adoption. It can be argued that much ordinary adoption practice amounts to removing children from poor families and handing them over to prosperous ones, and that it could be better instead to help the poor families to become more prosperous.

Box 9.3 'Internet adoption'

Alan and Judith Kilshaw, the Welsh couple who tried to adopt twins from America after finding them on the internet, made the children suffer and would have caused continuing harm if allowed to keep them, a judge ruled.

He said the couple's craving for media attention had shown their lack of suitability as parents to the twins. By engaging with the media, 'indeed by courting media attention', they maintained the high profile of the case to the ultimate detriment of the twins.

The judge found that they had not given the welfare of the twins the priority it should have had. He noted the report of a social worker who said that 'no affection towards, or interactions with, the twins by Mr and Mrs Kilshaw were observed' at the height of the case.

The judge was highly critical of the private home study report commissioned by the Kilshaws from an unqualified social worker to present to a US court. The report was 'dangerous, misleading, superficial and shallow'. He urged courts approving adoptions abroad to treat such reports with 'extreme caution' and to seek a certificate from the Department of Health that the would-be adopters were suitable.

Summing up their suitability as adoptive parents, he said: 'Taking together the known volatility of personality of Mrs K, the attitudes observed and expressed of Mr and Mrs K, their clear lack of empathy with, and recognition of the priority needs of, the twins, their apparently overriding preoccupation with the media, their past behaviour towards the twins and the circumstances and the continuing uncertainty they have created for the twins, I am fully satisfied of the likelihood of future harm to the twins in terms of impairment of their intellectual, emotional, social and behavioural development.'

Based on press reports in the *Daily Telegraph* and the *Guardian*, July 2001

The practice of intercountry adoption is now much better managed than it was, at least in the UK. Adopters have to be assessed and approved by an adoption agency at home, and there has to be clear evidence that the child's interests have been properly considered in the host country. Romania in particular has devoted considerable attention to improving practice in this area. The United Kingdom has now implemented the Hague Convention which regulates adoption between different countries. Partly as a result of these more effective controls and partly no doubt for other reasons, the incidence of intercounty adoption has fallen again, although it retains the ability to attract headlines.

Messages from research for practice

Roy Parker's review of Department of Health research (Department of Health 1999) draws attention to three particular aspects. First is the central import-ance of information, which is needed by social workers, adopters, children and birth parents. This includes: precision about children's past histories, in partic-ular their relationships with adults and other children; understanding of family composition and the likely dynamics of new families, as well as understanding of different parenting styles; and an understanding of the informal support available to adopters – friends, family, other adopters, churches and so on.

Second is the need for work to be much more child-centred and for practi-tioners to work directly with children, including the children already in the adoptive family. There is a tendency to concentrate too much on work with adults. Children need assistance in communicating, and adults cannot always represent their feelings. There is also a case for giving much more attention to child–child relationships, at home and at school.

Third, formal support after adoption needs to be much more extensive and demanding. Adopters need help and support in coping with challenging behav-iour. Social workers may not have the skills to give this advice, and specialised help is needed, for instance from mental health services. This support has to be 'on call' at times when families need it, and it has two dimensions – support for the adopters and direct support for the child. We should not assume that supporting the adopters is sufficient to support the child.

Thomas and Beckford (1999) spoke with children about their experiences of adoption and found that they had much to say about how it felt to go through the process. One of the strongest demands was for better information. One child's message to social workers was particularly clear:

> Explain to the children what's going on. Like, give them information about their parents, birth parents, foster parents ... And, oh, really help them understand what's going on. Encourage the parents to talk about it a bit more. Let the children talk to friends about it.

p. 140

Summary and conclusion

We have done two things, I hope, in this chapter. We have learned about the idea of 'permanence' – the different meaning that have been given to it, its relationship to ideas of attachment and 'psychological parenting', and the diff-erent ways in which it can be achieved. We have also learned about the insti-tution of adoption – not just as one of the ways in which children can achieve permanence, but as a mode of parenting that is both regulated and politically contested. We have seen that there is evidence that for many children, who are not going to return to their families of origin, adoption as the most secure and permanent option is clearly preferable to any other. We have also seen that for other children long term foster care can provide a satisfactory solution, if it is done with commitment and if families are given sufficient autonomy. However, the best way to provide permanence for most children is to maintain and strengthen their relationships with their own families, and this should be the object of most work with children and young people even when they are in care. Where there is uncertainty about whether or not this will be viable, 'concurrent planning' can be an effective response.

GUIDE TO FURTHER READING

Fahlberg (1994) is still essential reading on working with children through the journey to permanent placement. Jackson and Thomas (1999, 2001) offer a helpful introduction to issues of stability. There are very helpful guides to practice from British Agencies for Adoption and Fostering (1999c and 1999d). On concurrent planning, Monck, Reynolds and Wigfall (2003) is full of useful information about how it is done. On adoption, Triseliotis, Shireman and Hundleby (1997) is the best starting point for those who need to know more, and Hill and Shaw (1998) is a useful collection of recent papers. Fratter (1996) and Ryburn (1994) are both in their different ways good on the issues of contact and 'openness'. There is an interesting literature on what happens to parents who give up their children – for instance Howe (1993).

Leaving care and aftercare

Introduction

This chapter looks at work with young people before and after they leave the care system. In it all the central themes of this book are relevant.

- In relation to children's needs and 'best interests', we see how the needs of this group of young people must be broadly defined, and as far as possible self-defined
- Children and young people's rights and a 'listening' approach are hugely important in this area of practice. Leaving care services cannot work effectively without respect for the autonomy of young people, and we will see that some of the most effective leaving care services are those that create opportunities for young people to work collectively to improve their situation.

- Working with difference and oppression is a strong theme. We focus in this chapter on the needs of three particular groups of care leavers:
  - Black and ethnic minority care leavers
  - Young disabled care leavers
  - Refugees and asylum seekers leaving care
- In relation to issues of parenting and the state, we will need again to think about what 'corporate parenting' means, and also about what standards of care are being applied.

The chapter is heavily based on recent research, reflecting the extent to which this is a newly developing area of policy and practice in which the views of young people themselves, mediated through research, have had a major impact on how policy and practice have developed.

What do we mean by 'leaving care'?

'Leaving care' can mean a number of different things. It can mean returning home to the birth family; it can mean adoption; or it can mean moving on to some kind of 'independent' or semi-independent living. It almost always means both a change in living accommodation and a change in legal status, but not necessarily at the same time. Leaving care is usually a gradual process, but it can on occasion be a sudden event.

The first research to focus strongly on what happens to young people when they leave care was in the 1980s with the work of Mike Stein and colleagues in Yorkshire (Stein and Ellis 1983; Stein and Carey 1986). This research drew attention to the many difficulties faced by young people who were pushed out of the care system, often at a surprisingly young age, without the education, life skills or experience necessary for them to succeed. Since then a series of studies have drawn attention to the poor life chances of this group of young citizens, and to their relative neglect by those responsible for promoting their welfare. This has led to many projects aimed at improving services for care leavers, and a series of changes in legislation aimed at giving them stronger entitlement to support and assistance.

Most discussion of leaving care is centred, quite rightly, on this group of young people. In this chapter we will look at what is involved in helping them, and also at some of the changes in social provision for young people in general that may have left this group in a more exposed position. However, it is also important to remember that children may leave care at any age, and that care providers have responsibilities to even the youngest child returning home or moving on from care. Although the specific legal duties may only apply to young people after the age of 16, *all* children leaving the care system surely have a right to do so in a way that improves their chances of a healthy and happy life. This means ensuring that the arrangements for their care, by parents or whoever has parental responsibility, are satisfactory. It also means making appropriate arrangements for the continuation of relationships or interests which the child may have acquired while in care.

Young people leaving care in their teenage years

The main focus of leaving care policy and practice is on young people aged 15 to 18 years and over. It is a good idea to try to put the situation of this group into some context by considering what life is like for young people generally in this age group. It is often seen as a time of *transition* (see for instance Chisholm 1990). Between our mid-teens and our early twenties we all have to negotiate our way through a series of transitions – in sexuality and relationships, in educational achievement, in economic role and activity, and so on. At some point in this period we also make a major change in our living arrangements, usually from living with our parents to living independently of them.

It is arguable that these transitions have become more difficult in the last 50 years, as a result of wider social changes. The pressures on young people have become greater in a number of ways, for instance in relation to sexuality or education, while the social structures or 'niches' into which they can fit have become less clear. The period of economic dependence has become much longer, with the gradual replacement of employment by education and training. Most young people have the continuing support of parents and other family members throughout this period – not just financial support, but practical help, advice and emotional support.

For young people leaving the care system without these family supports, these transitions may be much more difficult and threatening. If the transitions are also telescoped together, instead of being spread over a number of years as Coleman's 'focal theory' (see Box 10.1) suggests is the case with most young people, then this adds greatly to the task – and to the risk that things will go wrong. In particular, if young people are pushed into 'independent living' sooner than usual, then their personal resources may be severely challenged. Very few young people from secure homes with good education and skills venture to live independently from their families at the age of 16 or 17 – yet young people in care, whose backgrounds may be quite unsettled and whose educational accomplishments are generally poor, have often been expected to do so.

In addition a proportion of young people leaving care in their teenage years have particular needs and vulnerabilities because of their background and the circumstances that brought them into care in the first place. This may mean that some of them are exceptionally susceptible to risks such as those of

---

Box 10.1   Focal theory of adolescence

Over 20 years ago, one of us (Coleman 1974, 1978) put forward a model of adolescent development which has come to be known as the focal model. In essence, this argued that an issue or difficulty arising from a particular relationship pattern comes into focus at a particular stage and, in time, comes to be replaced with another focal issue. The model is similar to a stage theory, in that it proposes a progression from one focal concern to another, but it does emphasise that no fixed sequence is envisaged. An important implication is that those young people who have to deal with more than one issue at a time might be considered to be more at risk than those for whom issues are well spaced out. A young person who has to cope with family breakdown, for example, as well as having to adjust to a change of school and to a new peer group, may be particularly vulnerable.

Coleman and Roker (1998), p. 593

---

homelessness and unemployment, drug and alcohol abuse, mental illness and sexual abuse and exploitation.

If we understand the situation of young care leavers in the context of their age group as a whole, we see that this has important implications for how to provide services that are helpful, sensitive and accessible to young people.

First, if we want to help young people to move on successfully from care we have to consider three distinct areas of service provision:

- services that are provided for care leavers directly;
- services that are provided for all young people in the age group;
- services that are provided for young people in care *before* they leave.

Second, service providers must recognise that young people will have their own views about what services they need; they will not simply accept whatever is provided for them. The services provided must respond to young people's needs as they define them for themselves, and they must be provided in ways that promote young people's self-esteem. Services that are experienced as stigmatised or demeaning will of course do the opposite – and they will be rejected.

What we can learn from research

Stein (1997) reviews leaving care research in terms of its value for practitioners. He suggests that it is helpful to look at the research with three distinct areas of focus:

- the *needs* of care leavers;
- the *processes* by which services are provided;
- the *outcomes* for young people.

Needs

The needs of young carers vary widely between individuals and groups. Later in this chapter we will focus on the needs of three such groups – black care leavers, disabled care leavers, and care leavers who are refugees. Each of these groups has its own distinct pattern of needs; and individuals within those groups will also have their own distinct needs. However, a series of research studies have painted a common picture of the kind of needs that do arise for many young people leaving care.

For instance, a Save the Children study that was actually carried out by a group of young people (West 1995) revealed that common problems and experiences included insufficient income, poor employment prospects, lack of educational qualifications, poor accommodation or lack of choice, homelessness, health problems, lack of social activities, unhappiness, feelings of stigmatisation and labelling, lack of life skills or preparation for leaving care and lack of support after leaving care (see Box 10.2).

Box 10.2 You're on Your Own: young people's research on leaving care

- 'Young people from care do not have enough income to live on. Many have experienced times with no money at all. Most are unemployed, living on income support rates or less. Many 16–17 year olds have been destitute. The needs of young people who have left care here are similar to other independent young people who have, for example, had to leave the family home.
- Young people leave care generally with poor employment prospects. Most have not had any help to find work or understand the range of employment opportunities. Those who have worked, have often been low paid with disposable income no higher than benefit. Lack of choice means YT [*youth training*] is taken up by 16–17 year olds in order to get an income – which is even lower than the 18–24 years benefit level.
- Young people in care were often treated differently by other pupils and teachers at school. Many had no support in school life. Nearly half left school with no qualifications. Most were not encouraged to stay in education after 16 years.

- Many did not choose their first home after care and found it unsuitable. Most moved home at least once, many over four times. Several had been homeless. Many did not get a leaving care grant towards setting up home; the amounts some received varied widely, and they often had no choice in how it was spent.
- Many had no support at all after leaving care, particularly young black people. Care leavers want support (listening, advice, advocacy) to be there when they need it, for as long as they want it after care.
- Many found leaving care affected their health badly, linked to diet and mental health. Several were underweight and more women than men were not eating enough. Health preparation in care was inadequate.
- Many were not involved in social activities or happy with their present situation. Happiness depended to an important extent on income, housing, work and prospects.
- Most would never or rarely tell anyone about being in care because public perception revolves around stigmatisation and labelling (often as criminals). The public needs education about care and young people in care.
- Many had contact with the police in care, but not since leaving. Most had been a victim of crime. Most found the police less than understanding towards them.
- Most were lacking in skills, especially money management, when they left care. Many were not ready to leave care when they did. Most did not have leaving care planning meetings. Preparation for leaving could be improved.'

From West (1995), p. 36

This is a depressing picture, and it is important to remember that life is not always bleak for all care leavers. Many do well, and some do very well, either despite their disadvantages or because they are given better chances. Parsons et al. (2002) refer to a report from CHAR (1996) that claimed that two thirds of young people leaving care experienced homelessness. However, the raw statistic may conceal a variety of different situations. It is not unusual for young people to experience periods when they do not have a settled place to live. Provided that this is not prolonged, it need not necessarily be seen as a negative or problematic experience. What may be of more concern is that many care leavers lack the resources or support that they need to move on from this situation in a productive way, or that they are put in accommodation that they have not chosen or do not 'feel OK' about.

Stein's 1997 review of the research concluded that 'young people leaving care have to cope with the challenges and responsibilities of major changes in their lives – in leaving foster and residential care and setting up home, in leaving school and entering the world of work or, more likely, being unemployed and surviving on benefits, and in being parents – at a far younger age than other young people. In short, they have compressed and accelerated transitions to adulthood' (Stein 1997, p. 26). Because young people leaving care have often started with powerful disadvantages – poverty, family disruption, abuse – they are likely to need more support than others in managing the transition to adult life. If they get less support, both in the years before they leave care and at the point when it happens, then it is not surprising that things go wrong.

> 'If you bring up a child, when it comes to 18 you don't just say "Cheerio, here is a couple of quid to buy some clothes with", do you? If you have a child ... when they get to 18 you are not going to get them in a little flat and get them sorted out and say "Right see you" and that is how I feel about social services.'
>
> Young woman quoted in Cambridgeshire County Council study
> Garnett (1992), p. 4

Processes

Research into the processes of providing services for young carers can in principle tell us a good deal about what appears to work well and what does not. Definitive answers to 'what works' are more elusive because of the difficulty in controlling all relevant variables, as we see below. In any case, it is arguable that the views of young people about what they find most helpful are as important as any measures of effectiveness.

Stein (1997) asked 'what works in practice' and reviewed the evidence in terms of (1) preparation for moving on (2) accommodation (3) personal and financial support, and (4) education, employment and training.

(1) He found that successful preparation depended on good assessment, on support and participation, and on gradual opportunities to learn skills in the context of a stable placement.

(2) Young people's accommodation needs appeared to be best met by approaches that involve them in planning and decision making, that assess their needs and prepare them, that offer a choice in type and location of accommodation, and that move young people in a planned way with a contingency plan, a package of support, a financial plan and relevant

information (see Hutson 1995). *Supported lodgings* work well when there is clarity of purpose, good staff input, a thorough approval system, training and support, clear funding arrangements, review and monitoring, and planning for moving on. *Independent tenancies* are most likely to work well when there is good assessment, preparation and support, so that young people are ready to move on with a degree of confidence. *Schemes* offering hostel-based accommodation and support, and *'foyers'* which provide accommodation along with structured support in gaining employment, also appear to work well for some groups of care leavers.

(3) Stein concluded that the foundation for support to the young person leaving care should be the review process prior to them leaving care. When this worked well the young person was engaged in planning their move together with their social worker, their carers and specialist leaving care services, in a way that could provide continuity through the transition. Specialist leaving care teams could add significantly to the support available, for instance, by providing:
- help and advice on getting financial support;
- drop-in centres;
- group work;
- mentors and volunteers.

He quotes an earlier work in which he and Frost argued that personal support should be *planned and negotiated* with young people, *proactive* rather than just responding to crises, *flexible* because of the variety of needs, and should address practical, financial and emotional needs.

(4) In relation to education, employment and training, Stein concluded that focused work was needed to overcome the disadvantages faced by young people as a result of the frequent neglect of their education in the care system. Examples include reading projects and initiatives designed to encourage social workers, teachers and carers to actively promote young people's education. In relation to individual young people he suggests that the most helpful interventions involve:
- gathering detailed information about the young person's achievements and potential, carefully assessing their capabilities for employment and working with a young person creatively to increase their employability;
- ensuring that employment initiatives are flexible, forging links with local community services and being creative in opening up opportunities;
- adequate emotional and financial support, and raising awareness of social work departments about the needs of young people.

Bob Broad (1998) distinguishes three broadly different models of leaving care work which he calls the 'social justice', 'social welfare' and 'technical assistance' models. The 'social justice' model is characterised by an emphasis on empowerment and on campaigning against oppression, the 'social welfare' model by a focus on individual care and welfare, and the 'technical assistance' model by a concentration on training and skills to promote independence through employment. When Broad analysed the recommendations from research studies of leaving care projects, which were based on young people's responses, he found that the overwhelming majority fitted the 'social justice' or 'social welfare' models, and only a few could be placed in a 'technical assistance' frame. However, government intervention often tends to be based on a 'technical assistance' model.

Outcomes

Stein (1997) points out the methodological problems in assessing outcomes, in part because of the range of factors that may influence the outcomes for any young person. As he points out, a diagram used by Nina Biehal and colleagues in *Moving On* (Biehal et al. 1995) illustrates this well (Figure 10.1). Research on outcomes is reviewed more generally in Chapter 11.

Some issues may affect care leavers more than other groups of young people. One is becoming a parent: Biehal et al. (1995) found a 'marked tendency to early parenthood' among their care leavers. In 18–24 months a third

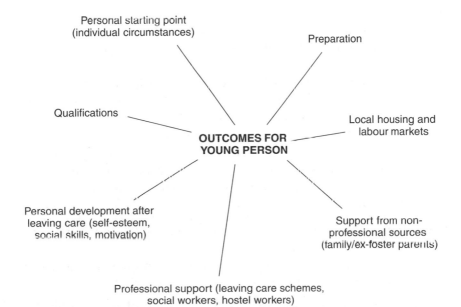

Source: Biehal et al. (1995), p. 251

Figure 10.1 Factors influencing outcomes for care leavers

of the sample had become parents (and nearly half of the young women). Nearly one third of these births were planned, and three quarters of young mothers lived with their partners at some stage. The researchers suggested that the level of young pregnancy indicated gaps in personal and social education, and considered that preparation for parenthood was uneven.

Young carers are sometimes typecast as particularly vulnerable to problems with drug and alcohol use and with offending. In fact, Biehal et al. found that most care leavers did not have problems in these areas. Where they did, offending and heavy drug use tended to go together, and were often associated with histories of rejection and instability. Other research has apparently found higher levels of drug and alcohol problems among care leavers (Wade 2003).

The law on leaving care services

Since 1948 the law in the United Kingdom has required care providers to plan for the welfare of young people leaving care, and to some extent to provide aftercare. The powers and duties contained in the Children Act 1948 were extended by the Children Act 1989 in England and Wales and the Children (Scotland) Act 1995 in Scotland, but not by as much as campaigners had hoped. Further research, much of it based on leaving care projects, showed how the system was still failing young people, and demands continued to be made for further reform of the legislation. The result in England and Wales was the Children (Leaving Care) Act 2000, which came into force in 2001.

The new law defines the young people who are entitled to services: 'eligible children' are young people aged 16 and 17 who have been looked after for a prescribed period; 'relevant children' are eligible children who leave care; 'former relevant children' are young people over the age of 18 who were previously eligible or relevant children. The new law also defines who should provide those services. The 'responsible local authority' is whichever local authority last looked after an eligible or relevant young person. The responsible local authority is under a duty:

- to assess and meet the care and support needs of eligible and relevant children and young people; and
- to assist former relevant children, in particular in respect of their employment, education and training.

The responsible local authority is also under a duty to keep in touch with all its care leavers who qualify for these new support arrangements, including those aged 18–21 (and in some cases beyond).

All eligible, relevant and former relevant children and young people must have a *pathway plan*. This takes over from the existing care plan and should run at least until the young person is aged 21. It encompasses education, training, career plans and any support that may be needed. It is envisaged that pathway plans will be reviewed every six months or more frequently as needed. All eligible, relevant and former relevant children and young people must also have a *personal adviser* who helps to draw up the pathway plan and to make sure that it develops with the young person's changing needs – and is implemented. The personal adviser is also responsible for keeping in touch with the young person after leaving care and for ensuring that they receive the advice and support to which they are entitled.

The Act also gives the responsible local authority other duties in relation to former relevant children: to assist care leavers in higher education; to assist with costs associated with employment, and with costs of education and training up to the end of an agreed programme even if that takes the young person past the age of 21, and to give the young person assistance in kind, or exceptionally in cash 'to the extent that his welfare requires it'. Local authorities have the power to give similar assistance to other care leavers who do not qualify as former relevant children.

'Eligible' and 'relevant' children are no longer eligible for income support, housing benefit or income-based job-seekers allowance. Instead local authorities are under a statutory duty to support them. There are exceptions for cases such as lone parents and disabled children, who could claim benefits if they were living with their parents.

As Wade (2003) writes:

> The Children (Leaving Care) Act provides a new framework for leaving care services. Its purpose is to delay transitions, improve preparation, planning and consistency of support for young people, and to strengthen arrangements for financial assistance. At its heart are new duties to assess and meet needs, provide personal advisers and develop pathway planning for young people up to the age of 21 (or beyond if continuing in education).
>
> p. 3

In Scotland, new regulations made under the Regulation of Care (Scotland) Act 2001 and the Children (Scotland) Act 1995 come into force in 2004. The Support and Assistance of Young People Leaving Care (Scotland) Regulations 2004 are designed to establish a very similar system to that set up in England and Wales, although the terminology is different – 'currently looked after person', 'compulsory supported person' and 'discretionary supported person' rather than 'eligible children', 'relevant children' and 'former relevant children'. However, the definition of 'responsible authority' is the same, as is the requirement for a pathway plan. What Wade writes about the new legislation in

England and Wales therefore applies just as well in Scotland:

> Pathway planning is envisaged as a multi-agency task, co-ordinated by the personal adviser, and subject to regular review. Regulations and Guidance specify the core areas that must be addressed. The need for comprehensive assessments and pathway planning should help to bring a sharper focus at the leaving care stage. Whether or not they continue to be accommodated, every young person will have an assessment, a personal adviser and a pathway plan as soon as practicable after they reach 16. Pathway planning should identify immediate needs and look forward to a longer-term future beyond care. It will need to be continually monitored, reviewed and adjusted in the light of experience. The role of the personal adviser is pivotal in helping to construct the plan, in providing continuity of support for the young person through transition and identifying the resources and services required to meet their needs. The plan will need to address all the core areas of young people's lives – personal support, accommodation, education and training, employment, family and social relationships, life skills, financial assistance, health and contingency planning.
>
> Wade (2003), p. 3

Focus on practice

The first half of this chapter has been about the theory of leaving care. In the second half we focus more directly on the practice. We will look at some of the needs of particular groups of care leavers, at some alternative pathways to success, and at some of the things that social workers and their agencies can do to support young people when they leave care.

Young black people leaving care

Biehal et al. (1995) found that the largest ethnic minority group were young people of mixed heritage. Black, Asian and mixed-heritage young people tended to enter care earlier and stay longer. There appeared to be little major difference in post-care careers – black young people were slightly more likely to make good educational progress than white care leavers, while their early housing patterns were similar. Biehal et al. point to the importance of focusing on young people's cultural and self-care needs and suggest that positive role models and images can make a real difference. They also point to the importance of giving space for young people to define their own ethnic identity, together with opportunities for contact with other young people of similar backgrounds.

Lynda Ince's study of young black care leavers points to the strong link between the 'care careers' of black children and young people and their ability to cope with the experience of moving on from the system (Ince 1998, 2004). Her research was based on talking to young people, and she analyses some of their individual 'career trajectories' (see Box 10.3).

Box 10.3 David's story

Despite facing a long prison sentence and an uncertain future, David (19) is surprisingly relaxed and willing to talk openly about his life in care. Yet the care path that led him to prison is one filled with abuse, rejection and violence. David's connection with the care system was cemented almost from birth. At the age of one month he came to the local authority's attention when his father abused him. Although the subject of a Place of Safety Order under the Children and Young Persons Act 1969, he was still returned to his parents, a white English mother and African-Caribbean father.

By the age of six months he had been taken into care following serious neglect by his mother. He and his sister were then adopted by a white couple living in an all white suburb where they had no contact with black people. David was subsequently physically abused by his adoptive parents which led to his return to the care system. While in a residential home, he was abused by a staff member. No support was forthcoming, instead he was moved from one residential placement to another.

With each move, David became more rootless, disturbed and aggressive. Over time he became virtually unmanageable. His care records show clear signs of psychological trauma stemming from his early abusive experiences. Attempts to manage his challenging behaviour through placements in Community Homes with education and socio-therapeutic units failed. Labelled as maladjusted, he was expelled from junior school. From this point on he never gained a significant foothold in education.

David's racial identity was only addressed when he was 14 years old. That was when he requested to be sent to a black-run residential project for young black people. Somehow, he managed to develop a significant relationship with a black couple who became his informal support and he responded to them positively.

But contact with his birth family was virtually non-existent. He was, in his view, well and truly institutionalised. When he left care he was unable to cope. The only real family he had was his sister who had also been abused by the adoptive parents. She became an underage mother and had regular contact with the police. At the time of interview, David had limited contact with her.

No formal attempt was made to appropriately prepare David for leaving care. But he had had the benefit of living, albeit briefly, in a preparation unit at a children's home. Afterwards he went to live with a family as a lodger, an arrangement that soon broke down. His next home was a self-contained flat with a resident landlord, but he was unable to cope with independent living.

His survival in the community was short lived as he was arrested and detained in custody and is now serving a long term prison sentence. He says that the only way he can live is in an institution. That is all he knows.

From Ince (1998), p. 38

Ince claims that for all the young people in her study prolonged exposure to a 'white Eurocentric model of care' adversely affected their self-perception and ability to cope after leaving care, while restricted contact with black family, friends and wider community made it harder for them to reintegrate with that community. In addition some of the young people had experienced considerable movement and disruption, which led to a sense of rootlessness and instability that continued after leaving care – in some cases combined with feelings of rejection and powerlessness. Those young people who had experienced a stable foster placement, or who had remained in their family until their teenage years, were more optimistic about the future. Poor education also made it harder for these young people to find employment or enter further education.

Ince concludes by suggesting that preparation for young black people leaving care should attend not just to life skills (as in Broad's 'technical assistance' model), but also to the emotional and psychological impact of individual and institutional racism (as in the 'social welfare' and 'social justice' models). This, she argues, means building bridges to the black community and proactively recruiting black carers, volunteers, and 'social aunts and uncles'; it also means:

- providing placements that reflect the needs of black children
- representation of black people in agency decision making
- attention to the educational needs of black children
- advocates and independent visitors for young black people
- enabling young people to test out living independently
- work on identity and helping young people explore their racial origins
- addressing racial harassment and abuse in care and education
- not placing black children in mainly white areas.

from Ince (2004)

Young disabled people leaving care

Broad (1998) found that 9 per cent of care leavers were affected by learning difficulties or physical disabilities. Bichal et al. (1992) reported a figure of 13 per cent; they found that young disabled care leavers were more likely to be homeless or unemployed, and were unlikely to receive support from their local authority, or even to be in contact with them.

Biehal et al. (1995) concluded from their small sample of young people with special needs that disabled young people need opportunities to acquire skills and confidence gradually. This work should not all be left to carers; specialist input may be needed, and formal assessment of skills and abilities should take place well before young people with disabilities or mental health problems leave care. Long term advance planning is crucial for success in independent living.

It should be obvious that young people leaving care who are disabled are likely to need more help and support than others. However, there is some evidence that they actually receive less. Harris, Rabiee and Priestley (2002) point to anomalies in the legal provision for disabled care leavers – particularly in relation to those in regular respite care, who are mainly excluded from the leaving care provisions even though in some cases they may spend more time in respite placements than at home. Extra work may be needed with these young people to ensure that they are fully involved in planning, that they have real choices and options in relation to their accommodation, that their educational needs are met (and they are not put on courses simply as a way to occupy them). A key point for young disabled people is transitional planning as they move from the school system into adult services including further education and training, and it is important for social workers and leaving care workers to be actively engaged with this process.

> They didn't tell me I was going to have a review. They just did it without me knowing. I'd get to know in the last day ... If they'd put it, to what it was all about, I'd have gone with them, sat down and listened to them.
>
> Harry, young person quoted in Harris, Rabiee and Priestley (2002), p. 163

Young people leaving care who are refugees and asylum seekers

This is a group who have begun to feature more strongly in the population of children in need and looked after in recent years. Their entitlement to the full range of statutory services has from time to time been questioned, by people including government ministers. However, at the time of writing the position is clearly that these children and young people are subject to the powers and duties in the Children Act 1989, the Children (Leaving Care) Act 2000 and the Children (Scotland) Act 1995 as amended by the Regulation of Care (Scotland) Act 2001. Furthermore, they are very specifically covered by the United Nations Convention on the Rights of the Child.

Strictly speaking, *refugees* are people who have been granted refugee status and *asylum seekers* are those whose status as refugees is still undetermined. Children and young people in both groups may need local authority services including accommodation, or may be committed to care, for all the same reasons as any other group of children and young people. However, they are in many ways especially vulnerable, and none more so than unaccompanied asylum-seeking or refugee children, who are also of course the most likely to find themselves in the care system.

Kidane (2002) reminds us that

> Unaccompanied refugee children have the same essential needs as all other children. As with other children in need, local authorities have the responsibility to ensure the safety and protection of refugee children as well as the promotion of their welfare, as stated in section 17(1) of the Children Act …
>
> However, it is clear that unaccompanied refugee children constitute a particularly vulnerable group of children in need. Their primary attachment base and most of their networks have been severed suddenly, often unexpectedly, and under traumatic circumstances … Therefore unaccompanied refugee children leaving local authority care are more likely to be in need of extra support than most of their peers.
>
> p. 133

For these young people uncertainty is likely to be a continuing feature of life, including in many cases uncertainty about their entitlement to remain in the country. Kidane continues:

> Successful care arrangements and leaving care packages need to be constructed in a way that helps unaccompanied refugee children and young people to form a secure enough base from which they can make the transition from childhood to adulthood. This needs to happen within the context of secure, lasting and appropriate relationships that can be maintained through time and across geographical space enabling the children to experience both permanence and security. Therefore, it is particularly important that wherever possible relationships and support arrangements are stable and enduring over time. This will ensure ample opportunities for appropriate and lasting relationships that, in the absence of other networks (e.g. familial or peer), the young people could rely on for support into adulthood.
>
> Kidane (2002), p. 133; see also Kidane (2001a, 2001b)

Pathways to success

Just as young people leaving care have many different needs, so there are many different pathways to success after leaving care.

For some it is to *return home*, at least in the short term. *Going Home* is the title of a major research study conducted by the Dartington Social Research Unit in the early 1990s (Bullock et al. 1993a). It showed that most young people, even those who have become completely separated from their families while in care, do at some stage return home. This may happen immediately on leaving care or later; it may be for a brief or an extended period; but in whatever way, the overwhelming majority re-establish contact with their families. There are a number of things that social workers can do to help make this return home successful, of which almost certainly the most important is to put real effort into helping children and young people to maintain links with their families during their time in care. A follow-up study by the same team found that among the strongest indicators of successful return home were 'that the family relationships were of a fairly high quality' and 'that the family was prepared for the anxiety generated by return and the disputes which were likely to occur' (Bullock et al. 1998, p. 203). Biehal et al. (1995) point to the need to make a proper assessment of the quality of support to be expected from a young person's own family *long before* they leave care – and that this should include members of the extended family.

For many the key is a continuing relationship with *foster parents* (see Fry 1992). Most children and young people in care are placed in foster homes, and many of those who do not have strong relationships with their birth families do have important relationships with their foster families. O'Mairthini, herself a foster carer turned leaving care worker, puts it vividly:

> Think back to the first time you had a place to call your own, the exhilaration, the excitement and happiness of going it alone. Can you recall the first crisis you had to cope with, and who did you turn to for advice and help? Your parents perhaps, or a trusted family member or friend ... Who do young people who leave care turn to when they have left the protective network of social services?
>
> O'Mairthini (2002), p. 74

She points out that young people often feel that their social worker is too busy and are reluctant to ask them for help, they may not be able to rely on birth family members, while advice lines or drop-in centres may involve talking to strangers. Foster carers, she suggests, are in a unique position to help, especially as 'they usually have intimate knowledge of the personality, likes, dislikes, habits and attitudes of the young people they have cared for' (p. 74).

The more that foster parents can offer continuing support to young people in the same way that most ordinary families do, the better the chances of those young people succeeding in their lives after care. Some foster parents will do this whatever the obstacles in their way. However, most need support themselves if they are to support young people properly. This may mean continuing financial support and other practical resources from the social work agency. It may mean that planning of future placements has to take account of foster homes' continuing obligations to young people who have officially 'left'. Most of us when we leave our parental home know that if we're stuck we can go back. We also know that we can always turn up for a meal, a chat, perhaps even a loan. Simply knowing that this support is available can sometimes make the difference between feeling safe and confident and feeling isolated and bewildered. If foster parents are to take on a similar role, they need to know that this is recognised by the agency – and they may also need help and support in dealing with the implications for taxes and benefits.

The same applies in a different way to *residential care*. If a children's home is where a young person has spent their teenage years, that is often where they will naturally look for support and guidance as a young adult. They need a clear message that this is OK, and not a feeling that they are being pushed out. They may even need to come back to stay if things go wrong for them. If homes or agencies have rules that make this impossible, they are not doing their job as 'corporate parents'.

As we have already seen, *education* can be a key element in a pathway to success. When Sonia Jackson and Pearl Martin studied a group of care leavers who had been successful in education and in other aspects of their lives, they found that

> Among the protective factors that were identified as most strongly associated with later educational success were: (i) stability and continuity; (ii) learning to read early and fluently; (iii) having a parent or carer who valued education and saw it as the route to a good life; (iv) having friends outside care who did well at school; (v) developing out-of-school interests and hobbies (which also helped to increase social skills and bring them into contact with a wider range of non-care people); (vi) meeting a significant adult who offered consistent support and encouragement and acted as a mentor and possibly role model; and (vii) attending school regularly.
>
> Jackson and Martin (1998), p. 578

Many of these factors may of course be related to what happens to children early on in their lives in care. However, there is still much that can be done during adolescence to support young people's education and encourage them to do well.

What helps in practice

Before leaving – 'pre-aftercare'

What happens before a young person leaves care is critically important. The Children Act 1989 says that 'where a child is being looked after by a local authority, it shall be the duty of the authority to advise, assist and befriend him with a view to promoting his welfare when he ceases to be looked after by them' (Section 24(1)). The Children (Scotland) Act 1995 makes a similar provision – as indeed did the Children Act 1948. The law does not impose any age limit on this duty. It implies that for any child in care, even those whose stay is only expected to be short, one eye should always be on the future. It is not enough just to deal with immediate problems or needs – being a 'corporate parent' means taking a parent's responsibility for planning ahead and for giving a child the best start in life. Calling this phase 'pre-aftercare' may help to remind us that what happens after a child or young person leaves care is not simply an afterthought, but an essential part of the whole story.

I suggested earlier that we think in terms of three distinct areas of service provision: services that are provided for care leavers directly; services that are provided for all young people in the age group; and services that are provided for young people in care before they leave. The second and third areas may sometimes tend to be overlooked in concentrating on leaving care projects and what they can offer. However, the second area is important because care leavers do not necessarily want services that are set apart from those provided for other young people, and because many of their needs are also the needs of other people in their age group. The third area is also very important – indeed, in some ways the key to good leaving care provision is in how young people are looked after in the care system.

We see this if we look at the question from the perspective of Broad's three 'models'. The 'technical assistance' model would point to the need for young people to acquire the skills they need for the future – both educational achievements and everyday living skills. The 'social welfare' model would emphasise the need for close and supportive relationships to be developed in this period, which will be a resource for the young person in the future. Meanwhile the 'social justice' model might remind us of the importance of empowering young people to recognise their common interests, to work together to tackle difficulties, and to speak up and expect to be listened to about issues that concern them. This of course includes being heard in relation to the plans for them to leave care. (The 'social justice' model might also remind us of the need to ensure that the best services are available for young people in care, which might help avoid abrupt ejections from the system.)

Accommodation and maintenance

From a social worker's point of view, accommodation and maintenance are of course the key issues in work with care leavers. Parsons et al. (2002) point out that the situation is simpler in Britain now that local authorities have unambiguous responsibility for maintenance and accommodation. There is no longer a financial incentive to push young people out early, and leaving care plans should be based on needs rather than resources. It is important to collaborate effectively with local housing providers to ensure that care leavers have the best choice from the range of accommodation types available.

This range is likely to include local authority and housing association tenancies, private sector accommodation, voluntary sector schemes, and supported lodgings. Broad and Fry (2002) argue for positive use of supported lodging, not as a cheap option but as a resource which properly managed and supervised can offer something of real value to many young people. For some young people the options may include returning to friends or relatives, or an extended stay in a foster or residential placement; for others a *foyer*, offering support with employment and training as part of the package, may be the answer. On occasion short term emergency accommodation may be needed, and the system should include some provision for this.

As the Department of Health says in its guidance:

> Young people living in and leaving care are a diverse group whose needs will vary according to their care experience, ethnicity, gender, sexuality, contact with their families, degree of preparedness for leaving and any disability that they may have. It follows that their accommodation needs will be equally diverse.
>
> Department of Health (2001c), 5.2

The same guidance also says:

> Councils should take steps to make sure that young people have the best chance to succeed in their accommodation. They should:

- Avoid moving young people who are settled unless it is unavoidable or offers clear advantages.
- Assess young people and prepare them for any move.
- Where practicable, offer a choice in the type and location of accommodation.
- Set up a package of support to go with the accommodation.
- Have a clear financial plan for the accommodation.
- Have a contingency plan in case the proposed accommodation breaks down.

- Ensure that the accommodation meets any needs relating to physical and/or sensory impairment and/or learning disability.

Department of Health (2001c), 5.27–8

It is interesting to note that this reproduces almost exactly Stein's summary of the points made by Hutson, with the addition of the first and final points. However, it omits any reference to involving young people in planning and decision making!

Perhaps the most important task is to ensure that the young person has good information on the choices open to her or him, and real support in securing accommodation and making a success of it; and that the timing of any move is right for the individual. As Biehal et al. (1995) say, 'There is a need to challenge informal practices and formal policies which create pressure for young people to move on before they are ready to do so.' They also note that moves are often precipitated by the breakdown of foster placements – even apparently stable ones – and conclude that 'particular attention should be given to supporting foster placements as young people reach their mid-teens' (p. 42).

Although social services authorities now have the primary responsibility for financial support of care leavers, young people may still need advice and support in claiming additional benefits to which they may be entitled. Many of them will also need help and advice with budgeting.

I thought it would be easy when I got the flat with my son   I thought all the bills were just paid, I never realised that I'd have to pay them.

Partridge (1989)

Other than accommodation, there are a number of other particular issues that young people may often need help with. We address some of these briefly in the next few subsections.

Education and employment

As we have seen, much of the work in relation to education has to be done long before children and young people leave care. If they have had a successful experience of education and want to continue learning and gaining qualifications, they will still need information about what might be available, and support and encouragement to take advantage of it. If their experience has been poor, then it is much more difficult for them to see what they might gain from further education. There are projects and services that can help with this, and it is important for staff working with care leavers to be aware of these. Equally important is to have someone who the young person can see is really taking an interest in their progress and achievements, preferably someone who can model a successful use of educational opportunities. Careers advice and support is equally important, as is help with the practicalities of getting and keeping work – help preparing for interviews, support with costs of transport, smart clothes and so on.

Local authorities are able to provide help through employability and mentoring schemes. As corporate parents, they have a responsibility to assist young people in producing effective CVs and preparing for interviews, and to provide employment experiences for them.

Emerging identities

Biehal et al. (1995) are not alone in pointing to the importance of knowledge of one's past for a sense of identity, which means that young people may need opportunities to explore their personal histories *before* and *after* they leave care. Biehal et al. also point to the importance of maintaining family links, even when family relationships are poor, and to the importance of young people having opportunities to participate in decision making and to take risks in a supported environment before they leave care.

Drug and alcohol use

Biehal et al. found that for those who had problems in this area, successful outcomes were usually associated with finding 'an incentive to stabilise their lives' – for example parenthood, or rapprochement with a parent. Harm reduction strategies could also be helpful, and social workers should make sure they know about these and where to get help with them locally.

Becoming a parent

Based on the experiences of the young people they spoke to, Biehal et al. recommend that a range of options for accommodation need to be available, and suggest that the support offered by leaving care schemes can be particularly important for care leavers who are parents. They found that social work support often tended to switch to focus on the new child, at a time when young people still needed help in their own right. Poverty was a major problem for this group, and help was needed with return to education, as well as access to social and parenting groups. As McAuley (2002, p. 101) says,

> It is not the end of a young person's life if they become a parent at a young age. As parents we would ensure we supported our child through this stage in their lives – as corporate parents we must do the same for looked after children and care leavers.

Exercise 10.1   Annie prepares to leave care

Annie's placement with Mr and Mrs Farmer broke down after three years, without the planned adoption being completed. After a period in a children's home she was placed with a specialist adolescent foster carer, Liz Green. She is now 17 and recently finished school with two GCSEs (an E in English and a D in Art). She has expressed some interest in pursuing studies in childcare.

Liz Green is fond of Annie, but plans to give up fostering shortly and move to the West of Ireland to pursue her interests in painting and marine ecology. On two occasions recently Annie has been brought home by the police after being found drunk in town with a group of older friends.

What are likely to be the key components of a leaving care plan for Annie?
What are the responsibilities of the local authority and others?
What would be the result of a SWOT analysis (strengths, weaknesses, opportunities, threats) of Annie's situation?

The role of the specialist leaving care team

One of the most notable developments in this field of practice in the past 20 years has been the creation of specialist leaving care teams and projects. Research has already shown that these can make a major contribution to improving services for young people, by promoting awareness of their needs, by acting as advocates, and by providing services directly. As Wade (2003) puts it, 'The informality of schemes is valued by young people and may therefore assist them to stay in touch or return for help when it is needed.' However, leaving care schemes should not be a substitute for good social work services, or for planned support from familiar figures such as foster parents or residential workers – the 'prime carers'. Mike Stein wrote in 1990:

> If a child care strategy was resourced and implemented which achieved placement stability and high quality substitute care for all young people who needed it, then preparation for adulthood would become the responsibility of the prime carers ... the role of a specialist leaving care team would not be to provide intensive support but to assist the prime carers, their social workers and their young people by packages of resources.
>
> Stein (1990), p. 82

Seven years later, the same author's review of 'what works in practice' concluded:

> The research evidence reviewed in this report gives overwhelming support to that view. Placement stability, continuity and family links are all essential to achieving positive outcomes for care leavers. Specialist schemes should work in a way that, as far as is possible, is able to build upon these foundations. If this is not possible, and the evidence suggests that may be the case for too many young people, then a more intensive supportive role will be needed.
>
> Stein (1997), p. 53

Support groups and mentoring

I want to conclude by returning to the point that young people leaving care have to be respected as autonomous, and that effective ways of helping them depend on letting them lead the process and develop and use their own personal resources – both as individuals and as a group of people with shared interests and concerns.

One way to harness those resources is through a leaving care support group. Carol Floris (2002) distinguishes two different kinds of leaving care support group, which she calls the 'preparation group' (short term, adult-led, focused on skills) and the 'working group' (longer term, young person-led, often focused on information and self-advocacy). She finds advantages and problems with both kinds of group, and argues that there may be a need for a properly resourced amalgam of the two. Although some agencies have resisted identifying care leavers as a group with common interests, practical experience of support groups suggest that young people can often be a powerful resource for each other.

Another approach to support is through mentoring schemes – which may use professionals or volunteers. Cathcart (2002) gives a useful account of how these can work. Again, one advantage of this approach is that it helps to put young people in the driving seat and to allow them to define the degree and type of support and advice they need.

Summary and conclusion

We began this chapter by thinking about what is meant by 'leaving care', and what are social workers' responsibilities to all children and young people moving on from the care system. We then looked at the particular needs of young people leaving care in their teenage years, and the implications for providing services to them that are helpful, sensitive and accessible. We considered what is to be learned from research in leaving care, including what it can tell us about young people's views. We looked at the thinking underlying recent legislation on leaving care, which has itself been heavily influenced by research. One of the messages of the chapter is that not all care leavers are the same, and we focused on the needs of particular groups of care leavers – those from ethnic minorities, those who are disabled, and refugees and asylum seekers. Finally, we looked at key messages for practice and at the importance of inter-agency working in this area.

In conclusion, the key to success in this area of practice seems to be a combination of good general services with targeted specialist services that are accessible to young people when they need them, and practitioners who have a real commitment to working in partnership with young people, listening to them and taking notice of what they have to say.

GUIDE TO FURTHER READING

The best sources for research on leaving care are probably Bichal et al. (1995), Broad (1998), Stein (1997) and West (1995). The Department of Health *Quality Protects* briefing (Wade 2003) is a good summary and a source of further reading. There is some good up-to-date practice guidance in the collection edited by Wheal (2002).

CHAPTER 11

Conclusion: outcomes, effectiveness and good practice

Introduction

In this final chapter I want us to think about the results of all our work with children and young people in care. We will review more of the evidence from past and recent research into the *outcomes* of care for children and young people, some of which we considered in the previous chapter. In this chapter we will also reflect on what this research actually tells us, on what we mean by outcomes, and what is being compared with what. Following this I want to focus on the idea of *effectiveness* and 'what works', before looking more generally at what constitutes good practice with children and young people in care. I will conclude by arguing again for a particular approach to practice, one that prioritises an active relationship with the child or young person.

Outcomes for young people in care – the evidence

What happens to children when they are in care or accommodation? Is the system giving them the welfare, and the life of relative normality, which has been its explicit aim for the last half century? In too many cases the answer is clearly no. Let us briefly review some of the evidence.

Stability and continuity

One of the chief aims of the system is to offer stability and continuity to children who in many cases are desperately in need of this. In the period leading up to the legislative reforms of the early 1990s, research revealed that children were experiencing repeated changes of placement and loss of contact with their families. It is not clear that this has improved much following the Children Act and other legislation – in fact, there has been some evidence to suggest that instability may actually have increased (Jackson and Thomas 1999, 2001).

The most substantial research evidence relating to stability relates to breakdown in permanent placement, and it is probably too soon to say how this has changed in recent years. Major studies like those by Berridge and Cleaver (1987) and Fratter et al. (1991) showed what a complex set of factors are involved in placement disruption, and it is possible that some causes of instability are improving while others may be worsening. (Indeed, Fratter et al. suggested that future research might concentrate on particular groups of children, since the implications for practice are likely to be different in different cases.)

In 1999 in England the number of children who experienced three or more placements in one year (the government's main performance indicator in this area) ranged in different authorities between 3 and 44 per cent. Instability for children who are not in permanent placements continues to be produced by organisational factors, some of which may have worsened. System-produced instability includes the built-in instability of many placements, especially residential placements, where 'because of shift patterns, staff turnover, and the use of agency and contract staff, a child may be faced with different carers every day' (Jackson and Thomas 1999, p. 39). It also includes changes of social worker or periods without a social worker, moves dictated by financial considerations, closures of establishments, and organisational disruption and upheaval. Advocacy services are frequently asked to help children who face being moved for financial reasons, often related to the use of private fostering agencies and private residential establishments (Jackson and Thomas 1999, p. 40).

As long as children are moving around, it is difficult to ensure that the 'ordinary needs' of children and young people are met. Nonetheless this is also a key objective of the system. How well does it appear to be doing? Let us look at two of the most important 'ordinary needs' of children – their health and their education.

Education

A recurring theme throughout this book has been the importance of educational achievement for young people's success in other areas of life, and for their self-esteem. In fact research consistently shows the educational attainments of care leavers falling far below that of the general population. It is not uncommon to find studies that report more than 75 per cent of young people in care leaving school with no qualifications at all, only 3 per cent achieving GCSE grades A–C (the basic measure of success for most of the school population), and no more than one in 300 reaching university. Other studies indicate that 60 per cent of looked after children do not attend school regularly, that children in residential care are 80 times more likely to be excluded than the average, and that there is a link between school problems and placement breakdown (Jackson 2001 and elsewhere).

In short, children and young people in local authority care typically achieve below their potential in school, and are at high risk of leaving without any useful qualifications. This leaves them with less chance of finding stable or satisfying employment, and can have negative effects on all aspects of their lives. Low attainment has been a consistent research finding over many years, but recently attention has been focused on behavioural problems and on school exclusion, which is increasingly denying educational opportunities to children in care.

Research interest in the education of children in care is quite recent, suggesting a lack of awareness among childcare specialists and perhaps indicative of a damaging split between the care and education systems. Sonia Jackson, who first opened up this topic to discussion and research in the 1980s, suggests that the chief problem is the low priority given to education by social workers and social work managers, coupled with the failure of social services and education authorities to work together for the benefit of children and young people. There is some indication that the situation is now improving (see for instance Maclean and Gunion 2003).

A consistent thread in the research into educational attainment of children in care has been the difficulty of attributing poor performance to the experience of being in care or to children's previous background. The evidence does not suggest that in general admission to care actually depresses children's educational achievement, except perhaps in the short term after admission (and also for adolescents admitted in a crisis where examination work may be disrupted). Although children and young people in care do much worse than the general population, their performance is comparable to that of children in similar circumstances who remain with their families. The question then becomes one of why the care system is failing to raise children's level of educational success, even when they spend many years in stable placements. Heath et al. (1994) argue on the basis of their research that 'greater-than-average' educational inputs are needed if children and young people who have suffered early deprivation are to catch up with their peers. There is some evidence to suggest that children who are adopted may do rather better than those in foster care or residential homes.

Health

In the 1980s in Britain serious problems were also identified for children and young people in care in accessing adequate healthcare. Immunisation rates were sometimes as low as 17 per cent, much lower than the general population. Routine surveillance was often overlooked, and there was a high incidence of sight and hearing problems together with a poor level of general health. Dental treatment and other preventative health measures were also often overlooked, and children appeared to be missing out on health education, possibly reflected in high levels of smoking and of teenage pregnancy.

This situation appears to have improved since attention was focused on it, and on some measures the system appears to be doing much better. For 73 per cent of looked after children in England in 2002 their immunisations were up to date; 72 per cent had a dental check, and 71 per cent had an annual health assessment. (Of course, these figures also mean that more than a quarter of children and young people did not have these checks.) Other research has suggested that in terms of general physical health young people in care may now be getting quite a good service, but that their mental health is still an area of high concern. A high proportion of children in care have difficulties that can lead to mental health problems, if they have not already done so, but the services available to meet these needs are very limited indeed.

Other indicators of wellbeing

We saw in the previous chapter how young people leaving the care system are still at an exceptionally high risk of unemployment, homelessness and relationship difficulties. Despite the improvements that have been made in leaving care entitlements, these problems have not gone away. As we saw, they are a result of what happens long before children and young people leave care, at least as much as they are a result of what happens at that stage.

What is meant by outcomes

'Outcomes' can be used in more than one sense. When applied to children and young people in care it is sometimes used to mean what happens to them after they leave care; in other words, the outcome of a life in care. It is largely in this sense that we were looking at outcomes in the previous chapter. On the other hand, it is also used to mean what happens to children and young people when they are still in care; in other words, the outcomes of the provision of care. In Britain since the early 1990s there has been a strong focus on measuring outcomes in both these senses, but particularly the second one. The aim has been to provide clear and accessible information to agencies on how well they are serving the young people for whom they have responsibility, and then to set objectives and targets for improvement. The *Looking After Children* package (originally entitled 'Good parenting, good outcomes') was an important part of this, as we saw in Chapter 6. Government initiatives like *Quality Protects* in England and *Children First* in Wales built on this, by setting a series of targets and performance indicators which local authorities were expected to achieve in order to qualify for additional funding.

However, measuring outcomes and interpreting the results is not always a simple or straightforward matter, as we noted in the previous chapter in relation to young people leaving care. We need to be sure that we are comparing things that really are comparable, and great care must be taken in drawing conclusions about the reasons for particular research findings. For instance, when we read that 10 per cent of looked after children aged 10 or over were cautioned or convicted for an offence during a year, three times the rate for all children of this age (Department of Health 2003), are we to interpret this as an indication of how badly the care system is looking after young people, or as a reminder that the young people it is looking after are already at a high level of risk of poor outcomes when they come into care?

In England the Department of Health outcome indicators for looked after children for the 12 months to 30 September 2002 showed that their educational performance still compared unfavourably with the general population.

- The percentages of looked after children reaching the expected level of educational attainment at 'key stages' were 50 per cent at KS1, 40 per cent at KS2 and 22 per cent at KS3 (compared to 85 per cent, 78 per cent and 66 per cent of all children).
- In year 11, 53 per cent of looked after children obtained at least one GCSE or GNVQ (compared with 95 per cent of all school children), and 42 per cent did not sit an examination.
- Only 8 per cent obtained at least 5 GCSEs or equivalent at grades A*–C (compared with 50 per cent of all children).
- At the end of year 11, 56 per cent remained in full-time education compared to 72 per cent of all school-leavers, and 24 per cent were unemployed in the September after they left school, compared to 6 per cent of all school-leavers.

Department of Health (2003)

On the other hand the same report reveals that 27 per cent of looked after children of school age had statements of special educational needs. This alone would lead one to expect that the average level of achievement of looked after children would be lower than that of the general population. If we also 'factor in' social class and other background factors, the performance of children and young people in care starts to appear much closer to that of their peers.

This means that we have to think about what the objects of the care system are for children and young people. It brings us back to the issues about standards, and about the relationship between children, parents and the state, that we flagged up at the start of this book. It even brings us back to issues that were alive in the postwar years when modern child care services were being established along with the rest of the welfare state, and which have never really been resolved. On the one hand, the Poor Law doctrine of 'less eligibility' was replaced with the idea of care as a service to children and families on the basis of need, just as the National Health Service and universal secondary education were founded on the principle that everyone should have access to the same life chances regardless of ability to pay. On the other hand, the setting of national assistance (later 'social security', 'supplementary benefit', and 'income support') at a minimal level close to subsistence suggested that, for those families who could not provide for themselves, only a basic safety net would be provided. Since then there has been a continuing ambivalence about the aims of the care system for children and young people, who mainly enter it from backgrounds and social circumstances where their life chances have been curtailed in all sorts of ways. Is the aim to bring them up according to the standards of the communities from which they have come? to those of the 'respectable working class', or of some average of the population? to the best standard available? or perhaps to the level that those providing the service would expect for their own children?

The message underlying the rhetoric of *Quality Protects* and *Looking After Children* is that children in care should expect, and be expected, to do as well as everyone else. But this ignores the fact that 'everyone else' is a very mixed group indeed, and that all children and young people do not have the same opportunities or achieve the same outcomes. If the expectation is that the care system will undo all the disadvantage that children and young people bring with them when they enter it, then it will need to be resourced to a very much higher level than it currently is. Furthermore, it will be hard to justify not setting out to achieve the same objectives for children who do not come into care. Indeed, the rhetoric of modern governments often is about extending the same life chances to all children and young people; but at the same time the huge inequalities of income and other resources that make that impossible are not challenged – in fact they are often maintained and exacerbated by economic and fiscal policy.

Exercise 11.1 Annie revisited

Return to the example of Annie when we first met her in Exercise 6.1.

(1) As if you were meeting Annie for the first time, ask yourself:
   How would you ensure that Annie has:
      continuity and quality of education?
      continuity and quality of health care?
      continuity of relationships?
      stability of placement?
   What work, skills and resources would be needed to achieve this?
   What obstacles might there be? How would you overcome them?
(2) With the benefit of hindsight after reading the subsequent examples, ask:
   What could have been done differently to ensure better outcomes for Annie?

These unresolved issues over outcomes and objectives can leave the poor social worker in a difficult situation. If what is being expected of the practitioner or the agency is not actually achievable, and yet practitioners and agencies are held to account for failing to deliver, then morale is likely to suffer. It is arguable that much of the poor morale that has been a feature of child care services in recent years is a result of just such a double bind. Until a real national commitment is made to give the interests of children and young people from poor families a much higher priority, this is unlikely to change.

I am not suggesting that attention to outcomes is misplaced. Clearly it is important to measure and record outcomes, if we are to do better by children and young people. I would also argue that we should in principle be setting the highest standards for children who are cared for by the state. However, in doing so it is important to recognise that the care system on its own cannot make up for all the deficiencies and inequalities in the wider society.

What is meant by effectiveness

Much current analysis of social work is couched in terms of effectiveness and 'what works'. There has been a strong movement for 'evidence-based practice', on the principle that one should not intervene in people's lives without having demonstrable reasons for believing that the intervention will be helpful and effective, and in the belief that there is evidence from research which can provide such reasons (see Alderson et al. 1996). This approach underlies much of the work by governments in disseminating research findings to practitioners.

This approach to evaluation can be criticised. Randomised controlled trials, which advocates of the evidence-based approach see as the 'gold standard' for research that provides a sound basis for practice, are not suitable for many aspects of social welfare. They can be difficult to set up, and there may be ethical problems. Much social work is highly context-sensitive, making it hard to standardise interventions or to generalise findings. The context is continually changing, and many aspects of intervention are not understood well enough for controlled trials to be undertaken (see Lewis 1998).

It can also be argued that 'evidence-based practice' is a misguided attempt to reduce the complexities of social work intervention to simple formulae of success and failure (see for instance Shaw 2003 and elsewhere). Much of what goes on in any social work encounter is not simply about delivering predefined objectives. It is also about exploring different perspectives on a situation, defining shared aims collaboratively (or sometimes through conflict), and even transforming the ways in which both practitioner and client see the situation. The client – whether an adult or a child – may have quite different objectives from those of the agency or the government, and the social worker's task in this situation is not easily or simply defined.

However, I am not suggesting that attention to effectiveness, any more than attention to outcomes, is misplaced. As Sonia Jackson and I wrote some years ago:

> It may be that the reality which can be expressed in terms of evidence-based practice does not represent the whole of what is involved in social work intervention; but this is not a reason for failing to use the approach in settings where it is appropriate. 'What works?' is a deceptively simple question, and the answer will often be rather complicated. ... However, anyone who intervenes in people's lives, especially those who are relatively vulnerable and powerless, has a responsibility to make full use of available knowledge about the effects of alternative kinds of intervention.
>
> Jackson and Thomas (1999), pp. 7–8

There are a number of ways of finding out about what makes for effectiveness in practice. These include learning from the experience of other practitioners, learning from what children and young people and their families have to say, and learning from research (which may itself tell us about the experience of other practitioners and about what children and young people and their families have to say). In recent years researchers and policy makers have paid much more attention to disseminating the findings of research to practitioners. In the UK the work of the Department of Health and other government departments, and of research institutions such as the Dartington Social Research Unit, have made major contributions to this process. In the Guide to Further Reading at the end of this chapter I give some examples of this work.

Using research in practice

The good practitioner in any field tries to be aware of research and what it can tell us – whether this be 'hard' research that demonstrates the effectiveness of different kinds of intervention, or 'soft' research that helps us to understand the processes involved in intervention and the perspectives of different actors. This can be a challenge in a field like childcare social work, where the level of research activity and the quantity of published work is very high. When I moved from practice into academic work in the early 1990s, it seemed possible to read most of the key research in the field, at least in Britain. Today it is certainly not; and the range of recent published research I have drawn on in writing this book has been very selective, in part because I have simply been unable to keep up with it all. If that is the case for a full time academic (and speed reader), how on earth is a busy practitioner meant to cope?

Part of the answer, of course, is to be selective, and also to make full use of the digests and summaries produced by government, by childcare organisations and by research centres. However, it is also important to insist on making space in one's working time for reading, thinking and keeping abreast of research and new ideas. To an extent research represents the accumulated wisdom and experience of our colleagues, and to work in ignorance of it is irresponsible. Any employing agency that fails to understand this, or fails to enable and encourage staff to use some of their time in this way, is due for some rethinking.

I would also argue that practitioners, especially the more experienced ones, have a responsibility to contribute to research and the exchange of ideas – by undertaking their own research, perhaps in collaboration with academics, and by publishing some of the fruits of their experience. Clinical psychologists use the concept of the 'scientist-practitioner' to reflect the idea that the skilled practitioner is constantly experimenting and testing ideas and hypotheses in the course of his or her work. Schön's (1983) similar conception of the 'reflective practitioner' applies to social work as it does many other professions. Artificial barriers between researchers and practitioners are unhelpful, because we should be working together to share knowledge and experience, in order to improve the life chances of children and young people.

What is known about good practice

Effectiveness is an important element in good practice, but it is not the only one. Being responsive to the needs of children and families, and working in an ethical way, are also of critical importance. If we return to the principles we set out in Chapter 1, this may remind us of some important points about listening to children and young people and working with difference and oppression.

Again, in the Guide to Further Reading you will find some references to good advice on these issues.

The previous discussion of effectiveness suggests that there may sometimes be difficult issues about accountability in work with children and young people in care. On the one hand social workers and their agencies are expected to be 'good parents' to the children and young people who have been entrusted to their care. This means providing care and supervision to a high standard. It means ensuring that children are in stable situations with people to whom they are securely attached. It means maintaining secure boundaries within which they can develop autonomy. It means looking after their health, and supporting their education. It means giving them love. The assumption is that we will do this as part of a team, with colleagues both within and outside the agency, working together to promote the interests of the child or young person.

At the same time we have to acknowledge that all is not always sweetness and light. Other agencies, and our own agency, may not always put the interests of individual children and young people first. There may be individuals who are pursuing objectives which are not in the interests of children and young people – and this includes adults who are abusers. The system itself may work in ways that run counter to the interests of children and young people.

In these circumstances we have a responsibility to speak up for children and young people, even if this means going against our own employer. It is part of the role of any good parent to be an advocate for their child at times, and it is part of the job of a social worker to be an advocate for her or his clients. In social work with young people in care these two obligations come together in a double responsibility to be an advocate for the children and young people whose lives depend so much on our professional practice. If we put our own convenience, or our duty to our employers or our colleagues, before the interests and the wishes of young people, we are letting them down.

A famous report into the death of a child in care took the title *A Child in Trust* (Blom-Cooper 1985). When we take on the responsibility for looking after children and young people in the place of their parents we take on a trust, as individuals and as organisations; a trust that we can not lightly put aside. The attitude reported by Garnett (1992) shows a lack of comprehension or acceptance of this responsibility that is unfortunately too common:

> As one social worker said of a young woman with whom she had been involved with for some years prior to leaving care and who contacted her on leaving her foster home some months after discharge, 'Susan was an adult with a housing problem. I advised her to contact her local housing office, and asked the duty officer to deal with her case as I didn't think it was appropriate for a child care worker to deal with this.'
>
> Garnett (1992), p. 109

But if part of the responsibility for the quality of practice with children and families lies at the door of individual social workers, part of it emphatically does not. Social work agencies are accountable for the quality of services, as is the government. In recent years government has done a great deal to raise the quality of practice and to improve outcomes for children and young people. However, real improvements in practice are dependent on having a workforce with the skills, and the morale, to absorb new learning and put it into effect. Gilligan (2000b) has argued forcefully that to a large extent childcare social workers in the British Isles do not at present have the ability to do all that is being asked of them. Jones (2001) also points out that much discussion of social work practice at the level of research and policy is blind to the reality of life for many social workers and the families with whom they work.

There are alternative models of practice to that followed in the British Isles. In much of continental Europe the model is one of *social pedagogy*. This includes elements of social work and elements of education, but is arguably more child-centred than either. The training includes technical knowledge and skills in areas such as psychology, but also includes a powerful stress on building and working in relationships with children and young people. It has been argued, for instance by Moss and Petrie (2002), that the English-speaking world has much to learn from this model. At a time when both social work education and training and the structure of children's services are under review, and when employment patterns are becoming more fluid between countries, perhaps we should be finding out more about how our neighbours do things.

Conclusion – the social worker's role with young people

A study for the British Association of Social Workers (2003) reviewed the role of the field social worker with looked after children, in response to a recommendation made by Utting (1997). The report, by Keith Bilton, suggests that the key elements of the social worker's role *on behalf of the agency* are:

- to maintain a direct relationship with the child;
- to advocate for the child;
- to work with family and carers;
- to coordinate assessment and planning;
- to ensure compliance with statutory requirements and to act on any non-compliance;
- to coordinate service provision;
- to ensure that case records are maintained.

The report then looks at the social worker's role *as seen by the child*, based mainly on the studies by Bell (2001) and Munro (2001). The key points

---

Box 11.1 'My ideal social worker'

When Claire O'Kane and I talked to children and young people in care about decision making in their lives, we asked them to tell us about their ideal social worker. This is what they said they looked for:

- *Good communication skills* – someone who is easy to talk to and who understands, and explains well.
- *A good listener* – listens to what you have got to say, let you have more say, don't butt in.
- *Understanding* – understands what you feel and your view of things.
- *Personal style* – the way they talk, not strict or boring, generally happy, their personality, good sense of humour, friendly, doesn't lose their temper, doesn't stare, similar interests, polite, fashionable.
- *Giving you time* – giving you information and time to think about decisions.
- *Helpful* – they sort things out, get you good foster parents, set boundaries, arrange things, put things into action, can help give you ideas.
- *Caring* – has time for us, kind, calms us down, like a friend, generous, determination, dedication, good at general conversation.
- *An advocate* – willingness to say difficult things on your behalf
- *Someone you can trust.*
- *Being fair* – they don't take sides, listen to all sides and negotiate, honesty not favouritism.
- *Taking you out & treats* – visiting and taking you out, giving you chocolate!

From Thomas and O'Kane (1998a)

---

identified are:

- the importance of the social worker's relationship with the child;
- continuity in this relationship – children actually complained more about changes of social worker than they did about changes of placement;
- reliability and availability;
- confidentiality;
- advocacy;
- doing things together.

Similar points are made in Box 11.1, which is based on research with children aged between eight and twelve.

Let us finish this book with a simple message. If good social work practice with children and young people in care means anything at all, it means above all being on the child's side and being committed to children as people. Children and young people soon know whether this commitment is really there. If it is not, whatever skills and knowledge we have will not count for very much. If it is there, then we will also be committed to developing our skills and knowledge to work as effectively as we can with these often complex and difficult situations.

GUIDE TO FURTHER READING

For up-to-date research findings on outcomes, journals such as *Child and Family Social Work* and *Adoption and Fostering* are valuable. Specially commissioned research reviews such as those by the Department of Health (1998 and 1999) and Aldgate and Statham (2001) are also extremely helpful, as are the publications of '*research into practice*' at the Dartington Social Research Unit. The latter also produce a series of very accessible audiotapes – see the website www.rip.org.uk/. For studies of effectiveness and 'what works', the series of that name from Barnardos is invaluable; in particular Stein (1997), Jackson and Thomas (2001), Thoburn, Sellick and Philpot (2004) and the digest by McNeish et al. (2002).

References

Adcock, M. (2001) 'The core assessment: how to synthesise information and make judgements' in Horwath, J. (ed.) *The Child's World: assessing children in need*, London: Jessica Kingsley.

Ainsworth, F. and Maluccio, A. (2003) 'Towards new models of professional foster care', *Adoption and Fostering* 27(4), 46–50.

Alderson, P., Brill, S., Chalmers, I., Fuller, R., Hinkley-Smith, P., MacDonald, G., Newman, T., Oakley, A., Roberts, H. and Ward, H. (1996) *What Works? Effective social interventions in child welfare*, Barkingside: SSRU/Barnardos.

Aldgate, J. (1991) 'Attachment theory and its application to child care social work – an introduction' in Lishman, J. (ed.) *Handbook of Theory for Practice Teachers in Social Work*, London: Jessica Kingsley.

Aldgate, J. and Statham, J. (2001) *The Children Act Now: messages from research*, London: The Stationery Office.

Aldgate, J., Bradley, M. and Hawley, D. (1997) *Supporting Families through Short Term Accommodation: draft report for Department of Health*, University of Leicester.

Allen, N. (1999) *Making Sense of the Children Act: a guide for social and welfare services*, 3rd edition, Harlow: Longman.

Alston, P. (ed.) (1994) *The Best Interests of the Child: reconciling culture and human rights*, Oxford: Clarendon Press.

Ball, C., McDonald, A. and McGhee, J. (2002) *Law for Social Workers*, 4th edition, Aldershot: Ashgate.

Banks, N. (1999) 'Direct identity work' in Barn, R. (ed.) *Working with Black Children and Adolescents in Need*, London: British Agencies for Adoption and Fostering.

Barn, R. (1999) 'Racial and ethnic identity' in Barn, R. (ed.) *Working with Black Children and Adolescents in Need*, London: British Agencies for Adoption and Fostering.

Barn, R. and Sinclair, R. (2001) 'Black families and children: planning to meet their needs', *Research Policy and Planning* 17(2), 5–11.

Bebbington, A. and Miles, J. (1989) 'The background of children who enter local authority care', *British Journal of Social Work* 19(5), 349–68.

Beckett, C. (2003) *Child Protection: an introduction*, London: Sage.

Bell, M. (2001) 'Promoting children's rights through the use of relationship', *Child and Family Social Work* 7(1), 1–12.

Berridge, D. (1985) *Children's Homes*, Oxford: Blackwell.

Berridge, D. (1994) 'Foster and residential care reassessed: a research perspective' *Children and Society* 8(2), 132–50.

Berridge, D. (1997) *Foster Care: a research review*, London: Stationery Office.

Berridge, D. (2002) 'Residential care', in McNeish, D., Newman, T. and Roberts, H. (eds) *What Works for Children? Effective services for children and families*, Buckingham: Open University Press.

Berridge, D. and Brodie, I. (1997) *Children's Homes Revisited*, London: Jessica Kingsley.

Berridge, D. and Cleaver, H. (1987) *Foster Home Breakdown*, Oxford: Blackwell.

Biehal, N., Clayden, J., Stein, M. and Wade, J. (1992) *Prepared for Living? A survey of young people leaving the care of three local authorities*, London: National Children's Bureau.

Biehal, N., Clayden, J., Stein, M. and Wade, J. (1995) *Moving On: young people and leaving care schemes*, London: HMSO.

Blom-Cooper, L. (1985) *A Child in Trust: report into the death of Jasmine Beckford*, London: Borough of Brent.

Brammer, A. (2003) *Social Work Law*, Harlow: Longman.

Brandon, M., Schofield, G. and Trinder, L. (1998) *Social Work with Children*, London: Macmillan (now Palgrave Macmillan).

Braye, S. and Preston-Shoot, M. (1997) *Practising Social Work Law*, 2nd edition, Basingstoke: Macmillan (now Palgrave Macmillan).

Brayne, H. and Carr, H. (2003) *Law for Social Workers*, Oxford: Oxford University Press.

Bridge, C. and Swindells, H. (2003) *Adoption: the modern law*, Bristol: Family Law.

British Agencies for Adoption and Fostering (1999a) *Contact in Permanent Placement*, London: BAAF.

British Agencies for Adoption and Fostering (1999b) *Making Good Assessments*, London: BAAF.

British Agencies for Adoption and Fostering (1999c) *Assessment, Preparation and Support: implications from research*, London: BAAF.

British Agencies for Adoption and Fostering (1999d) *Contact in Permanent Placement*, London: BAAF.

British Association of Social Workers (2003) *Be My Social Worker: the role of the child's social worker*, Birmingham: Venture Press.

Broad, B. (1998) *Young People Leaving Care: life after the Children Act 1989*, London: Jessica Kingsley.

Broad, B. (ed.) (2001) *Kinship Care: the placement choice for children and young people*, Lyme Regis: Russell House.

Broad, B. and Fry, E. (2002) 'Sustaining supported lodgings: a golden opportunity for growth' in Wheal, A. (ed.) *The RHP Companion to Leaving Care*, Lyme Regis: Russell House.

Broad, B., Hayes, R. and Rushforth, C. (2001) *Kith and Kin: kinship care for vulnerable young people*, London: National Children's Bureau.

Bronfenbrenner, U. (1979) *The Ecology of Human Development: experiments by nature and design*, Cambridge, Massachusetts: Harvard University Press.

Brown, E., Bullock, R., Hobson, C. and Little, M. (1998) *Making Residential Care Work: structure and culture in children's homes*, Aldershot: Ashgate.

Brown, H. C. (1998) *Social Work and Sexuality: working with lesbians and gay men*, Basingstoke: Macmillan (now Palgrave Macmillan).

Bryer, M. (1988) *Planning in Child Care: a guide for team leaders and their teams*, London: British Agencies for Adoption and Fostering.

Bullock, R., Gooch, D. and Little, M. (1998) *Children Going Home: the reunification of families*, Aldershot: Ashgate.

Bullock, R., Little, M. and Millham, S. (1993a) *Going Home: the return of children separated from their families*, Aldershot: Dartmouth.

Bullock, R., Little, M. and Millham, S. (1993b) *Residential Care for Children: a review of the research*, London: HMSO.

Butler, I. and Roberts, G. (1997, 2nd edition 2003) *Social Work with Children and Families: getting into practice*, London: Jessica Kingsley.

Butler, S. and Charles, M. (1998) 'Improving the quality of fostering provision: a thematic and dynamic approach' in *Exchanging Visions: papers on best practice in Europe for children separated from their birth parents*, London: British Agencies for Adoption and Fostering.

Cairns, K. (2002a) *Attachment, Trauma and Resilience: therapeutic caring for children*, London: British Agencies for Adoption and Fostering.

Cairns, K. (2002b) 'Making sense: the use of theory and research to support foster care', *Adoption and Fostering* 26(2), 6–13

Calder, M. and Hackett, S. (eds) (2003) *Assessment in Child Care: using and developing frameworks for practice*, Lyme Regis: Russell House.

Camis, J. (2001) *We Are Fostering: an interactive guide for children who are fostering*, London: British Agencies for Adoption and Fostering.

Cathcart, J. (2002) 'Volunteer mentoring for care leavers' in Wheal, A. (ed.) *The RHP Companion to Leaving Care*, Lyme Regis: Russell House.

CHAR (1996) *Inquiry into Preventing Youth Homelessness*, London: CHAR.

Chisholm, L. (1990) 'A sharper lens or a new camera? Youth research, young people and social change' in Chisholm, L., Büchner, P., Krüger, H.-H. and Brown, P. (eds) *Childhood, Youth and Social Change: a comparative perspective*, London: Falmer.

Cleaver, H. (2000) *Fostering Family Contact*, London: Stationery Office.

Cleaver, H., Unell, I. and Aldgate, J. (1999) *Children's Needs – parenting capacity: the impact of illness, problem alcohol and drug use, and domestic violence on children's development*, London: Stationery Office.

Cliffe, D. and Berridge, D. (1991) *Closing Children's Homes*, London: National Children's Bureau.

Coleman, J. (1974) *Relationships in Adolescence*, London: Routledge.

Coleman, J. (1978) 'Current contradictions in adolescent theory', *Journal of Youth and Adolescence* 7, 1–11.

Coleman, J. and Roker, D. (1998) 'Adolescence: a review', *The Psychologist* December, 593–5.

Colton, M. (1988) *Dimensions of Substitute Child Care: a comparative study of foster and residential child care practices*, Aldershot: Avebury.

Colton, M. and Hellinckx, W. (1993) *Child Care in the EC*, Aldershot: Arena.

Colton, M., Sanders, R. and Williams, M. (2001) *An Introduction to Working with Children: a guide for social workers*, Basingstoke: Palgrave (now Palgrave Macmillan).

Corby, B. (1993) *Child Abuse: towards a knowledge base*, Buckingham: Open University Press.

Cox, A. and Bentovim, A. (2000) *The Family Pack of Questionnaires and Scales*, London: The Stationery Office.

Cull, L.-A. and Roche, J. (2001) *The Law and Social Work*, Basingstoke: Palgrave (now Palgrave Macmillan).

Dalrymple, J. and Burke, B. (1995) *Anti-Oppressive Practice: social care and the law*, Buckingham: Open University Press.

Daniel, B., Wassell, S. and Gilligan, R. (1999) *Child Development for Child Care and Protection Workers*, London: Jessica Kingsley.

Davies, E. (1994) *'They All Speak English Anyway' – Yr Iaith Gymraeg ac Ymarfer Gwrth-Orthrymol (The Welsh Language and Anti-Oppressive Practice)*, Caerdydd/Cardiff: CCETSW Cymru.

Davies, E., Siencyn, S. and Owen, G. (1999) *Nid Ar Chwarae Bach: pecyn hyfforddiant ac adnoddau ar gyfer gweithio gyda phlant yng Nghymru*, Caerdydd/Cardiff: CCETSW Cymru.

Department of Health (1988) *Protecting Children: a guide to comprehensive assessment for social workers*, London: HMSO.

Department of Health (1991a) *Patterns and Outcomes in Child Placement: messages from current research and their implications*, London: HMSO.

Department of Health (1991b) *The Children Act 1989 Guidance and Regulations Volume 3: Family Placements*, London: HMSO.

Department of Health (1991c) *The Children Act 1989 Guidance and Regulations Volume 4: Residential Care*, London: HMSO.

Department of Health (1992) *Choosing with Care (the report of the committee of inquiry into the selection, development and management of staff in children's homes)*, London: HMSO.

Department of Health (1998) *Caring for Children Away from Home: messages from research*, Chichester: Wiley.

Department of Health (1999) *Adoption Now: messages from research*, Chichester: Wiley.

Department of Health (2001a) *Studies Informing the Framework for the Assessment of Children in Need and Their Families*, London: The Stationery Office.

Department of Health (2001b) *Children's Homes at 31 March 2000, England* (Statistics Division Bulletin 2001/9), London: Department of Health (accessed online at www.doh.gov.uk/public/sb0109.htm#16, 6 July 2003).

Department of Health (2001c) *Children (Leaving Care) Act 2000 Regulations and Guidance*, London: The Stationery Office.

Department of Health (2001d) *Adoption: draft practice guidance to support the National Adoption Standards for England*, London: Department of Health.

Department of Health (2003) *Outcome Indicators for Looked-after Children: twelve months to 30 September 2002*, London: Department of Health.

Department of Health and Department for Education and Employment (2000) *Guidance on the Education of Young People in Public Care*, London: DH/DfEE.

Department of Health, Department of Education and Employment and Home Office (2000) *Framework for the Assessment of Children in Need and their Families*, London: The Stationery Office.

Donaldson, M. (1978) *Children's Minds*, London: Fontana.

Doolan, M., Nixon, P. and Lawrence, P. (2004) *Growing up in the Care of Relatives or Friends: delivering best practice for children in family and friends care*, London: Family Rights Group.

Dumaret, A.-C. (1988) 'The SOS Children's Villages: school achievement of subjects reared in a permanent foster care', *Early Child Development and Care* 34, 217–26.

Dunn, J. (1988) *The Beginnings of Social Understanding*, Oxford: Blackwell.

Fahlberg, V. (1994) *A Child's Journey Through Placement*, London: British Agencies for Adoption and Fostering.

Farmer, E. and Parker, R. (1991) *Trials and Tribulations: a study of children home on trial*, London: HMSO.

Fisher, T., Gibbs, I., Sinclair, I. and Wilson, K. (2000) 'Sharing the care: qualities sought of social workers by foster carers', *Child and Family Social Work* 5(3), 225–33.

Fletcher, B. (1993) *Not Just a Name: the views of young people in foster and residential care*, London: National Consumer Council.

Floris, G. (2002) 'Leaving care support groups', in Wheal, A. (ed.) *The RHP Companion to Leaving Care*, Lyme Regis: Russell House

Fox Harding, L. (1997) *Perspectives in Child Care Policy*, 2nd edition, Harlow: Longman.

Fraser, M. (ed.) (1997) *Risk and Resilience in Childhood: an ecological perspective*, Washington, DC: NASW Press.

Fratter, J. (1996) *Adoption with Contact*, London: British Agencies for Adoption and Fostering.

Fratter, J., Rowe, J., Sapsford, D. and Thoburn, J. (1991) *Permanent Family Placement*, London: British Agencies for Adoption and Fostering.

Frost, N., Mills, S. and Stein, M. (1999) *Understanding Residential Child Care*, Aldershot: Ashgate.

Fry, E. (1992) *Aftercare: making the most of foster care*, London: National Foster Care Association.

Gambe, D., Gomes, J., Kapur, V., Rangel, M. and Stubbs, P. (1992) *Improving Practice with Children and Families: a training manual*, Leeds: Central Council for Education and Training in Social Work.

Garbarino, J., Stott, F. and Faculty of the Erikson Institute (1992) *What Children Can Tell Us*, San Francisco: Jossey-Bass.

Garnett, L. (1992) *Leaving Care and After*, London: National Children's Bureau.

Garrett, P. M. (1999a) 'Questioning the new orthodoxy: the *Looking After Children* system and its discourse on parenting', *Practice* 11, 53–64.

Garrett, P. M. (1999b) 'Mapping child-care social work in the final years of the twentieth century: a critical response to the Looking After Children system', *British Journal of Social Work* 29(1), 27–47.

Garrett, P. M. (2003) *Remaking Social Work with Children and Families: a critical discussion on the 'modernisation' of social care*, London: Routledge.

Gill, O. and Jackson, B. (1983) *Adoption and Race*, London: British Agencies for Adoption and Fostering.

Gilligan, R. (2000a) 'Adversity, resilience and young people: the protective value of positive school and spare time experiences', *Children and Society* 14(1), 37–47.

Gilligan, R. (2000b) 'The key role of social workers in promoting the well being of children in state care – a neglected dimension of reforming policies', *Children and Society* 14(4), 267–76.

Gilligan, R. (2001) *Promoting Resilience: a resource guide on working with children in the care system*, London: British Agencies for Adoption and Fostering.

Goffman, E. (1963) *Stigma: notes on the management of spoiled identity*, Harmondsworth: Penguin.

Golding, K. (2003) 'Helping foster carers, helping children: using attachment theory to guide practice', *Adoption and Fostering* 27(2), 64–73.

Goldstein, J., Freud, A. and Solnit, J. (1973) *Beyond the Best Interests of the Child*, New York: Macmillan.

Gorin, S. (1997) *Time to Listen? Views and experiences of family placement*, Report no. 36, Portsmouth: Social Services Research and Information Unit, University of Portsmouth.

Grimshaw, R. and Sinclair, R. (1997) *Planning to Care: regulation, procedure and practice under the Children Act 1989*, London: National Children's Bureau.

Grotberg, E. (1997) *A Guide to Promoting Resilience in Children: strengthening the human spirit*, Amsterdam: Bernard Van Leer Foundation.

Harris, J., Rabiee, P. and Priestley, M. (2002) 'Enabled by the Act? The reframing of aftercare services for disabled young people' in Wheal, A. (ed.) *The RHP Companion to Leaving Care*, Lyme Regis: Russell House.

Hayden, C., Goddard, J., Gorin, S. and Van Der Spek, N. (1999) *State Child Care: looking after children?*, London: Jessica Kingsley.

Heath, A., Colton, M. and Aldgate, J. (1994) 'Failure to escape: a longitudinal study of foster children's educational attainment', *British Journal of Social Work* 24(3), 241–60.

Hegar, R. L. and Scannapieco, M. (eds) (1999) *Kinship Foster Care: policy, practice and research*, New York: Oxford University Press.

Hendrick, H. (2003) *Child Welfare: historical dimensions, contemporary debate*, Bristol: Policy Press.

Herbert, M. (2002) *Typical and Atypical Development*, Oxford: Blackwell.

Hershman, D. and McFarlane, A. (2002) *Children Act Handbook*, Bristol: Family Law.

Hess, P. and Proch, K. (1993) *Contact: managing visits to children who are looked after away from home*, London: British Agencies for Adoption and Fostering.

Hicks, S. and McDermott, J. (1998) *Lesbian and Gay Fostering and Adoption*, London: Jessica Kingsley.

Hill, M. and Shaw, M. (1998) *Signposts in Adoption*, London: British Agencies for Adoption and Fostering.

Hitchman, J. (1966) *The King of the Barbareens*, Harmondsworth: Penguin.

HM Government (2003) *Every Child Matters* (Cm 5860), London: The Stationery Office.

Holland, S. (2004) *Child and Family Assessment in Social Work Practice*, London: Sage.

Holman, R. (2002) *The Unknown Fostering: a study of private fostering*, Lyme Regis: Russell House.

Holmes, J. (1993) *John Bowlby and Attachment Theory*, London: Routledge.

Horwath, J. (ed.) (2001) *The Child's World: assessing children in need*, London: Jessica Kingsley.

Howe, D. (1993) *Half a Million Women*, Harmondsworth: Penguin.

Howe, D. (1995) *Attachment Theory for Social Work Practice*, London: Macmillan (now Palgrave Macmillan).

Howe, D. (ed.) (1996) *Attachment and Loss in Child and Family Social Work*, Aldershot: Avebury.

Howe, D., Brandon, M., Hinings, D. and Schofield, G. (1999) *Attachment Theory, Child Maltreatment and Family Support*, London: Macmillan (now Palgrave Macmillan).

Hutchby, I. and Moran-Ellis, J. (eds) (1998) *Children and Social Competence: arenas of action*, London: Falmer.

Hutchinson, B. (2003) ' "Skills protect": towards a professional foster care service', *Adoption and Fostering* 27(3), 8–13.

Hutson, S. (1995) *Care Leavers and Young Homeless People in Wales: the exchange of good practice*, Swansea: University of Wales Swansea.

Ince, L. (1998) *Making it Alone*, London: British Agencies for Adoption and Fostering.

Ince, L. (2004) 'Young black people leaving care' in Lewis, V., Kellett, M., Robinson, C., Fraser, S. and Ding, S. (eds) *The Reality of Research with Children and Young People*, London: Sage.

Ivaldi, G. (1998) *Children Adopted from Care*, London: British Agencies for Adoption and Fostering.

Jack, G. (2001) 'Ecological perspectives in assessing children and families' in Horwath, J. (ed.) *The Child's World: assessing children in need*, London: Jessica Kingsley.

Jack, G. and Gill, O. (2003) *The Missing Side of the Triangle: assessing the importance of family and environment factors in the lives of children*, Barkingside: Barnardos.

Jackson, S. (1998) 'Looking after children: a new approach or just an exercise in form-filling? A response to Knight and Caveney', *British Journal of Social Work* 28(1), 45–56.

Jackson, S. (ed.) (2001) *Nobody Ever Told Us School Mattered: raising the educational attainments of children in public care*, London: British Agencies for Adoption and Fostering.

Jackson, S. and Kilroe, S. (eds) (1996) *Looking After Children: good parenting, good outcomes*, London: HMSO.

Jackson, S. and Martin, P. (1998) 'Surviving the care system: education and resilience', *Journal of Adolescence* 21, 569–83.

Jackson, S. and Thomas, N. (1999) *On the Move Again? What works in creating stability for looked after children*, Barkingside: Barnardos.

Jackson, S. and Thomas, N. (2001) *What Works in Creating Stability for Looked after Children*, 2nd edition, Barkingside: Barnardos.

James, A. and Prout, A. (1997) *Constructing and Reconstructing Childhood: contemporary issues in the sociological study of childhood*, 2nd edition, London: Falmer.

James, A., Jenks, C. and Prout, A. (1998) *Theorizing Childhood*, Cambridge: Polity.

Jenkins, J. and Tudor, K. (1999) *Being Creative with Assessment and Action Records*, Rhondda Cynon Taf Borough Council.

Jones, C. (2001) 'Voices from the front line: state social workers and New Labour', *British Journal of Social Work* 31(4), 547–62.

Jones, D. (2003) *Communicating with Vulnerable Children: a guide for practitioners*, London: Gaskell.

Kahan, B. (1994) *Growing up in Groups*, London: HMSO.

Kahan, B. and Levy, A. (1991) *The Pindown Experience and the Protection of Children*, Stafford: Staffordshire County Council.

Kamerman, S. B. and Kahn, A. K. (1978) *Family Policy: government and families in fourteen countries*, New York: Columbia University Press.

Katz, L. (1996) 'Permanency action through concurrent planning', *Adoption and Fostering* 20(2), 8–13.

Katz, L. and Robinson, C. (1991) 'Foster-care drift: a risk-assessment matrix', *Child Welfare* LXX(3), 347–58.

Kellmer Pringle, M. (1974, 1986) *The Needs of Children*, London: Hutchinson.

Kent, R. (1997) *Children's Safeguards Review* (Report for the Scottish Office Home Department), Edinburgh: The Stationery Office.

Kidane, S. (2001a) *I Did not Choose to Come Here: listening to refugee children*, London: British Agencies for Adoption and Fostering.

Kidane, S. (2001b) *Food, Shelter and Half a Chance: assessing the needs of unaccompanied asylum seeking and refugee children*, London: British Agencies for Adoption and Fostering.

Kidane, S. (2002) 'Asylum seeking and refugee children in the UK' in Wheal, A. (ed.) *The RHP Companion to Leaving Care*, Lyme Regis: Russell House.

Kiddle, C. (1999) *Traveller Children*, London: Jessica Kingsley.

Kirkwood, A. (1993) *The Leicestershire Inquiry 1992*, Leicester: Leicestershire County Council.

Knight, T. and Caveney, S. (1998) 'Assessment and Action Records: will they promote good parenting?', *British Journal of Social Work* 28(1), 29–43.

Lansdown, G. (1995) *Taking Part: children's participation in decision making*, London: Institute for Public Policy Research.

Lewis, J. (1998) 'Building an evidence-based approach to social interventions', *Children and Society* 12, 136–40.

Lewis, V. (2003) *Development and Disability*, 2nd edition, Oxford: Blackwell.

Lloyd, P. (1990) 'Children's communication' in Grieve, R. and Hughes, M. (ed.) *Understanding Children: essays in honour of Margaret Donaldson*, Oxford: Blackwell.

Lowe, N. and Murch, M. (2002) *The Plan for the Child: adoption or long term fostering*, London: British Agencies for Adoption and Fostering.

Luxmoore, N. (2000) *Listening to Young People in School, Youth Work and Counselling*, London: Jessica Kingsley.

Maccoby, E. (1980) *Social Development: psychological growth and the parent–child relationship*, New York: Harcourt Brace Jovanovich.

Maclean, K. (2003) 'Resilience: what it is and how children and young people can be helped develop it', *In Residence* 1 (accessed online via International Child and Youth Care Network, *CYC-online* 55, 8 January 2004).

Maclean, K. and Gunion, M. (2003) 'Learning with care: the education of children looked after away from home by local authorities in Scotland', *Adoption and Fostering* 27(2), 20–31.

Mallon, G. (2000) *Let's Get This Straight: a gay- and lesbian-affirming approach to child welfare*, New York: Columbia University Press.

Maluccio, A. N. and Fein, E. (1983) 'Permanency planning: a redefinition', *Child Welfare* 62(3), 195–201.

Maluccio, A. N., Fein, E. and Olmstead, K. A. (1986) *Permanency Planning for Children: concepts and methods*, London: Tavistock.

Marsh, P. and Triseliotis, J. (eds) (1993) *Prevention and Reunification in Child Care*, London: Batsford.

Maximé, J. (1993) 'The importance of racial identity for psychological well being of black children', *Association of Child Psychology and Psychiatry Newsletter* 15(4), 173–9.

McAuley, K. (2002) 'Becoming a parent: good practice in prevention strategies and support services for looked after young people and care leavers' in Wheal, A. (ed.) *The RHP Companion to Leaving Care*, Lyme Regis: Russell House.

McNeil, P. (1998) *Adoption of Children in Scotland*, 3rd edition, Edinburgh: Green/Sweet and Maxwell.

McNeish, D., Newman, T. and Roberts, H. (eds) (2002) *What Works for Children? Effective services for children and families*, Buckingham: Open University Press.

McNorrie, K. (1995) *Children (Scotland) Act 1995 – annotated version*, Edinburgh: Green/Sweet and Maxwell.

Middleton, L. (1999) *Disabled Children: challenging social exclusion*, Oxford: Blackwell.

Millham, S., Bullock, R., Hosie, K. and Haak, M. (1986) *Lost in Care: the problems of maintaining links between children in care and their families*, Aldershot: Gower.

Milner, J. and O'Byrne, P. (2002) *Assessment in Social Work*, 2nd edition, Basingstoke: Palgrave (now Palgrave Macmillan).

Monck, E., Reynolds, J. and Wigfall, V. (2003) *The Role of Concurrent Planning: making permanent placements for young children*, London: British Agencies for Adoption and Fostering.

Morris, J. (1995) *Gone Missing: a research and policy review of disabled children living away from their families*, London: Who Cares? Trust.

Moss, P. and Petrie, P. (2002) *From Children's Services to Children's Spaces*, London: Routledge.

Mullender, A. (1999) *We Are Family: sibling relationships in placement and beyond*, London: British Agencies for Adoption and Fostering.

Munro, E. (2001) 'Empowering looked after children', *Child and Family Social Work* 6(2), 129–38.

National Assembly for Wales (2000) *Framework for the Assessment of Children in Need and their Families*, Cardiff: The Stationery Office.

National Society for the Prevention of Cruelty to Children (1997) *Turning Points: a resource pack for communicating with children*, Leicester: NSPCC.

Neil, E. (2003) 'Accepting the reality of adoption: birth relatives' experiences of face-to-face contact', *Adoption and Fostering* 27(2), 32–41.

O'Hagan, K. (2001) *Cultural Competence in the Caring Professions*, London: Jessica Kingsley.

O'Mairthini, P. (2002) 'Foster caring and throughcare or aftercare: a personal and professional view' in Wheal, A. (ed.) *The RHP Companion to Leaving Care*, Lyme Regis: Russell House.

O'Quigley, A. (2000) *Listening to Children's Views: the findings and recommendations of recent research*, York: Joseph Rowntree Foundation.

Oliver, M. (1990) *The Politics of Disablement*, Basingstoke: Macmillan (now Palgrave Macmillan).

Parker, R. (1990) *Away from Home: a history of child care*, Barkingside: Barnardos.

Parker, R., Ward, H., Jackson, S., Aldgate, J. and Wedge, P. (eds) (1991) *Looking After Children: assessing outcomes in child care*, London: HMSO.

Parsons, K. with Broad, B. and Fry, E. (2002) 'Accommodation issues arising from the Children (Leaving Care) Act 2000' in Wheal, A. (ed.) *The RHP Companion to Leaving Care*, Lyme Regis: Russell House.

Parton, N. (1991) *Governing the Family: child care, child protection and the state*, Basingstoke: Macmillan (now Palgrave Macmillan).

Partridge, A. (1989) *Young People Leaving Care in Oxford: a report for Oxfordshire County Council*, Oxford: Oxfordshire County Council.

Penn, H. and Gough, D. (2002) 'The price of a loaf of bread: some conceptions of family support', *Children and Society* 16(1), 17–32.

Phillips, M. and Worlock, D. (1996) 'Implementing the Looking After Children system in RBK&C [Royal Borough of Kensington & Chelsea]', *Adoption and Fostering* 20, 42–8.

Philpot, T. (2001) *A Very Private Practice: an investigation into private fostering*, London: British Agencies for Adoption and Fostering.

Plumer, E. (1992) *When You Place a Child …*, Springfield, Illinois: Charles Thomas.

Plumtree, A. (1997) *Child Care Law Scotland: a summary*, London: British Agencies for Adoption and Fostering.

Pringle, K. (1998) *Children and Social Welfare in Europe*, Buckingham: Open University Press.

Putnam, R. D. (2000) *Bowling Alone: the collapse and revival of American community*, New York: Simon and Schuster.

Quinton, D., Rushton, A., Dance, C. and Mayes, D. (1998) *Joining New Families: a study of adoption and fostering in middle childhood*, Chichester: Wiley.

Read, J. and Clements, L. (2001) *Disabled Children and the Law: research and good practice*, London: Jessica Kingsley.

Richards, M. (1986) 'Behind the best interests of the child: an examination of the arguments of Goldstein, Freud and Solnit concerning custody and access at divorce', *Journal of Social Welfare and Family Law*, March, 77–95.

Richman, N. (2000) *Communicating with Children: helping children in distress*, London: Save the Children.

Riddell, M. (1996) *The Cornflake Kid*, Chippenham: Partnership Publications/ Antony Rowe.

Rowe, J. and Lambert, L. (1973) *Children Who Wait: a study of children needing substitute families*, Association of British Adoption Agencies.

Rowe, J., Cain, H., Hundleby, M. and Keane, A. (1984) *Long Term Foster Care*, London: Batsford.

Rowe, J., Hundleby, M. and Garnett, L. (1989) *Child Care Now: a survey of placement patterns*, London: British Agencies for Adoption and Fostering.

Ruxton, S. (1996) *Children in Europe*, London: NCH Action for Children.

Ryan, M. (1994, 1999) *The Children Act 1989: putting it into practice*, London: Arena.

Ryan, T. and Walker, R. (1993) *Life Story Work*, London: British Agencies for Adoption and Fostering.

Ryburn, M. (1992) *Adoption in the 1990s: identity and openness*, Leamington Spa: Leamington Press.

Ryburn, M. (1994) *Contested Adoptions: research, law, policy and practice*, Aldershot: Arena.

Sanders, R. (2004) *Sibling Relationships: theory and issues for practice*, Basingstoke: Palgrave Macmillan.

Scannapieco, M. (1999) 'Kinship care in the public child welfare system: a systematic review of the research', in Hegar, R. L. and Scannapieco, M. (eds) *Kinship Foster Care: policy, practice and research*, New York: Oxford University Press.

Schofield, G. (2003) *Part of the Family: pathways through foster care*, London: British Agencies for Adoption and Fostering.

Schofield, G., Beek, M., Sargent, K. and Thoburn, J. (2000) *Growing up in Foster Care*, London: British Agencies for Adoption and Fostering.

Schön, D. (1983) *The Reflective Practitioner*, London: Basic Books.

Scottish Office (1995) *The Children (Scotland) Act 1995 Regulations and Guidance Volume 2: children looked after by local authorities*, Edinburgh: HMSO.

Seden, J. (2001) 'Assessment of children in need and their families: a literature review' in Department of Health, *Studies Informing the Framework for the Assessment of Children in Need and their Families*, London: The Stationery Office.

Sellick, C. (1996) 'The role of social workers in supporting and developing the work of foster carers', *Adoption and Fostering* 20(2), 21–6.

Sellick, C. and Thoburn, J. (1996) *What Works in Family Placement?*, Barkingside: Barnardos.

Sellick, C. and Thoburn, J. (2002) 'Family placement services' in McNeish, D., Newman, T. and Roberts, H. (eds) *What Works for Children? Effective services for children and families*, Buckingham: Open University Press.

Shaw, I. (2003) 'Qualitative research and outcomes in health, social work and education', *Qualitative Research* 3(1), 57–77.

Sinclair, I. and Gibbs, I. (1998) *Children's Homes: a study in diversity*, Chichester: Wiley.

Spears, W. and Cross, M. (2003) 'How do "children who foster" perceive fostering?', *Adoption and Fostering* 27(4), 38–45.

Stainton Rogers, W. and Roche, J. (1994) *Children's Welfare and Children's Rights: a practical guide to the law*, London: Hodder and Stoughton.

Stein, M. (1990) *Living Out of Care*, Barkingside: Barnardos.

Stein, M. (1997) *What Works in Leaving Care?*, Barkingside: Barnardos.

Stein, M. and Carey, K. (1986) *Leaving Care*, Oxford: Blackwell.

Stein, M. and Ellis, S. (1983) *Gizza Say?*, London: National Association of Young People in Care.

Thoburn, J. (1994) *Child Placement: principles and practice*, Aldershot: Arena.

Thoburn, J., Murdoch, A. and O'Brien, A. (1986) *Permanence in Child Care*, Oxford: Blackwell.

Thoburn, J., Sellick, C. and Philpot, T. (2004) *What Works in Adoption and Foster Care?*, Barkingside: Barnardos/British Agencies for Adoption and Fostering.

Thomas, C. and Beckford, V. (with Lowe, N. and Murch, M.) (1999) *Adopted Children Speaking*, London: British Agencies for Adoption and Fostering.

Thomas, N. (1995) 'Child abuse and allegations of abuse in local authority foster care', *Practice* 7(3), 35–44.

Thomas, N. (2000) 'Listening to children' in Foley, P., Roche, J. and Tucker, S. (eds) *Children in Society: contemporary theory, policy and practice*, Basingstoke: Palgrave (now Palgrave Macmillan)/Open University.

Thomas, N. (2002) *Children, Family and the State: decision-making and child participation*, Bristol: Policy Press.

Thomas, N. and O'Kane, C. (1998a) *Children and Decision Making: a summary report*, University of Wales Swansea, International Centre for Childhood Studies.

Thomas, N. and O'Kane, C. (1998b) 'When children's wishes and feelings clash with their "best interests"', *International Journal of Children's Rights* 6(2), 137–54.

Thomas, N. and O'Kane, C. (1999a) 'Children's participation in reviews and planning meetings when they are "looked after" in middle childhood', *Child and Family Social Work* 4(3), 221–30.

Thomas, N. and O'Kane, C. (1999b) 'Children's experiences of decision making in middle childhood', *Childhood* 6(3), 369–87.

Thomas, N., Phillipson, J., O'Kane, C. and Davies, E. (1999) *Children and Decision Making: a training and resource pack*, University of Wales Swansea, International Centre for Childhood Studies.

Thompson, N. (2002) *Building the Future: social work with children, young people and their families*, Lyme Regis: Russell House.

Tolfree, D. (1995) *Roofs and Roots: the care of separated children in the developing world*, London: Save the Children/Arena.

Trevarthen, C. (1995) 'The child's need to learn a culture', *Children and Society* 9(1), 5–19.

Triseliotis, J. (2002) 'Long term foster care or adoption? The evidence examined', *Child and Family Social Work* 7(1), 23–33.

Triseliotis, J., Borland, M. and Hill, M. (2000) *Delivering Foster Care*, London: British Agencies for Adoption and Fostering.

Triseliotis, J., Sellick, C. and Short, R. (1995) *Foster Care: theory and practice*, British Agencies for Adoption and Fostering.

Triseliotis, J., Shireman, J. and Hundleby, M. (1997) *Adoption: theory, policy and practice*. London: Cassell.

Utting, W. (1991) *Children in the Public Care*, London: HMSO.

Utting, W. (1997) *People Like Us: the report of the review of the safeguards for children living away from home*, London: The Stationery Office.

Verhellen, E. (1992) 'Changes in the image of the child' in Freeman, M. and Veerman, P. (eds) *Ideologies of Children's Rights*, Dordrecht: Martinus Nijhoff.

Wade, J. (2003) *Leaving Care: Quality Protects research briefing*, London: Department of Health/Research in Practice (available at www.rip.org.uk/publications/).

Ward, A. (1993) *Working in Group Care: social work in residential and day care settings*, Birmingham: Venture Press.

Ward, A. (2004) 'Working with young people in residential settings' in Roche, J. and Tucker, S. (eds) *Youth in Society: contemporary theory, policy and practice*, London: Sage.

Ward, H. (ed.) (1995) *Looking After Children: research into practice*, London: HMSO.

Ward, H. and Rose, W. (eds) (2002) *Approaches to Needs Assessment in Children's Services*, London: Jessica Kingsley.

Waterhouse, R. (2000) *Lost in Care: report of the tribunal of inquiry into the abuse of children in care in the former county council areas of Gwynedd and Clwyd since 1974*, London: The Stationery Office.

Weisner, T. S. (2002) 'Ecocultural understanding of children's developmental pathways', *Human Development* 45(4), 275–81.

West, A. (1995) *You're on Your Own: young people's research on leaving care*, London: Save the Children.

Wheal, A. (1995) *The Foster Carer's Handbook*, Lyme Regis: Russell House.

Wheal, A. (2002) *The RHP Companion to Foster Care*, Lyme Regis: Russell House.

Whitaker, D., Archer, L. and Hicks, L. (1998) *Working in Children's Homes: challenges and complexities*, Chichester: Wiley.

Wilkinson, I. (1998) *Child and Family Assessment: clinical guidelines for practitioners*, 2nd edition, London: Routledge.

Willow, C. (1996) *Children's Rights and Participation in Residential Care*, London: National Children's Bureau.

Wilson, J. (1991) *The Story of Tracy Beaker*, London: Doubleday.

Woodhead, M. (1997) 'Psychology and the cultural construction of children's needs' in James, A. and Prout, A. (eds) *Constructing and Reconstructing Childhood: contemporary issues in the sociological study of childhood*, London: Falmer.

Woodhead, M. (1999) 'Reconstructing developmental psychology – some first steps', *Children and Society* 13(1), 3–19.

Index

Note: bold page numbers indicate a chapter, section or subsection devoted to the named subject.